Safe Haven

Interdenominational

Bible College
&
Training Institute

Bachelor's Degree Program Books
Volume 1

BACHELOR'S DEGREE BOOKS
VOLUME 1

FROM SALVATION TO YOUR CALLING

Accredited by National Bible College Association

PO Box 457
Zebulon, NC 275

From Salvation to Your Calling
Table of Contents

Lesson 1
Salvation
Romans 10:9-10; Matthew 5:4; 2 Corinthians 5:17

1. **(Romans 10:9)** Salvation is:
   a. Freedom from sin.
   b. Rescued from the old man.
   c. Brought out the old life into new life.

2. To receive salvation, one must:
   a. Confess with the mouth.
   b. Believe in the heart.
   c. Confession of Jesus Christ.
   d. Believing in Jesus Christ.

3. Salvation concerning *"Thou shall be saved." means:*
   a. It is a continuous process.
   b. You are continuously being rescued from something in your life.
   c. You are continuously being rescued from yourself.
   d. **(2 Corinthians 5:17)** You are continuously dying from your old man.

4. When receiving salvation, one must understand:
   a. That the wages of sin is death.
   b. The word wages in the Greek means "*payment for sin*".
   c. You will get paid for the good and the bad.
   d. Death means destruction or defeat.

5. Salvation:
   a. Is the beginning process for every believer.
   b. Is the beginning of freedom for an individual life.
   c. Is the beginning of the cleansing process of your life.
   d. If one is not cleansed by salvation first, then the Holy Spirit cannot come in.

6. Salvation:
   a. gives you open access to Christ.
   b. connects you to GOD through Christ Jesus.
   c. lets you pray unto Him, and He will hear you.
   d. Without Salvation, you can only pray the prayer of repentance.

e. **(Matthew 5:4)** Prayer for someone that has not confessed salvation is done through an Intercessor.

7. Salvation:
   a. When you receive salvation, you are covered under the blood of Jesus.
   b. Without salvation, you are only covered under the mercy of GOD.
   c. Salvation brings you to the table of GOD's true grace and favor.

8. Salvation:
   a. You can never work for it.
   b. You can never earn it.
   c. It is given through the grace of GOD.
   d. It is afforded to man through Christ's death on the cross.

9. Salvation:
   a. Salvation offers man the opportunity to go to heaven.
   b. Without salvation, man is doomed for hell.
   c. Salvation rescues man from the arms of Satan.
   d. Salvation places you back in the arms of GOD.

10. Salvation:
   a. Salvation gives you the right to all spiritual blessings.
   b. Spiritual blessings are love, joy, peace, hope, and many others.
   c. Salvation frees you from the natural curses of the world such as hatred, sadness, and confusion.
   d. Salvation connects you to the fruit of the Spirit so that you can have life.

11. Salvation/Born Again:
   a. Born again means to *"get GOD back"*.
   b. Through Adam and Eve's sin, we were separated from GOD.
   c. Salvation sets you free from sin.

Lesson 2
Conversion
Acts 3:9; John 12:40

1. **(Acts 3:19)** The first thing we will talk about concerning salvation is the *process of conversion.* What does it mean to be converted? To be converted means: "*GOD is now getting the sin or unrighteousness out of you.*" When you accepted Christ saved, you were rescued from sin. You were freed from the arms of Satan and placed in the arms of GOD. The process of getting sin out of your life begins now.

2. For example, if a person is put into a rehab center, first you rescue the person from their old surroundings and old friends. Once in the facility, the process begins of getting the taste of that old habit out of them. The conversion process is the beginning of the detoxification process.

3. **(Acts 3:19)** The conversion process is where true repentance begins. Notice, to get saved, you do not have to repent; you only have to confess and believe.

4. To be converted means "*to come again.*" GOD is always trying to get us back to our original state. This is the innocent state that Adam was in before he sinned.

5. Repentance starts GOD's process of helping us out of sin and forgetting about the things you have done. Repentance causes us to completely turn and go in a totally different direction.

6. Conversion is when you truly begin to change from the old man to the new man. You begin to look the other way.

7. **(Matthew 18:3)** Conversion starts the true humbling process of a person. Christ desires that we come to Him as a child. Once conversion starts, the person will release their heart to the Almighty GOD.

8. When a person allows themselves to be converted, they become teachable in the Kingdom. They will become available to hear the voice of GOD and learn from the written Word.

9. When people get saved, but reject conversion, they are rejecting the Word. They confess and accept Christ, but they refuse to accept the written Word which exposes

their short coming. They will not allow the written Word to get the sin out of them.

10. **(John 12:40) (Act 28-27)** When a person is willing to be converted, they then can begin a true healing process. The person can be physically, mentally, and spiritually healed.

11. **(Matthew 9:1-5)** When a person is converted, many physical conditions can be removed. Some sicknesses happen because of the sin in their lives. Many times, when true repentance comes, healing will come.

12. There are those who can be healed from generational curses and bitter roots. There are those who have curses from other family members and those whose conversion can deliver them from that curse. There are those who have spoken curses into their lives. This is a bitter root. Again, through conversion, deliverance can come.

13. This is why Jesus would tell many people to "***go and sin no more***" when they received their healing. Sin caused this sickness; therefore, He would insist that they would get and keep their conversion.

14. **(Isaiah 6:10)** There are those who have a hard heart. Healing can come to a hard-hearted person when conversion happens. Conversion will remove the condition that causes their hearts to be hard.

15. **(Psalm 19:7)** Then there is mental conversion. This is a person who truly needs mental deliverance. They are controlled by the thoughts of pornography, negativity, and serious mental bondage. This person may be depressed or suicidal.

16. Mental conversion is especially important. There must be a deliverance of the mind, or the mind could destroy you spiritually. You could be pulled back into the World if there is not mental deliverance. Many are still bound because of mental bondage.

17. **(Luke 22:32)** When a person is truly converted, they can strengthen or help others become converted.

18. A converted person will understand what it is to go beyond salvation. They understand they must rid their lives of sin to be able to stand against the devil.

19. A converted person will help build other individuals in faith. They have the ability to help others go through the detoxification process.

20. **(James 5:19-20)** When someone helps another individual towards conversion, he or she helps prevent a soul from dying and going to hell. Conversion again rescues that person from what is inside of them.

Lesson 3
Transformation
Romans 12:2

1. The third thing that a person must go through is **transformation.** The word transformed means "*to develop the mind and character of Christ.*"

2. **(Romans 12:2)** Many people get saved and converted, but have a difficult time being transformed because they must begin to think like the Word instructs them to think.

3. This is not necessarily a sinful mind; however, it is a worldly mind or a mind that is contrary to the Word. The person will still handle money, marriage, and many things in life like the world handles things.

4. You must be able to think like Christ and act like Christ to be effective in life and in ministry. Your mind must be transformed from the world's system to totally go against the principles of the world. The things of the Word will be foolish to man. Therefore, your mind must be transformed to walk and act according to the word.

5. **(Galatians 5:22)** The character of Jesus is the Fruit of the Spirit. They come in when you receive Christ, but they will not manifest unless there is a transformation of the mind first.

6. You will not be able to long suffer, have peace, joy, and love properly without a transformation of the mind. That is why you have angry Christians. Christians who do not have peace or Christians who are not available to endure longsuffering, have not conditioned their minds.

7. Many Christians never truly come into the transformation state because they mentally reject transformation. They refuse to let their mind reach that level in the Word.

8. **(James 1:22) Transformation** is the true saving and deliverance process of the mind. You will need transformation of the mind to properly fulfill ministry and purpose while destroying the old man.

9. **(Matthew 5:1-10)** In Jesus' first assignment, the Beatitudes, He taught transformation

of the mind in line with the Kingdom of GOD.

10. **(Philippians 2:5)** Jesus had no worldliness in His mind. His mind was totally transformed to the mind of His Father. He could never sell out on His Father. He could never sell out to Satan because His mind was totally disciplined. His mind was totally controlled by the Word of His Father.

11. **(Genesis 3:1-7)** When Satan tempted Eve, his temptation was on her mind. He eventually convinced her to ignore the will of her Father, GOD, and obey the will of Satan. At that point, her desires or her thought patterns became fleshly.

12. Once Adam and Eve sold out to Satan, their character and thought patterns became worldly. Their desires became worldly. Man's character began to be more emotional. It obtained hatred, impatience, jealousy, and no faith.

13. **(I Samuel 15:1-35)** So many ministers get in trouble because they have not been transformed once they go into ministry. This causes their ministry to fail in due time.

14. **(I Samuel 15: 1-35)** Saul had not been transformed. As you read the story of his life, you will see why he acted the way he did. Saul did not go through transformation. That is why he was disobedient to GOD. Saul did not have true mental transformation. He continued to attempt to do GOD'S business like he did in the world.

15. Transformation is the making of man. Transformation will make the ministry. Transformation causes your mind to set things in proper order in your personal life, ministry, and church.

16. You must embrace the transformation process in your mind, or you will continue to repeat the same mistakes over and over again. You will continue to do the same things while expecting different results.

17. You must ask GOD to reset your thinking pattern to be able to embrace life changes and prepare yourself for the process of ministry. Many people and denominations do not embrace or understand the fivefold ministry, because their minds have not been through a transformation. To be able to embrace different levels of ministry, you must embrace a mental transformation.

18. **(Ephesians 1:18)** Transformation of the mind takes you into a better level of

understanding of the Word. Every level of mental and spiritual transformation allows you to open up to GOD's Voice and His Will.

19. Transformation is needed to be trusted with GOD's anointing in the Kingdom. If your mind is not changed concerning the anointing power, you will abuse it or misuse it.

20. **(I Timothy 3:10)** A novice should not be put in position of power or authority too soon because of their mind. The word novice in Greek means *"immature, untrained, undisciplined, or unprepared."* A lot of young ministers must trust their leader to take them through the transformation process.

21. You must understand it is not the position or title that confirms you. It is your level of mental and spiritual transformation. True transformation brings maturity, discipline, and order.

22. Again, you must embrace the transformation process to be victorious in life and most ministries. The transformation is truly what prepares you to stand. If your character and mindset are properly transformed according to the Word, you will be properly armored for any battle.

Lesson 4
Transition
Romans 1:17; I Samuel 16:21

1. Now we will talk about *transition.* The word transition means to *"go from one phase of your walk to another."* It is also from "one work to another."

2. There is a spiritual transition and there is natural transition. Spiritual transition is when you go from basic salvation to sanctification.

3. **(Roman 1:17)** Many people do not understand that your walk in Christ never stops. You must continue to move from one phase of your walk to another. You are moving from faith to faith.

4. Many believers' lives are stunted because they do not realize they must keep moving in the Kingdom.

5. **(Matthew 16:16)** Jesus Himself went from being Savior, to becoming The Christ. He was continually transitioning in His spiritual life. The day will come that we bow down to Him as King of Kings and Lord of Lords. We, as people of GOD, and the world will recognize Him in His final transition.

6. **(I Samuel 16-31)** Every transition brings you closer to Christ. Every transition prepares you to handle GOD's power and the anointing. Every transition will equip you for what you are about to face.

7. Transitions increase your obedience because you are always accepting GOD's changes. You are always accepting the way GOD does things.

8. **(Genesis 33:28)** Jacob went through transitions continuously. His transition was so great that GOD changed his name from Jacob to Israel. Jacob had truly come to a place of transition.

9. Jacob changed from a man of trickery to a righteous and pure man. That is the spiritual transition that everyone must go through. We must go from that spiritually ugly person to that beautiful person of true spiritual holiness. We must go from being

a worm to a butterfly or from being a lemon to becoming lemonade.

10. **(I Samuel 16:21)** Then there is transition of works. Even though David was anointed king, he did not instantly assume his kingly position. David's first assignment was being an armorbearer for Saul.

11. A lot of people get confused and sidetracked because they do not understand the transitioning process. Even though they may be called to preach or to be a prophet, there is always a starting point.

12. GOD may have called you to be a prophet or be a great apostle, but your starting point may be cleaning the bathroom. You may start out having to be an usher or children's church worker.

13. Can you imagine how degrading it was to David to be anointed king over Israel and his starting point was to be the armorbearer for his enemy? David was anointed for the position of king, but the anointing for the work came in stages. David had to go through stages to prepare for the ultimate position of kingship.

14. **(I Samuel 17:1)** David transitioned to the next phase that began his fight with the giant. He began to transition to a place of favor. Through this transition David proved how much he believed and trusted GOD.

15. Your transitions will increase your assignment and it will increase your favor. David's assignments and power increased. Your assignments will be manifested in your next level of power.

16. **(I Samuel 18:7)** Your next level will increase your favor. You can miss moving to the next level of power and favor if you refuse to transition.

17. You cannot get comfortable in a position and refuse transition. You must transition to open the door for the next person, and you must transition for your power and favor.

18. Each level of transition continues to prove your faith. Your faith is proven as you are willing to accept each plan that GOD introduces into your life.

19. You cannot interrupt the levels of transition. Each phase of transition is needed for

empowerment. It is needed for your ultimate placement in the kingdom. If you become impatient and try to skip a level, you will not have the power, GOD's anointing or the favor for that level and the levels after that one.

20. Many times, people become ministers before they have mastered the foundation levels. They are not prepared. I have seen pastors fall because they skip transition levels. They blame the devil and others for their failure when it has nothing to do with others or the devil. Again, you must finish each transitional stage to be equipped. GOD knows when you have completed each transitional phase.

Lesson 5
Calling
Matthew 22:1-4, 13

1. What does it mean to be called? The word called means *"to be summoned by GOD."* Calling is an invitation or a personal invitation from GOD Himself. There are two types of calling. There is the calling for your specific place in the kingdom and your specific earthly works.

2. **(Matthew 22:1-4)** GOD summons us to take our place in His kingdom. Every time someone gets saved, they are in position to be summoned or invited into heaven. There was a young lady in a service one night in a revival who received Christ. She told me that she kept hearing something calling her to the altar. She was being summoned by the Holy Spirit.

3. **(Hebrews 3:1)** Each person will have a chance to make it into the kingdom by meeting certain standards. They must be willing to respond to the invitation by first accepting salvation. Then they must be willing to "dress" the part or be renewed by being righteous and holy. If they are not willing to dress the part through their lifestyle, they will not receive an invitation into the Kingdom. They have been called but they will not be chosen.

4. **(Matthew 22:13)** "Weeping and gnashing of teeth" means they will be sent to hell because they refused to comply with standards. This kind of disobedience causes a person to be called or invited to come to heaven, but that person may not be chosen.

5. **(Ephesians 1:18)** We must first get caught up in the hope of His calling. Again, calling is for us to know Him and most of all to see Him one day. Ultimately, we all desire to truly be in His presence.

6. **(Ephesians 1:18)** When you are enlightened about being called, you are made aware of how important it is to prepare yourself for heaven. You must prepare yourself to be absent from the body and present with the Lord.

7. **(II Timothy 1:9)** Now we will deal with your calling for the works of the Kingdom of GOD. Understand that your calling for the Kingdom is holy. It is sacred. We must not think of it as a calling or something you can choose not to do. You must get it in your mind and spirit, the calling of the Holy Ghost is a sacrifice. It is not to

be taken lightly. There are many today who are possibly dead or extremely sick because they did not realize their calling was holy.

8. **(II Timothy 1:9)** Your calling is not according to your work or works. People think their calling is according to a talent they have identified for themselves or what they are good at. Singing is an example. But that may have nothing to do with GOD's calling. Your talent at times can match your calling but that will not always be the case.

9. **(II Timothy 1:9)** Your calling is always according to purpose. Your calling is according to what GOD created you to do and where He knows you will be most effective. Many people walk into a calling that has nothing to do with the Will of GOD. Neither talents nor your work will bring you favor. Only your purposed calling will bring favor. Your talent brings you favor if it is purposed by GOD. Many people get very frustrated. They have a dream attached to a talent that will never come to pass. Favor is never guaranteed on just talents alone. Many times, people seek out opportunities that never come to pass. Sometimes, this causes discouragement.

10. Some people can be exceptionally good at something but ineffective in the Kingdom. When Jesus called the twelve, they all had different talents and gifts, but they were purposed by GOD to do totally different things.

11. Many people never even step into their calling because they falsely believe doing their *"own thing"* will yield the same results. That is such a trick of the devil, because he knows as long as you believe this, you will remain out of the will of GOD.

12. **(Romans 11:29)** The Bible states, *"The gifts and calling of GOD are without repentance."* We must get a clear understanding of this scripture. Sometimes people use this scripture to justify unrighteousness in their life while continuing to work in the Kingdom of GOD. This cannot be. Again, people must be willing to *"dress the part,"* which is being righteous and holy.

13. **(Romans 11:28)** In this scripture, it references God's chosen people, the Jewish people. They never accepted Jesus Christ as their Savior, therefore, they never repented. But because GOD loves them and they are His people, He still blessed them and covered them. He never stopped even though they had rejected Him. However, even in Israel's rejection they still had callings and gifts because of God's

favor.

14. **(Acts 9: 1-19)** Many receive the callings and gifts in their unsaved lives. These people may be very gifted or know they have been called to preach, but they have never repented of their sins. There are people who sing in the choir, teach Sunday school, and are ushers on the usher board, but they have never repented. They have callings and gifts with no repentance. These can be very traditional or religious people. These are law minded people like the Jewish people.

15. **(Romans 11:29)** This scripture states, *"The gifts and callings come without repentance."* This is usually used to represent someone who is practicing or operating in a gift or calling but are still continually active in a certain sin or unclean lifestyle. For example, this person may be the pastor of a large congregation and yet is heavily involved in adultery. They may be a powerful evangelist, leading people to get healed and delivered but they themselves are still involved in homosexuality.

16. GOD is no respecter of persons. Sin blocks the calling of GOD no matter what one's position is in the body of Christ. However, the gift will still manifest because the gift itself has its own anointing.

17. **(Romans 11:31-32)** Many times the gift is in full operation, yet the lifestyle does not match. The person is still coming up short in so many areas, but the power of the call can be very strong. This can be dangerous if the person will not repent. It is only through the mercy of GOD that this person is not destroyed.

18. **(John 13: 21-30)** The two other areas when a calling is working without repentance are when a person has iniquity in their heart, or they are being used by Satan. We will discuss both briefly below.

19. A person with iniquity in their heart is a person whose motives for doing the work are totally wrong. They are using the gift for their own gain. They are using the gift to become popular or to fleece the people. The word fleece means they actually use the gift to persuade people to give them certain things. I knew a man who only wanted the power of the Holy Ghost to get rich. There are people who only want to be pastors or other ministry "titles" to be recognized or be blessed financially.

20. Ministry has become popular with the world and, unfortunately, it has become about status, titles, and positions instead of about GOD and fulfilling His Will and Purpose. Your calling must be to glorify GOD only. You must check your ***motives*** at all times

when it comes to your calling.

21. Then there are times when a person's calling is used by Satan. There are many people, preachers, teachers, pastor, prophets, and apostles totally under the control of Satan. They perform signs and wonders just like the true pastor or apostle, yet they have yielded their calling to the control of Satan.

22. This is why the scripture states, *"There will be many false prophets and apostles in the last day."* They will be workers of Satan. In these last days you must have a strong discerning spirit to be able to recognize the difference. Many will fall into the hands of Satan because this generation is extremely impressed by signs and wonders. This generation is very influenced by what something looks like on the outside. Because the church compares itself so much to the world, we are always looking for something that is as much compatible to the world as possible. Many people of today will be used by Satan because of their own personal desires. Judas was used by Satan against GOD because of the desires of his heart.

Lesson 6
Calling
(Continued)

1. **(I Corinthians 7:20-24)** It is important that every man comes to a place where he learns to abide or be comfortable in his own calling. Each person has been called to do a certain purpose. Once you understand your purpose and calling, that should be your focus. Your calling is where your favor and anointing are. We will deal with this in more detail when we talk about the anointing. Many times when people do not appreciate their calling, they attempt to walk in someone else's calling. They will not be effective because they are not favored or anointed in that calling.

2. **(Acts: 1-7)** Peter knew to stay in his specific calling. He was not anointed in the administrative, day-to-day operations of the church. Peter said, "Find me seven good men full of the Holy Spirit who can do that job." Peter's job was evangelism and he remained there without confusion.

3. You must remain faithful in each level of your calling until GOD makes a shift in your life. Your calling is only effective when you are truly faithful.

4. **(2 Peter 1:10)** It is important that you make your calling sure. The word *"sure"* in Greek means *"stable, firm, or steadfast."*

5. You cannot be unstable in your calling. You must have balance and consistency in your calling. When you are unstable in your calling, you will become unfruitful. You may have the gift; however, productivity will be lacking because of the lack of faithfulness.

6. If you lose focus in your calling, the body will lose trust in you and your ability in the calling. When you remain stable and focused, you will be productive continuously.

7. **(2 Thessalonians 1:11)** God's greatest desire is to count every saint worthy in His calling for their lives. To be counted worthy means that GOD can trust you. It means He can release His power to you, and He can be glorified. GOD will not share His glory with anyone. Therefore, to be counted worthy means that anyone who is called will always recognize that the power comes from Almighty GOD.

8. **(Matthew 22:14)** The scriptures states, "Many are called but few are chosen." What is it to be chosen? Chosen means "to be available."

9. Even though there are many who will be called to make it to heaven and many who will be called to work in the Kingdom, only a few will be available to meet the requirements.

10. **(Ephesians 5:27)** Jesus is coming back for a church without a spot or wrinkle. How many will come up to par? How many will allow themselves to be cleansed and thoroughly washed until they are spotless and without wrinkle?

11. Jesus called many to follow him, but few chose to meet the requirements necessary to be a follower or a disciple. Many walked away when Jesus asked, *"Who will eat my body and drink my blood?"*

12. There are so many in the body of Christ who are called to do so many different things. GOD had no respect of person, but only a few will meet the requirements to be a true prophet or a true apostle.

13. Moses was called and chosen because he was available totally to GOD. Moses led millions of people out of Egypt because he met the requirements to be that kind of leader.

14. There are three types of qualifications that everyone must meet to be chosen. They are: (1) life qualifications; (2) work qualifications, and (3) time qualifications. Life qualifications are your day-to-day walk for life requirements in the Kingdom. It is your integrity and character. It is how you handle your family and your money. Work qualifications are when you must properly learn how to handle the gift or the calling. You must be willing to be trained in each position. Time qualification is the amount of time that you must have to give to each assignment given to you as an individual in the Kingdom. For example, if you are a mother, you will not be time qualified to travel all over the world like a single person would be.

15. Jesus spent three years training the disciples on how to be life qualified and work qualified. I believe Jesus chose them according to time qualifications at that time. He knew that these men had to be extremely focused on him for three straight years with as few distractions as possible. They had to watch Jesus be a prophet, teacher, pastor, apostle, and evangelist. They watched him operate in all the revelation gifts and motive gifts. They also watched Jesus' time management skills.

16. They watched Jesus love His Father more than anything else and love His brother as Himself. They saw Jesus always qualify himself. He was always willing to be available to requirements.

17. GOD has no respect of persons. Therefore, everyone can have the opportunities, but not all will make themselves available or allow themselves to be qualified.

18. When Jacob and Esau were born, they both had the same opportunities. Esau refused to make himself available to Godly requirements. Jacob ended up receiving the blessings.

19. You must make yourself available to every requirement for your calling to be completed in the Kingdom. There are many avenues available to those who are willing to meet the requirements. There is much favor and opportunity for those meeting the requirements. You may ask yourself, *"Am I called or am I to be chosen?"*

Lesson 7
Sanctification - Jeremiah 1:5

1. **(Jeremiah 1:5)** Now we will deal with the word sanctified. The word sanctified means *"to be set apart."* There are two types of sanctification. Sanctified in life and sanctified in works.

2. Every believer should become a saint or one that is truly set apart from the world. People should see our light shining totally above sin. They should recognize we have nothing in common with the world.

3. **(Jeremiah 1:5)** There is one who is sanctified for works. When GOD chooses you for a specific calling, He sets you apart in your mother's womb as He did with Jeremiah. Many wonder why their lives seem to follow a certain path, or they may wonder why they are different from their other siblings. It is because that person has been set apart.

4. GOD knew Jeremiah in his mother's womb, and He sanctified him. He set Jeremiah apart in his mother's womb. He started directing Jeremiah's life from the very beginning.

5. **(Exodus 2:1-9)** Moses was sanctified by GOD in the beginning of his life. Pharaoh wanted all of the male children under the age of two to die when they were born, but GOD saved Moses' life. Not only that, but He placed Moses in the hand of the most important family in Egypt.

6. From birth Moses was chosen to be the Deliverer. When people have been chosen from birth for a specific assignment, their hearts are being conditioned from birth to be receptive.

7. **(I Peter 3:15)** When you are sanctified, it has already been pronounced from GOD that you are set apart for that special calling. Your life will follow a certain path to get to that calling. No matter what, when you have been specifically sanctified for a calling, you will not be able to do anything about the route you are on.

8. This is quite different from someone just speaking over a child what they would like for them to become. Yes, we should speak positive things over our lives and our children, but you cannot sanctify them.

9. **(Genesis 25:28)** Even though Esau was Isaac's favorite, and he was the older twin, he still could not sanctify him. GOD had already chosen Jacob for the position. GOD already knew that Jacob's heart could be conditioned for what needed to be done.

10. **(Genesis 16:15-16)** When Abraham had Ishmael, he was the joy of his father's life because he had no natural son of his own with Sarah. But Ishmael still was not the chosen or sanctified one. Isaac was the one that GOD had already conditioned to be The One. He was the one that God's bloodline would travel through.

11. **(Genesis 41:1-36)** GOD called Joseph to be sanctified. He set Joseph apart by allowing him to go to prison. Many people in prison are sanctified, GOD has separated them, and He is preparing them for a certain season.

12. We are not condoning anyone's wrongdoing. However, there are those that GOD knew would follow a certain path and end up in a set apart place. There are those who are really innocent, but they are in that place because they are being groomed and conditioned for the calling.

13. **(Genesis 37: 1-11)** We will use Joseph again as an example. He was hated by his brothers because he was his father's favorite. He was always different from his brothers. He was kept separated from them because he was sanctified. He did no wrong yet he ended up in prison.

14. There may be one sibling who is simply different from everyone else. They are hated by the others. The other siblings may be jealous and envious. Many times, that hated sibling will not understand what is going on because they are sanctified. That specific child has been chosen to be different.
15. When you are sanctified, you will never fit into the crowd. You are chosen to be different, separated and set apart. Your life has been selected for a specific purpose. Moses did not fit in Pharaoh's house. He was chosen as a child to be different, to be set apart. He had a specific calling on his life. He killed an Egyptian which caused him to rebel totally against the plan of Pharaoh. Still, he was set apart.

16. GOD is not fair; He is just. He knows the heart of every individual in creation. He knows whose heart can be conditioned for the call. Even though GOD allowed the people to choose Saul, He had already sanctified David for the position. (Remember our Associate class study of God's Perfect Will versus His Permissive Will.)

17. GOD knew that Saul would fall because his heart could not be conditioned for the position. Again, GOD is a just GOD. He looks at the heart, not the outer man. GOD chooses based on what is on the inside, not the outside. Israel chose Saul as their king because of his looks and military prowess, but GOD knew his heart.

18. **(Jeremiah 1:5)** Again, that is why GOD said to Jeremiah, "I knew you when you were in your mother's womb." He knew what was in Jeremiah's heart. He was already aware of the condition of Jeremiah's heart. He knew his heart would follow him and be submissive to Him. Jeremiah's heart was sold out to GOD.

19. **(Genesis 48:9-22)** When Joseph brought his sons, Manasseh, and Ephraim, to Jacob, his father, to be blessed, Jacob put his right hand on the second son. Joseph became offended because he knew the first son, or the older son should get the birthright. GOD then revealed to Jacob the hearts of his sons.

20. GOD had sanctified the second son for a specific purpose. GOD knew his heart. You are sanctified spiritually because you allow your heart to change. You are sanctified for works because of your heart. You have been specially selected for a certain calling. GOD knows it must be done, so He sanctifies different people from inception to get the job done.

Lesson 8
Ordained - Jeremiah 1:5

1. **(Jeremiah 1:5)** What does it mean to be ordained? Many times, when we hear that someone has been ordained, we assume that person has been given a ministerial license with privileges. Ordination allows a person to administer communion, perform weddings, and funerals. It does allow much freedom.

2. But what does it really mean when one is ordained? When GOD said to Jeremiah, *"I ordained thee a prophet unto the nations."* What was He really saying? The word ordained means *"to be charged to."* We should strive to reach the level where Jeremiah was when GOD said, "I charge thee a prophet unto the nations."

3. To be charged to do something means three things: 1) GOD excels you into the calling, 2) gives you the authority in the calling, and 3) makes you responsible. There are natural ordinations and spiritual ordinations. Ordination is a dangerous tool to bestow on a person if they are not ready.

4. First, when a person is ordained, they are activated to the call to be somewhat on their own. They are free to minister their calling without supervision. It is like saying someone is ready to fly a 747 plane with 200 passengers on it without the pilot who has 30 years of experience in the cockpit with them.

5. No one should be ordained as a layman or minister until they are truly ready to be released on their own. Zeal and excitement do not make you ready. Years of being in church do not make you ready. Saying you are ready does not make you ready.

6. **(John 20:21)** Jesus knew when to ordain or activate His disciples. Jesus would allow His disciples to minister while He was there with them, but they were always protected or under His covering. He knew they were not ready at certain times to be released on their own.

7. Leaders and pastors must know when saints or ministers are not ready to be released on their own. Sometimes you must be overprotective with ministers to keep them in order. However, you cannot do anything with those who choose to grow up too fast or rebel against the process. It is like having a natural child who just chooses to grow up too fast.

8. When you are ordained, it means that GOD gives you the authority to work. Remember, the word *"authority"* means jurisdiction. When you are ordained, your jurisdiction is expanded. You are no longer a local police officer or a county sheriff, you are a state trooper. Ordination is dangerous if you are not ready for authority.

9. Even though your jurisdiction has expanded, it does not mean you are now free to run wild. Even though you are ordained, you should still be covered, subject to authority, and accountable to others. Many people say that as long as they are subject to GOD that is enough. But I believe that all should have some earthly accountability. Many people get in serious trouble because they abuse their freedom. They abuse their authority.

10. The third thing you must understand is that you are now responsible for the calling. When a child is underage, their mistakes can be charged to their parents, but once that child becomes of age, he or she is subject to the law like any adult.

11. **(Matthew 17: 14-21)** When the disciples could not cast out a devil, Jesus was there to back them up. When the man came to Jesus and complained about the disciples, Jesus explained that this comes by fasting and praying. Jesus made the correction and finished the job. Jesus did this because the disciples were not yet ordained. They were not held responsible for that area of ministry.

12. When you are ordained, you are charged with great responsibilities. It is not just about carrying the title and position; it is about the responsibilities. When you do not act responsively, you get into serious trouble in the natural law and spiritual law.

13. When ministers conduct marriages and funerals, it is more than just quoting some scriptures or committing a body to the ground. Ordination is also the responsibility that goes along with the action.

14. There was once a show about a young lady who was on a psychiatric drug. A friend of hers, a rock star, convinced her not to take her medicines. When she stopped taking her medicine, she killed someone. Though the friend persuaded her, he was not convicted of any crime because he was only a lay person. If a doctor had given her that same advice he would have been imprisoned because he is considered a licensed professional with knowledge, power, and position.

15. When you are ordained, your responsibility level is greater. Everything you do and words you give are examined under spiritual and natural laws. Your prophetic

ministry is now measured against spiritual and natural laws.

16. There was a prophetess that I knew who had been ministering and prophesying to a young lady. The young lady and her husband sued the Prophetess for the word she spoke. Through her prophecy, the husband felt the prophetess had forced the young lady to do a lot of unnecessary things. They did not believe the spoken prophecy.

17. We have a spiritual responsibility to live up to the part. Every time we take on more responsibilities, we also take on spiritual responsibilities.

18. As an ordained man or woman of GOD, we wear a spiritual responsibility to be a first partaker of the Word. We cannot use that authority to justify wrongdoing. We are required to live up to spiritual standards.

19. **(I Timothy 3:1-6)** This scripture talks about two, major ordained positions: (1) the Bishop/ Pastor and (2) the deacon. The Word stresses the great spiritual qualifications it takes to walk in these positions. You cannot bypass the Word.

20. We cannot justify wrong by saying, *"I am just human."* That is why the leader must really take their time before ordaining deacons and pastors so quickly. They must be careful not to place responsibilities on them that they cannot handle.

21. Many people take on charges that they cannot keep. They take on authority that they cannot walk in. Leaders must not be afraid to say no to people who they know may not be qualified.

22. Do not be afraid to take your time. Leaders should encourage ministers to take their time while their natural and spiritual lives are developing.

Lesson 9
Anointing
I Samuel 26:9; Isaiah 61:1; Genesis 37:1-12

1. **(I Samuel 26:9)** Now we will deal with the words anointed and assigned. What does it mean to be *"anointed?"* To be anointed means, *"To be empowered to do."* The anointing comes from and through the Holy Ghost/Spirit.

2. **(Isaiah 61:1)** Once GOD has set you apart for any work and He calls you, He will anoint you. GOD will empower or anoint you to be kept performing the work. The anointing is ***in you***, ***with you***, and ***upon you***.

3. **(Luke 24:49, John 20:21)** The first anointing we will talk about is the "keeping anointing." When Jesus prepared to leave the disciples, He knew they had to be kept until they were filled with the anointing. When Jesus released the Holy Ghost on them, He empowered them to be kept until they could be filled with power. Once you accept Jesus Christ, he anoints you to be kept. Many times, you will hear people say *"You can be kept if you want to be kept."* In order to be kept, you must have the anointing.

4. When a person first gets saved, they receive the anointing to be kept. Jesus was with the disciples for three years and the eleven that wanted to be kept were kept by the anointing that was on Jesus' life.

5. **(Galatians 5:24-25)** Being filled with the Holy Ghost is the living anointing not, the working anointing. Many times, young converts attempt to work too fast and end up defeated. That was not anointing, that was zeal. The filling of the Holy Ghost is the anointing to encounter and overpower the enemy daily.

6. **(Galatians 5:16)** When you walk in the Spirit, you are walking in the anointing in the power of GOD to overcome the flesh. When you walk in the Spirit, you are walking in the anointing of His character and integrity. All you have to do is yield to that power.

7. **(Acts 9:17-19)** When GOD dealt with Paul on the road of Damascus, He anointed Paul in two areas at that time. He anointed Paul to be kept and He anointed him to live amongst the Galatians. Paul had spent 3 years in the Presence of GOD while He anointed Paul to work.

8. There comes a time when GOD will anoint you to work. There are 3 aspects of the working anointing: a) the anointing is *on the gift* b) the anointing is *in you*; and c) the anointing *will be upon you.*

9. All the gifts come from the Trinity, or GOD, Jesus, and the Holy Spirit. The gifts are anointed. Every gift has power already attached to it. It is most effective in a clean and ready vessel.

10. **(Genesis 37:1-12)** Your gift will make room for you because it is anointed. The gift can manifest without your approval because it is anointed. A novice can manifest a gift, because of the power of the gift itself. It is not based on the person.

11. A novice with a gift or a new convert must be kept under control when a gift manifests itself because the novice does not have the maturity to handle the anointed gift. They can abuse it, or they can be abused by others. It is like putting a loaded shotgun in a 6-year old's hand. They cannot handle all that power.

12. **(Mark 16:17)** The anointing is within us. This anointing is manifested through faith in what GOD has anointed you to do. That is why the scripture states, "These signs shall follow them that believe..."

13. The internal working anointing is manifested through faith. If you can believe in the power, the power will manifest.

14. **(Acts 28:1-7)** When the viper bit Paul on his hand, he was able to shake it off because of the power of the anointing in Paul. Paul believed no deadly thing would hurt him because of his faith in Jesus. His faith manifested working power.

15. The anointing can be manifested through faith. The anointing can work through faith. There are many who manifest power because of their faith.

16. **(Acts 1:8)** When the anointing is upon you, power is manifested whether you have the faith to believe or not. The Bible states that "you shall be witnesses." The word "witness" means "manifest or show evidence of the power." Many times, in services when the atmosphere has been properly set, God's anointing will be upon individuals in the very atmosphere.

17. The anointing will come upon an individual when they are pure and holy and when they have been fasting and praying. When you fast and pray, you deny the flesh and prepare yourself to become the perfect place for the Spirit.

18. When the anointing comes upon a person who possesses a certain gift to work, they can work at their fullest potential because of the anointing. Without the anointing, you are working from your own will.

19. The anointing will come upon you based on the timing of your gift. For example, you may have been called to be an apostle at the age of 26, but the apostle's anointing may not be manifested in you until you are 40. The manifestation of the anointing comes in levels.

20. David was anointed to be king at an incredibly young age, but the full manifestation did not come until almost 20 years later. That is why you meet people who were first called minister, then pastor or evangelist, then a prophet because their anointing is manifesting in levels.

21. It is a dangerous thing to attempt to operate in a level that your anointing has not reached. When this happens, you struggle unnecessarily. You will be operating on your own strength. You must stay in each level of your anointing to be effective.

22. You can lose your anointing. You may not lose your position, but you can lose your anointing. Many lose their anointing because of sin, disobedience, and totally being out of the Will of GOD.

23. Saul lost his anointing because of being out of the Will of GOD. He refused to obey the warnings of GOD, so he lost his anointing to David.

24. Your calling does not protect your anointing. Your title does not protect your anointing. Only a righteous, holy, and obedient life will protect your anointing. Many women and men today have lost their anointing because of their lifestyles.

25. Once GOD has truly anointed you for the calling, you can be assigned. You can now be placed in that specific location to go to work. You are now ready for your "duty station."

26. When you join the military, you go through 3 major processes: enlisting, basic training, and your specific schooling. Then you are allowed go to your duty station. You do not enlist and then go straight to your assignment. You must go through the process in the proper order first.

27. You must first enlist. For Christians, that's salvation. You must pass the physical test and then you are sent off to basic training.

28. Basic training is where you learn all the guidelines in the military. You learn the rules. You learn how to develop character and the right attitude about military life. You must have respect and honor for the military. It is the same way in your spiritual life. After you enlist, you must go through spiritual basic training. You must learn the fruit of the Spirit, how to give honor, and how to respect God's order.

29. Next the military sends you to a specific training school called your duty station. There you will learn all about your specific job and be trained in the details. The length of time you stay in basic school training is determined by the complexity of the job you will be assigned. Once your specific training is complete and you have passed all of the tests, you are ready for your next duty station. You are now ready for your assignment.

30. Your spiritual assignment is the same. You must go through the training. You must learn the craft well. Once you have learned it well and passed the tests, you are ready for your duty station. You are ready for your assignment. It does not mean that you know everything, but GOD has determined that you are ready for the next level.

31. You must meet the qualifications before you get the assignment. Sometimes, you may have to repeat some things until you can get it right. GOD is faithful. He will keep working on you until you are ready for the assignment. It is not enough to get the assignment. You must be ready for it.

Lesson 10
Transfiguration
Matthew 17:1-2; Genesis 5:24

1. **(Matthew 17:1-2)** The last point we will bring out is transfiguration. What does mean to be transfigured? To be transfigured in Greek means *"to be changed."*

2. There are 2 types of transfigurations that should go on in an individual's life. The **first transfiguration** is to become who GOD originally created man to be: immortal, innocent or perfect. This is when man will be transfigured into the heavenly body.

3. **(2 Corinthians 5:8)** To be absent from the body is to be present with the Lord. When Jesus comes back to rapture the Church, the Church will become immortal. We will be transfigured back to or into who GOD created us to be. Every man should desire to be in this place.

4. Paul always talked about leaving and being transfigured because he wanted to be in the presence of GOD. It is the greatest thing man could do.

5. **(Genesis 5:24)** Enoch was transfigured right into heaven. He never had to die. He just walked right into heaven and was transfigured into immortality.

6. **(2 King 2:1-12)** Elijah had that same opportunity. He was caught up into the presence of GOD and never saw physical death.

7. The Church will be like Enoch and Elijah. We will be transfigured out of this world during the Rapture. We will become immortal instantly. We will be transfigured in the air. This will be our *heavenly transfiguration*.

8. In the **second transfiguration**, *earthly transfiguration*, our earthly body becomes who GOD created us to be. Transfiguration is the last step. It is where you truly become a part of the family of GOD.

9. People are born into this world everyday and most people will never see their earthly transfiguration because they will never recognize or understand their purpose.

10. Moses was eighty years old when he was finally transfigured into his purpose. Moses was chosen as a baby to be the Deliverer of the children of Israel. Again, he

was transfigured, at the age of 80.

11. **(Matthew 17:1-12)** When Jesus went on the Mountain of Transfiguration, he was joined by those three disciples who He had purposed to be with Him. He was God's Almighty Son and there was no one like Him.

12. **(Genesis 40: 5-23)** When Joseph interpreted the king's dream, he was transfigured into his purpose. He became second in command to Pharaoh. He was called at 17. He was processed for 13 years and then he was transfigured.

13. The ultimate goal is to get each person to a place of transfiguration. Every person must be brought to a place of purpose. Once you come into your earthly transfiguration, you truly have found your purpose and destiny. You are now in the place of total favor.

14. **(Genesis 22:1-18)** When Abraham came off of that mountain, he was fully transfigured. He had become the man GOD had purposed him to be. He was that man of faith. There was no going back for Abraham at this time.

15. Many people will never get to that place of transfiguration because they will never finish the process. They will attempt shortcuts or try to be something or someone they are not called to be.

16. No matter how strong our will or desires are, you cannot be transfigured into someone GOD never called you to be. You must be who GOD purposed you to be. Sometimes this changes your natural job and your spiritual job.

17. Transfiguration will cost you greatly. It is not an overnight success plan. It may take years to get to that place of transfiguration.

18. When you have been transfigured, there is no going back. You have truly reached your spiritual and earthly place of success. From saved to transfiguration equals the total package of Salvation. When you reach Salvation, you have reached the ultimate life and the work of GOD.

Works Cited

Brand, C. O., Draper, C. W., & England, A. W. (2003). *Holman illustrated Bible dictionary*. Nashville, Tenn.: Holman Bible Publishers.

Rapids, M. (2002). *Holy Bible: King James Version.* Grand Rapids, Mich.: Zondervan.

Strong, J., Kohlenberger, J. R., & Swanson, J. A. (2001). *The strongest Strong's exhaustive concordance of the Bible* (Larger print Ed.). Grand Rapids, Mich.: Zondervan.

Cerullo, Morris, *"The Prophecy Bible."*

Process of Salvation
Workbook

Lesson 1

1. What is salvation?

2. To receive salvation what must one do?

3. When receiving salvation, one must understand ________________.

4. Without salvation, you are only covered _________________.

5. As far as receiving salvation, what are the two things you can never do?

Lesson 2

6. What does it mean to be converted?

7. The conversion process is where what begins?

8. Conversion is when you truly begin to change from _____________________.

9. What is mental conversion?

10. A converted person will understand what it is to go where?

Lesson 3

11. What does the word transform mean?

12. The character of Jesus is reflected in _______________.

13. Transformation is a true saving and _______________________.

14. Once Adam and Eve sold out to Satan, what happened?

15. Transformation is the making of what two things?

Lesson 4

16. What does the word transition mean? It is also from ____________________.

17. Transitions increase your________ because you are always accepting_______.

18. GOD may have called you to be a prophet or be a great apostle, but your starting point may be ___________________.

19. Your transitions will increase what two things?

20. Each level of transition continues to prove____________.

Lesson 5

21. What does the word called mean?

22. What is a Calling and what are the two types of calling?

23. Your calling is not according to__________. Your calling is always according to________________________.

24. Many people never even step into their calling because________________.

25. What blocks the calling of GOD?

Lesson 6

26. When you are unstable in your calling, what will you become?

27. God's greatest desire is to count every saint what?

28. What are the three types of qualifications that everyone must meet to be chosen?

29. What are work qualifications?

30. What is time qualification?

Lesson 7

31. What are the two types of sanctification?

32. When people have been chosen from birth for a specific assignment, their _______.

33. GOD set Joseph apart by allowing him to________.

34. When you are sanctified, you will never fit__________.

35. GOD is not_____________________; He is ________________.

Lesson 8

36. What does the word ordained mean?

37. To be charged to do something means what three things?

38. No one should be ordained as a layman or minister until ______.

39. Sometimes you must be overprotective with ministers to _________.

40. Ordination is also the responsibility that goes along_____________.

Lesson 9

41. What does to be anointed mean?

42. What type of anointing does a person need when they first get saved?

43. When you are filled with the Holy Ghost that is _______________.

44. When you walk in the Spirit, you are___________.

45. What are 3 aspects of the working anointing?

Lesson 10

46. The first transfiguration is to become who _________________.

47. When Joseph interpreted the king's dream, he was transfigured into _________.

48. Many people will never get to that place of transfiguration because they will __________.

49. No matter how strong our will or desires are, you cannot be transfigured into someone _______________________.

50. When you have been transfigured, there is _______________________. You have truly reached your _________________. From saved to transfiguration equals the ______________________.

Process of Salvation
Assignments

All homework, practical, and scripture information, must be on a separate sheet of paper. If it is written on this paper, there is a 50% deduction from your grade automatically.) Homework, practical, and Bible study observation must be a paragraph long or more).

Homework

Explain an area where your works have nothing to do with your calling?

Practical

You have a young man who now thinks he knows his calling; how would you keep him under control?

100 Word Essay

Please try and type all essays if possible. If you cannot type your essay, please make sure your teacher is aware of it. Your essay and Bible study lessons must be turned in with all of your homework. Your essay must be 100 words. Please be aware that your homework and essays count 20% each of your total of grades.

Write a 100-word paper on when you know that you are in your anointed place. Make sure that you use all three areas of the anointing in your paper.

Name ______________
Site ________________
Instructor ____________
Date ________________

Process of Salvation
Test
(Each Question is Worth 10 Points)

1. Explain “salvation”.

2. Explain “conversion”.

3. Explain “transformation”.

4. Explain “transition”.

5. Explain what is to be “ordained”.

6. Explained what is to be “called”.

7. Explain the three types of anointings.

8. Explain “sanctification”.

9. Explain “transfiguration”.

10. Explain how your calling is not according to your work or works.

CONCISE

STUDIES

Make Up of the Church I

*Accredited by National Bible College Association

CONCISE STUDIES
(Make Up of the Church 1)
Table of Contents

Lesson 1
The Sinner - Luke 7:36-50

1. The first person we will deal with in the church is the sinner.

2. Who or what is a sinner? A sinner is:
    a. One who practices sin.
    b. One who has not accepted Christ yet.
    c. One who still belongs to the devil.

3. Even though the sinner may not appear to be practicing sin, if he/she has NOT accepted Christ, he/she is still a sinner.

4. **(Luke 7:41-50)** "Then Jesus told him this story: "A man loaned money to two people—500 pieces of silver to one and 50 pieces to the other. [42] But neither of them could repay him, so he kindly forgave them both, canceling their debts. Who do you suppose loved him more after that?"[43] Simon answered, "I suppose the one for whom he canceled the larger debt. That's right," Jesus said. [44] Then he turned to the woman and said to Simon, "Look at this woman kneeling here. When I entered your home, you didn't offer me water to wash the dust from my feet, but she has washed them with her tears and wiped them with her hair. [45] You didn't greet me with a kiss, but from the time I first came in, she has not stopped kissing my feet. [46] You neglected the courtesy of olive oil to anoint my head, but she has anointed my feet with rare perfume. [47] "I tell you, her sins—and they are many—have been forgiven, so she has shown me much love. But a person who is forgiven little shows only little love." [48] Then Jesus said to the woman, "Your sins are forgiven."

5. The ultimate goal of Christ concerning the sinner is to:
    a. Forgive their sins.
    b. To give them salvation through their faith.
    c. To give them a life of freedom.

6. The purpose of the Word in the church is to:
    a. Convict them of their sins.
    b. Cause them to be drawn into the kingdom.
    c. Change the condition of their heart and renew their minds.

7. The Word is never preached to a sinner to make them feel good about themselves or their lifestyles.

8. **(Matthew 9:12-13NLT)** "When Jesus heard this, he said, "Healthy people don't need a doctor—sick people do." [13] Then he added, "Now go and learn the meaning of this Scripture: 'I want you to show mercy, not offer sacrifices. "For I have come to call not those who think they are righteous, but those who know they are sinners."

9. Jesus' main purpose for coming to Earth was not for the righteous, but to call the sinner to repentance.

10. Many sinners come to the church out of:
    a. Habit.
    b. Religion.
    c. Tradition.

11. That is why the Word must be preached from the unction, or direction of the Holy Spirit, so that it will affect the sinner.

12. **(Romans 5:8 NLT)** "But GOD showed His Great Love for us by sending Christ to die for us while we were still sinners."

13. We were all once sinners; therefore, we must understand the sinners who come to the church. We must embrace their situation, while helping them come out of a life of bondage.

14. Again, we must not judge the sinner because that was once us. However, we must believe in God's Power to draw the sinner to Him.

15. **(Luke 18:13-14 NLT)** "But the tax collector stood at a distance and dared not even lift his eyes to heaven as he prayed. Instead, he beat his chest in sorrow, saying, 'O GOD, be merciful to me, for I am a sinner.' [14] I tell you, this sinner, not the Pharisee, returned home justified before GOD. For those who exalt themselves will be humbled, and those who humble themselves will be exalted."

16. Satan's ultimate goal is to kill every sinner while they are still in sin. If he can kill a sinner, Satan has accomplished his ultimate goal: sending another person to hell.

17. Every sinner needs and receives God's mercy. They have a right to God's compassion and will receive that protection when they accept Christ into their heart.

18. Therefore, the compassion of GOD is needed. On the flip side, the sinner needs God's mercy, because GOD will not live among sin. Therefore, we need His compassion to filter through the mess that we have made.

19. Every sinner needs God's Grace. The sinner needs time to turn from a life of sin to a life of righteousness. Thank GOD for grace.

20. Every time a sinner comes to Church and leaves the same way he came in, he is gambling with his life. There is no guarantee that he will make it back to Church before Satan takes his life.

21. **(Galatians 2:21)** "I do not frustrate the grace of GOD: for if righteousness come by the law, then Christ is dead in vain."

22. Every sinner must be careful not to frustrate or abort the grace or time of GOD. They must not take advantage of the time that GOD has given them to receive His Son. Grace and mercy should not be played with.

23. **(Luke 15:7-10 NLT)** In the same way, there is more joy in heaven over one lost sinner who repents and returns to GOD than over ninety-nine others who are righteous and haven't strayed away! The Parable of the Lost Coin: [8] "Or suppose a woman has ten silver coins and loses one. Won't she light a lamp and sweep the entire house and search carefully until she finds it? [9] And when she finds it, she will call in her friends and neighbors and say, 'Rejoice with me because I have found my lost coin.' [10] In the same way, there is joy in the presence of God's angels when even one sinner repents."

24. A sinner giving his/her life to Christ is so important that the angels rejoice over any sinner who repents or comes into the Kingdom.

25. The angels praise GOD for a life that has been snatched out of the hands of Satan. They know that it is one less person that will spend eternity in hell.

26. The Church must rejoice whenever a sinner comes to Christ because God's greatest commission has been fulfilled.

Lesson 2
Saved - Romans 10:9

1. The next person we will talk about is the *"saved."*

2. **(Romans 10:9 NLT)** "If you confess with your mouth that Jesus is Lord and believe in your heart that GOD raised him from the dead, you will be saved." "The word saved means "to be rescued from or set free from."

3. The saved people in the Body of Christ are those who have been rescued from something or someone. They have been rescued from sin or situations in their life.

4. **(Romans 10:9)** When an individual goes through the process of salvation, they then begin the process of being rescued.

5. **(Romans 10:9)** Confessions are made unto salvation. When a person confesses their sins and faults to CHRIST, then they receive their freedom.

6. **(Romans 10:9)** The saved believe in CHRIST and they believe in the power of change. When saved people believe unto righteousness, they believe they are going to be different. They should also believe in the freedom they accepted through salvation. Freedom comes when you are rescued.

7. When people only grasp being saved, they believe in Jesus as Savior, but sometimes that is as far as it goes. Confession is made with the mouth, but the mind is not "rescued". It does not yet believe. Many people who get saved become repeat offenders. They keep coming back to be rescued again and again. (Romans 10: 9, 13) Both of these scriptures say, "They shall be saved". This means salvation is a continuous process. You are always getting saved or rescued from something in your life. When people don't truly understand being saved, they don't understand the power of their freedom.

8. **(Philippians 3:20 NLT)** "But we are citizens of heaven, where the Lord Jesus Christ lives. And we are eagerly waiting for him to return as our Savior."

9. Those who only know Jesus as Savior or rescuer, tend to only see Him as a rescuer. It is as though He is the lifeguard at a pool. They only notice Him when they are drowning.

10. Often people, who only have salvation, function on emotional experiences. They tend to lean heavily on their feelings. If they feel encouraged they remain saved. However, if they feel depressed or have a bad experience, they will suddenly need rescuing.

11. **(Romans 8:24NLT)** "We were given this hope when we were saved. (If we already have something, we don't need to hope* for it.)"

12. We are saved by hope. For salvation to be maintained properly, one must keep their expectations up at all times. But, if their expectations are emotional, he/ she will not be able to stay saved. Emotions will not sustain salvation.

13. **(Ephesians 2:8NLT)** "GOD saved you by His Grace when you believed. And you can't take credit for this; it is a gift from GOD."

14. We are saved through faith. For people to maintain salvation, their salvation or their faith cannot be just zeal. It cannot be a temporary excitement. Zeal alone is the reason why a lot of people who are saved have to be rescued over and over again.

15. The church is full of saved people. We do hope that people are getting saved at every opportunity possible. The Bible declares that angels rejoice for one soul getting saved or rescued from their old life in the world. We must hope that the soul knows JESUS CHRIST for more than just their Savior or their rescuer. HE wants to be so much more than just their rescuer.

16. Because of the cross, we now have the opportunity to be saved by His Grace. Salvation is the beginning process for everyone. No one can be rescued from sin without salvation.

Lesson 3
Unbeliever - Romans 3:3; John 10:38

1. The next person we will talk about in the Church is the *"unbeliever."*

2. What or who is the unbeliever? The unbeliever is that person who refuses to accept Biblical laws or principles that must be obeyed.

3. The unbeliever is a person who has gotten saved, confessed Christ, but still will not accept or practice certain Biblical laws or principles.

4. The unbeliever is a person who lacks:
   a. Faith.
   b. Trust.
   c. Obedience.

5. The Church is full of unbelievers. They come into the Church, but they turn a deaf ear to much of the Word.

6. Unbelievers refuse to believe the Word concerning certain areas such as tithing. They lack the faith to believe GOD for their every need. There are those who do not want to pay their tithes and offering. They justify it by giving and working in other areas because of their unbelief. They join the choir, usher board or give to a special cause to justify unbelief and disobedience to the Word.

7. **(Romans 3:3)** For what if some did not believe? shall their unbelief make the faith of GOD without effect?"

8. When a person is an unbeliever, they make the faith of GOD ineffective. They even make His life here on earth and His death in vain. Jesus worked and suffered on the cross that we might believe everything about Him, His Word and His works.

9. **(John 10:38)** "But if I do, though ye believe not me, believe the works: that ye may know, and believe, that the Father is in me, and I in him."

10. That is why He said in His Word, "Believe in Me for my works' sake." Many times in the church, miracles and blessings cannot come forth because of unbelievers. They

lack the ability to believe in the impossible. Because miracles and blessings are the works of Jesus, they must be believed in order to see their true manifestation.

11. **(John 20:25)** "The other disciples therefore said unto him, We have seen the Lord. But he said unto them, Except I shall see in His Hands the print of the nails and put my finger into the print of the nails, and thrust my hand into His side, I will not believe."

12. The unbeliever is one that operates on sight, not faith. They must first understand or see it before they accept it. That is why the unbeliever will be limited in faith, because they operate in the five senses (taste, touch, hearing, smelling and sight) mainly sight.

13. **(John 5:47)** "But if ye believe not His writings, how shall ye believe my words?" Even though the Word may say that GOD can do certain things, unbelievers cannot trust the fact that His Word said it, because they cannot see it.

14. **(John 6:36)** "But I said unto you, that ye also have seen me, and believe not." There are many unbelievers who do not TRUST the manifestation of GOD and still refuse to believe in His omnipotence. Because of their own belief, they refuse to accept certain things, no matter what.

15. **(John 10:38)** "But if I do, though ye believe not me, believe the works: that ye may know, and believe, that the Father is in me, and I in him." The unbeliever refuses to accept the true power of GOD. They cannot trust His ability to do what He said He can do.

16. **(Psalm 78:22)** "Because they believed not in GOD and trusted not in His salvation:" The people of Israel were considered unbelievers because they refused to accept who GOD was. Their disobedience to God's Word caused them to miss several blessings and miracles. They refused to accept Jesus (God's Son) and the power and knowledge He walked in. Jesus could do very few miracles among them because of their unbelief."

17. Again, it is exceedingly difficult for the unbeliever to obey God's Word or His Voice because they cannot comprehend how the results are going to be manifested.

18. Most unbelievers are:
    a. Traditional.
    b. Religious.

c. Legalist.
d. Stubborn to the Word.
e. Rebellious to the Word.

19. **(Exodus7:3)** "And I will harden Pharaoh's heart and multiply my signs and my wonders in the land of Egypt" A person who is an unbeliever has a hard heart or what we call a "Pharaoh's heart" concerning certain areas of the Word. Their heart finds it difficult to accept all of the truths of the Word of GOD.

20. Unbelievers place great limitations on themselves because of their unbelief. Their unbelief limits their spiritual growth and the ability to enjoy the full benefits of the Kingdom of GOD.

21. Many people who are unbelievers are what we call professional students; they just come to church and learn a lot of Word. However, they never graduate into or from anything. They are ever learning but they will never embrace truth.

22. You will see these same people ten years later and nothing has really changed. Again, they are just professional students. In church they know how to ask the right questions, they even know how to give the right answers, but they themselves are useless to the Kingdom because of their unbelief. Normally, they are very challenging people because of their negative attitudes and lack of faith toward the Word.

23. These people are like the Pharisees and Scribes. They are very smart, most of the time. They know the Word or the laws very well, but are of no value to the Kingdom because of their unbelief.

24. All you can do for an unbeliever is pray for them. However, as a leader you must be careful not to let that spirit of unbelief spread throughout the church.

25. It is a spirit that can be contagious if you don't have a praying church. Unbelief is the main spirit of the enemy that can stop all progress in every area of an individual's life, and the body of Christ.

26. When you recognize the spirit of unbelief in an individual, you may have to take them out of certain positions because of the damage that can be done through their unbelief. They will kill the increase of anything.

27. Unbelief is what we call a "*SILENT KILLER.*"

Lesson 4
Born Again - John 3:3

1. The next person we will talk about is the person who is born again.

2. **(John 3:3 NLT)** "I tell you the truth, unless you are born again, you cannot see the Kingdom of GOD." What does it mean to be born again? Who are those that are born again?

3. To be born again means to get GOD back or to receive God's Spirit back within your life. When Adam and Eve sinned, they lost the most precious thing they ever had; God's Presence inside of man. Their sin destroyed that personal relationship with GOD himself.

4. Many would say, "Isn't being saved the same as being born again?" Some people get saved because of a situation, even from sin, but they don't really allow GOD into their lives.

5. To truly embrace being born again, you must accept Him as Savior and Lord. GOD consists of three major roles or personages:
    a. Savior.
    b. Christ.
    c. Lord.

6. Again, Savior means to be rescued. *"Christ "means the anointed one with the ability to destroy every yoke (a yoke is that thing that one is entangled by) and "Lord" means in control of everything.*

7. When people only get saved, they embrace the rescuer, yet tend to be repeat offenders. To be born again they must get Christ and Lord. When people get born again, they embrace Christ's yoke destroying power. The enemy must totally let go. The born again will accept Him as Lord and they will begin to give Him total control over every area of their lives.

8. **(1 John 5:18)** "We know that whosoever is born of GOD sinneth not; but he that is begotten of GOD keepeth himself, and that wicked one toucheth him not."

9. When people are truly born again, they struggle with sin less and less because they have Christ in them, and the yokes are being destroyed. They truly understand that

He is Lord or in control of everything. As he is Lord in their lives, they are able to recognize that Satan has no more control of their lives unless they allow him to.

10. As a leader, you cannot see inside of their hearts, but it will eventually show in their actions if they are truly born again, especially in their level of commitment.

11. **(1 John 5:4)** "For whatsoever is born of GOD overcometh the world: and this is the victory that overcometh the world, even our faith."

12. Whosoever is born again has the power to overcome the world. They have the power to defeat everything concerning the flesh, if they will use the power within.

13. **(1 John 2:29)** "If ye know that he is righteous, ye know that every one that doeth righteousness is born of him." When a person is born again, righteousness becomes their focus, not just staying out of sin. Their day-to-day battle is not trying to stay out of sin, but their entire focus becomes walking right and most of all being in the perfect will of GOD.

14. Their desire is truly based on who is inside of them and that is Jesus Christ. They began to learn how to manifest the fruit of the Holy Spirit. You will see the character of Jesus Christ starting to come forth more and more. The born again will start to manifest more love, joy, and peace in their everyday lives.

15. When we are truly born again, we become anchored in Him because He is in our lives. Stability will be present. We will begin to get off of the spiritual roller coaster.

16. Leaders must recognize when people have only been saved and not truly born again. When you see people who cannot remain consistent in their walk, they are usually people who only got saved and are not born again.

17. When people truly are born again, they have a repentant heart. They really have turned from sin and turned toward a righteous life. Repentance means to turn and truly go the other way.

18. **(2 Corinthians 5:17)** "Therefore if any man be in Christ, he is a new creature: old things are passed away; behold, all things are become new." People who are born again embrace being a new creature. All you have to do is work on bringing the newness out of them.

19. Christ, the Anointed One, is in control. The yoke of bondage is so much easier to break because Christ has come into their heart.

20. As you look at yourself and people around you, you will be able to see through their actions and where they stand. You may have to deal with them based on being saved or born again.

21. Remember, you must be born again to be stable. It is in being born again that the Holy Spirit is given the right to take over.

22. **(John 3: 3-5)** "Jesus answered and said unto him, Verily, verily, I say unto thee, Except a man be born again, he cannot see the kingdom of GOD. [4] Nicodemus saith unto him, How can a man be born when he is old? can he enter the second time into his mother's womb, and be born? [5] Jesus answered, Verily, verily, I say unto thee, Except a man be born of water and of the Spirit, he cannot enter into the kingdom of GOD." This means that when you are born again, you are born of the Spirit.

23. Your spirit is renewed and taken over by the Holy Spirit. The water is an outward showing that you have received Christ.

Lesson 5 – The Believer

1. The fifth person we will talk about is the *"believer."*

2. Who or what is the believer? The believer is one that:
    a. Accepts the Word.
    b. Agrees with the Word.

3. **(John 2:22)** "When therefore he was risen from the dead, His disciples remembered that he had said this unto them; and they believed the scripture, and the word which Jesus had said."

4. The believer is one that has accepted Jesus Christ as their personal Savior. They have truly accepted Christ as Lord. They have been born again.

5. **(Proverbs 14:15)** "The simple believeth every word: but the prudent man looketh well to his going." The believer comes and hears the Word. He or she has no problem accepting the Word of GOD at face value.

6. **(Matthew 9:28)** "And when he was come into the house, the blind men came to him: and Jesus saith unto them, believe ye that I am able to do this?"

7. Believers position themselves for the miracles and the promises of GOD. The believer embraces the true work of the Kingdom. In many ways the believer is part of the starting place of Kingdom work because of their belief.

8. **(Mark 9:23)** "Jesus said unto him, If thou canst believe, all things are possible to him that believeth." Nothing is impossible for a true believer. The believer accepts and agrees with the written and the spoken Word of GOD. The believer is in the position for every opportunity possible for their individual lives and those around them.

9. **(Romans 4:11)** "And he received the sign of circumcision, a seal of the righteousness of the faith which he had yet being uncircumcised: that he might be the father of all them that believe, though they be not circumcised; that righteousness might be imputed unto them also:" GOD becomes the Father of those that believe. You truly belong to Him when you are a believer. He is the headship of the believer's life.

10. **(Psalm 23:1)** "The Lord is my shepherd; I shall not want." GOD becomes the true Chief Shepherd of the believer. He knows the believer's hopes and desires rest in Him.

11. **(Romans 9:33)** "As it is written, Behold, I lay in Sion a stumbling stone and rock of offence: and whosoever believeth on him shall not be ashamed."

12. The true believer has nothing to be ashamed of. They don't have to make excuses for their belief. The believer does not have to work in condemnation or guilt, for being a believer. The believer will have to believe some very strange things that the average person would not dare attempt to believe. Therefore, the world may attempt to make the believer feel guilty for their beliefs.

13. **(Hebrews 10:9)** Then said he, Lo, I come to do thy will, O GOD. He taketh away the first that he may establish the second." Believers, first of all, create an atmosphere for the saving of souls. If there were more true believers in the church, the unsaved could not just come and go without feeling the conviction of GOD. They would desire immediate change.

14. **(Acts 4:34)** "Neither was there any among them that lacked: for as many as were possessors of lands or houses sold them and brought the prices of the things that were sold."

15. When there are a multitude of believers, it represents unity. It creates a true working atmosphere for the Holy Spirit to move. That is why in certain types of services, multitudes of people get healed and delivered. People get out of wheelchairs because of the multitude of believers. Again, the believer has created an atmosphere for the work of the Kingdom of GOD.

16. **(1 Peter 2:6)** "Wherefore also it is contained in the scripture, Behold, I lay in Sion a chief corner stone, elect, precious: and he that believeth on him shall not be confounded."

17. No believer will be confounded, which means they will not be dishonored or disgraced. GOD will honor or uphold the believer. Every believer will be showed the honor of the power of GOD because of their belief. GOD honored many in the Bible because of their strong belief. He gave such reference to the woman with the issue of blood and the woman who was willing to accept the crumbs from the table because of their belief.

18. **(John 1:7)** "The same came for a witness, to bear witness of the Light that all men through him might believe." All believers should be the method for other people to believe. They should have the ability to increase other believers' confidence through their believing. The world should accept as true through the believer. People should be eager to follow the church because of belief. People followed Jesus not just because of miracles but because of His Belief in His Father.

19. **(Romans 10:14)** "How then shall they call on him in whom they have not believed? and how shall they believe in him of whom they have not heard? and how shall they hear without a preacher?"

20. The greatest believer should be the preacher. He/she should be the first partaker of the Word. The preacher is the presenter of the belief in the Word and all should believe through the preacher.

21. GOD chooses a preacher, not because of their talents and abilities, but because they should be a true believer.

22. The pulpit is full of preachers who are not truly believers. They preach a Word that they themselves don't believe. How can they convince others, when they themselves have not truthfully been convinced? Many miracles of GOD can't come forth in the church today because of the unbelieving preachers. They stand in fear and doubt yet holding the greatest tool to success in their hand: total belief on God's Holy Word.

23. **(1 Corinthians 7:12-14)** "But to the rest speak I, not the Lord: If any brother hath a wife that believeth not, and she be pleased to dwell with him, let him not put her away. [13] And the woman which hath an husband that believeth not, and if he be pleased to dwell with her, let her not leave him. [14] For the unbelieving husband is sanctified by the wife, and the unbelieving wife is sanctified by the husband: else were your children unclean; but now are they holy."

24. A believing spouse can draw an unbelieving spouse. Most spouses don't change because there is so much doubt in the so-called believing spouse. Therefore, they place a limit on GOD concerning their spouse's salvation. At times the believing spouse will act like the unbelieving spouse therefore, causing the spirit of rejection to be in the unbeliever. The so-called believing spouse will speak negative words out of their mouths totally contrary to the Word yet expecting the unbeliever to still want to come to Christ. That believing spouse has the power to change their home, even the very atmosphere of their home because of their belief.

25. **(John 10:38)** "But if I do, though ye believe not me, believe the works: that ye may know, and believe, that the Father is in me, and I in him". Every believer must believe in God's works. That is His ability and capability. To believe in God's ability means that you actually believe He can do what He said He can do. To believe in His capability means you believe He knows how to do it the right way. Because a believer believes in His abilities and capabilities, the believer trusts GOD. He allows the responsibility to be totally in the hands of GOD.

26. **(1 Timothy 4:12)** "Let no man despise thy youth; but be thou an example of the believers, in word, in conversation, in charity, in spirit, in faith, in purity." Again, a believer should be an example. They should be a sign of the acceptance and agreement to the Word of GOD. One of the greatest things you will see in a believer's life is peace. Again, because they believe and trust in GOD, they can just rest. Because Jesus was such a believer, in the midst of the storm on the boat he could just go to sleep.

27. However, some believers can believe but sometimes they have a difficult time acting out. The believer must move to the next level, which is faith, to be a true believer. They cannot just believe and refuse to act out what they believe.

28. Sometimes believing may be enough, but in many cases, there has to be some acting to see results.

29. Again, believing is that starting point. If you can become a believer you have crossed over a great hurdle in your spiritual life. Every time you can believe, you have made your journey as a believer a little less complicated.

Lesson 6
Christian - Acts 11:26

1. The next person we will talk about is the *"Christian."*

2. **(Acts 11:26)** "And when he had found him, he brought him unto Antioch. And it came to pass, that a whole year they assembled themselves with the church, and taught much people. And the disciples were called Christians first in Antioch." Even before the disciples became disciples, they were called Christians.

3. What are or who are Christians? The word Christian in the Greek means a follower of Christ or one who has chosen to be Christlike.

4. The church and the world are full of Christians. Christians are or should be beautiful people in the Lord.

5. They are people who are faithful to the life of Christ. Christians are very faithful to the likeness and order of Christ, but not necessarily the work of Christ.

6. The church may be full of Christians, but many have little work going on because they are not necessarily workers in the Kingdom.

7. Most Christians are faithful church members and pay tithes, but they lead their own lives. Many times, they carry no titles or positions in the church.

8. **(Matthew 5:6)** "Blessed are they which do hunger and thirst after righteousness: for they shall be filled." These are people who truly do represent Christ and win souls by their righteous lives, not necessarily works. Christians truly do live up to the part. They carry a righteous name in the community, on their jobs, and in their families.

9. **(Matthew 5:15)** "Neither do men light a candle, and put it under a bushel, but on a candlestick; and it giveth light unto all that are in the house." People see them for their lives and their light. They are drawn to them because of their lives, not necessarily anything they say. They are salt and light, they add flavor and create an atmosphere for people around them to want to be in. They manifest Jesus through their life style.

10. **(Galatians 5 :22-23)** "But the fruit of the Spirit is love, joy, peace, longsuffering, gentleness, goodness, faith, [23] meekness, temperance: against such there is no law."

Christians truly carry the characters of the fruit of the Spirit. They truly do have love, joy, peace, longsuffering, temperance, faith or gentleness, goodness, and meekness."

11. Every born-again believer should be a Christian. They should be Christlike. They should be followers of Christ.

12. Another name for a Christian is sheep. A sheep is led by the shepherd. They know the voice of their Shepherd. They listen to the Shepherd which is Jesus Christ Himself. They listen to the Shepherd because they always have a desire to be pleasing to the Shepherd.

13. **(Matthew 10:16)** "Behold, I send you forth as sheep in the midst of wolves: be ye therefore wise as serpents, and harmless as doves." When sheep are sent out among wolves, they must be wise and harmless. That is the same as the Christians. They must be aware of what is going on around them at all times. However, they must be harmless.

14. The word harmless means he/she must remain innocent at all times. He/She cannot allow himself/herself to get caught up in all of the things going on around him/her. He/She/ must stay focused. He/She will be tempted to fall into all kinds of things because he/she is a Christian. He/She is a target for the devil because he/she is a Christian. The Christian represents Christ; therefore, the devil hates him/her.

15. **(John 10:3-5)** "To him the porter openeth; and the sheep hear His voice: and he calleth His own sheep by name, and leadeth them out. [4] And when he putteth forth His own sheep, he goeth before them, and the sheep follow him: for they know His voice. [5] And a stranger will they not follow but will flee from him: for they know not the voice of strangers." Again, the Christian knows the voice of the Lord, just as the sheep knows the voice of the Shepherd. He is very aware of following the right thing because the Christian truly wants to imitate Christ.

16. The Christian will be challenged for his/her faith. He/she will be challenged for what he/she believes. But the Christian must stand strong. Just saying, *"I am Christian"* will never be enough. One truly must be a part.

17. **(1 Peter 4:16)** "Yet if any man suffer as a Christian, let him not be ashamed; but let him glorify GOD on this behalf." Also understand the Christian will suffer because of doing right. They will suffer for being like Christ. It is a wonderful thing to know you are only suffering because of being a Christian.

18. Many people have died because of being a Christian. There are those who have been put in jail, beaten, and burned because of being a Christian. Because the disciples were first seen as Christians, many were killed because of their Christianity. They were burned, stoned, and even hung because of being a Christian.

19. Many Christians in other countries do not have the freedom we have to go to church as often as we do. To pray and carry Bibles here in the United States is a blessing. What an honor it is to be a true Christian to be Christlike every day of your lives, never having to hide or feel guilty about it. Thank GOD for being a Christian.

20. Yes, we will suffer as Christians, but we also will be rewarded for being a Christian. Because the Christian lives a life of obedience, there are many blessings in store for the Christian. Christians not only have the fruit, they also have the Beatitudes. They know how to be merciful and compassionate. Therefore, they will be rewarded in that area.

21. As leaders, we must teach all to be Christians. Christians have a forgiving heart. They are people that could draw *MANY* to Christ just by their lifestyles. Again, Christians draw or attract others to Christ by their lifestyle, not by works.

Lesson 7
The Disciple - Matthew 5:1-2

1. The seventh person we will deal with is the *"disciple."*

2. Who or what is the disciple? The disciple is one that can be:
    a. Disciplined
    b. Taught
    c. A follower
    d. A keeper of the Word
    e. Subject to His will

3. **(Matthew 5:1-2)** "And seeing the multitudes, he went up into a mountain: and when he was set, His disciples came unto him: [2]and he opened His mouth, and taught them, saying,"

4. **(Matthew 10:24)** One of the first things a disciple has to be is teachable. They must be taught the principles of the Word of the GOD. A disciple is not above his master. A disciple always remains disciplined. Everyone who gets saved must remain a disciple because they must remain teachable at all times.

5. Many would say, "What is the difference between a Christian and a disciple because they seem to be so much alike?" ***The Christian is one being prepared to live the life. The disciple is one being prepared for the life and the work***. Disciples will end up carrying positions and doing great work. That is why the disciples went from being disciples to being apostles.

6. Apostles are ones that are sent out to work. Again, the Christian is one that is developed to live the life; the disciple is developed to live the life and discipline for life and the work. And then they will be able to move into their specific call. However, no matter what position you end up in you must stay in a trainable place. GOD is always trying to teach us through His Word, the Spirit, and others.

7. The church is full of people who cannot be disciples because they are not teachable. They are not trainable. Many traditional or religious people are not trainable or teachable for the work of the Kingdom. They have a one-track mind. They are very law oriented instead of Word oriented. Their focus seems to be more on a set of rules written by their doctrine than the Word.

8. Disciples must be followers. When Peter and the other disciples were chosen, immediately they left what they were doing and followed JESUS. Again, they were first Christians, but they were made disciples because they were trainable. Many who at first claim to be disciples could not remain because of not being able to be taught.

9. The word follow means to: "*imitate or be willing to obey the leader.*" A follower must be able to deny their own will and pick up the Will of Christ.

10. **(Matthew 8:21-22)** "And another of His disciples said unto him, Lord, suffer me first to go and bury my father. [22] But Jesus said unto him, Follow me; and let the dead bury their dead." When the disciple in this scripture wanted to go back and bury his father, Jesus had to make him aware of what was important first and that was following Him.

11. Even the death of his father was not more important than following Jesus. Jesus wasn't being insensitive, but He had to set immediate order in His life. Even his emotions could not overpower obedience. A disciple must embrace the discipline principles of the Kingdom of GOD. The discipline principles are not easy that is why so many people stop at Christianity.

12. **(Matthew 8:23)** "And when he was entered into a ship, His disciples followed him." Following Jesus is a total assignment of every disciple. It is not a choice; it is a command.

13. **(Matthew 11:1)** "And it came to pass, when Jesus had made an end of commanding His twelve disciples, he departed thence to teach and to preach in their cities". A disciple must be able to follow commands. That is why there are only a few disciples in the church. Others have a difficult time following leadership and the Word. They must come into disciple principles because they are being prepared for works.

14. **(Matthew 16:24)** "Then said Jesus unto His disciples, If any man will come after me, let him deny himself, and take up his cross, and follow me." Every disciple must be able to deny himself and pick up his individual cross. The cross is the denying of flesh, or your own will. The cross seems to be so difficult because it is denying self. It is denying what you have believed and been used to all of your life.

15. Again, to be a disciple, your own personal will must be surrendered. The Will of GOD must be the most important thing. Many could not deny themselves; therefore they could not follow Jesus.

16. Many people in the church cannot be disciples because they cannot deny their own wants or personal desires. Because we are such a worldly society, it is very difficult to denounce the natural things of the world and embrace the spiritual things of GOD. Because of so much of our success, we are determined to get what we can touch and see. So much success is based on where we live and what we do. It is very difficult to walk in a lifestyle of *"taking no thought."*

17. Jesus told His disciples to take no thought. They did not have to be concerned about how they were going to survive because He would take care of them. That is extremely difficult for those who must know where their survival is coming from.

18. Every disciple will have their own cross. Every disciple will have their own personal struggles. Things that you must carry, you must give up, or you must surrender.

19. Every disciple will have their own assignment or their own anointing with this assignment. But with the anointing, there will be a cross. There will be a struggle and a price to pay.

20. You are known as a disciple when you can embrace the Word. You will know that you are a disciple when you are teachable and are able to deny yourself and follow Christ. You are known as a disciple when you can pick up your cross and follow.

21. Being a disciple requires a process of discipline. Discipleship sets your life in true spiritual order or the order of GOD. You must be disciplined to be a disciple. You would hope that every church member's desire is to be a disciple. But that is not always true because of sacrifices that must be made.

22. Discipleship is a mindset. Because of its being a mindset, everybody will not surrender to that type of mind. It will take much reconditioning of the mind by the Word to truly accept discipleship.

23. Again, that is why Jesus started out with a multitude. However, he ended up with twelve disciples. Every one of them could not meet the standards because of personal mindset and heart.

24. It is the desire to have a church full of disciples. A church full of disciples will usually mean that church will produce laborers, who will be discussed in Lesson 10 of this module.

Lesson 8
The Saint

1. What is a saint? The word saint in Greek means *hagios,* which means to be consecrated and pure. It means to be set apart or separated because of a righteous and holy life.

2. A saint is one who is sanctified. It is that person who has truly separated themselves totally from the things of the world. He/she is separate for a righteous life and for the work of the Kingdom.

3. When Christ returns, He will return for a sanctified or holy church. He will return for a sanctified body. A people that is clean, pure, and holy.

4. **(2 Corinthians 6:17-18)** "Wherefore come out from among them, and be ye separate, saith the Lord, and touch not the unclean thing; and I will receive you, [18] and will be a Father unto you, and ye shall be my sons and daughters, saith the Lord Almighty."

5. The Word states for us to separate ourselves and come out from among anything that is unclean. The saint is one who will not entangle themselves anymore with anything that could come between them and their relationship with Jesus Christ.

6. **(Romans 1:7)** "To all that be in Rome, beloved of GOD, called to be saints: Grace to you and peace from GOD our Father, and the Lord Jesus Christ." We are called to be saints. The ultimate goal of the church is to bring every born-again believer to a place of being a saint, or one who is set apart totally for the kingdom of GOD.

7. A saint is one who is willing to be blameless and consecrated totally for the Father. It is one who is willing to stay pure. Again, GOD is coming back for a pure church. Therefore, everyone's ultimate goal should be to be a saint of GOD. Because you desire to be a saint, then your primary desire is to make it to heaven. Being a saint places you in the very forefront of your life.

8. **(1 Corinthians 6:2-3)** "Do ye not know that the saints shall judge the world? and if the world shall be judged by you, are ye unworthy to judge the smallest matters? [3] Know ye not that we shall judge angels?" Because of the purity of the saints, saints shall judge:
   a. The world
   b. The sinner
   c. Angels

9. **(Ephesians 4:11-12)** "And He gave some, apostles; and some, prophets; and some, evangelists; and some, pastors and teachers; [12] for the perfecting of the saints, for the work of the ministry, for the edifying of the body of Christ:"

10. The office gifts are in place to perfect or complete the saints. As the saints are being perfected, the church is being perfected. As the church is being perfected so is the body of Christ. As the body of Christ is being perfected so is the bride of Christ. Everything must be in order concerning the bride when CHRIST returns. Therefore, He sent the gifts specifically for the saints or those who chose to separate themselves for the Kingdom of GOD.

11. **(1 Corinthians 16:15)** "I beseech you, brethren, (ye know the house of Stephanas, that it is the firstfruits of Achaia, and that they have addicted themselves to the ministry of the saints,)" Saints have a ministry of their own. Every saint has a ministry of steadfastness, faith, strength, and spiritual maturity. Yes, you may have a separate work or office position in the Kingdom, but all saints have the above corporate ministry.

12. **(Revelation 5:8)** "And when he had taken the book, the four beasts and four and twenty elders fell down before the Lamb, having every one of them harps, and golden vials full of odours, which are the prayers of saints." GOD truly receives or inhabits the prayers of the saints because of their purity and holiness. Because of the life and righteousness of a saint, their prayers are effectual. Saints always release righteous prayers. The saints' prayers are unselfish. The saints' prayers will work. The saints should pray more than anything else.

13. **(Romans 8:27)** "And he that searcheth the hearts knoweth what is the mind of the Spirit, because he maketh intercession for the saints according to the will of GOD." The Holy Spirit makes intercession for the saints. This actually means He prays for the saints because of holiness and righteousness. The saint has a pure heart. That is why the Holy Spirit can do anything for a saint.

14. When a saint does not know the Will of GOD, the Holy Spirit knows the perfect will and, therefore, stands in the gap. He does not do that for everybody.

15. **(2 Thessalonians 1:10)** "When He shall come to be glorified in His Saints, and to be admired in all them that believe (because our testimony among you was believed) in that day." He is glorified in a saint. Because a saint's life is taken over by the

power of purity, holiness, and righteousness, GOD is glorified. The world is able to truly see the light of GOD in the life of a saint.

16. **(Psalm 37:28)** "For the Lord loveth judgment, and forsaketh not His saints; they are preserved for ever: but the seed of the wicked shall be cut off." GOD never forsakes His saints. He will keep them forever. No matter what comes up against a saint, GOD will always keep them. A saint totally belongs to GOD because of their life. The devil hates a saint because they are so close to GOD.

17. **(Psalm 116:15)** "Precious in the sight of the Lord is the death of His saints." The death of a saint is always precious to GOD because of their life and destination. A saint will die in two areas: flesh to the nature of sin and in the natural body. The greatest thing is the dying to flesh, not so much in the flesh.

18. The true saint dies to their sins and fleshly desires. That is why GOD rejoices in the death of a saint. They are pure, holy, and righteous. They show GOD that He means more to them than the desires of the flesh.

19. The saint should rejoice because they will always make GOD proud. The saint declares that Jesus' Death was not in vain.

20. The saint declares to the world that we can be separated from sin, and be holy, righteous, and pure.

21. **(Genesis 5:24)** "And Enoch walked with GOD: and he was not; for GOD took him. The saint has an Enoch spirit. They have an earthy walk with GOD and with time they will be raptured out to have a heavenly walk with GOD. They continuously walk in the Spirit and in GOD'S presence because of their purity and holiness.

22. Saints please GOD.

Lesson 9
The Hypocrite - Matthew 23:27

1. **(Matthew 23:27)** "Woe unto you, scribes and Pharisees, hypocrites! for ye are like unto whited sepulchres, which indeed appear beautiful outward, but are within full of dead men's bones, and of all uncleanness." The church is full of hypocrisy or hypocrites.

2. The word hypocrisy or hypocrite means false or halted between two opinions.

3. There are many in the church who are false or trying to serve two gods.

4. **(Matthew 13:25-26)** "But while men slept, his enemy came and sowed tares among the wheat, and went his way. [26] But when the blade was sprung up, and brought forth fruit, then appeared the tares also." Another name for hypocrisy is tare. This is one who is among the true saints, but they are false.

5. **(Isaiah 32:6)** "For the vile person will speak villany, and his heart will work iniquity, to practise hypocrisy, and to utter error against the Lord, to make empty the soul of the hungry, and he will cause the drink of the thirsty to fail."

6. Hypocrites are workers of iniquity. They practice a false life. They may appear to be a Christian, but their hearts are far from GOD.

7. The hypocrite speaks lies and gives out false information.

8. The hypocrite is very resistant to the truth. They make excuses to avoid the real truth.

9. The hypocrites are tares that will grow up in the church with the real saints and it is God's job to bring true separation.

10. The hypocrite attempts to live a double life. They are very attached to the world while they try to be a so-called Christian.

11. Hypocrites justify sin because they are still so involved with sin themselves.

12. Scribes and the Pharisees are called hypocrites because they were all about themselves.

13. The Scribes and the Pharisees saw religion and Christianity as self-gain and self-gratification.

14. **(Matthew 6:16)** "Moreover when ye fast, be not, as the hypocrites, of a sad countenance: for they disfigure their faces that they may appear unto men to fast. Verily I say unto you, they have their reward."

15. Jesus expressed to us not to be like the hypocrite, or not to put ourselves on display. We are to keep ourselves humble and submitted to GOD at all times. Hypocrites want you to recognize them more than GOD. They are always trying to impress man. They want you to recognize when they are fasting and praying. They put all of their religious experiences on display.

16. **(Job 36:13)** "But the hypocrites in heart heap up wrath: they cry not when he bindeth them." The hypocrites bring wrath and confusion. They are very damaging to the body of Christ.

17. The hypocrites bring mockery to the body. They live very compromising lives. Many people are turned off to the church because of the hypocrite. The world will see their compromising lives, therefore rejecting the church all together.

18. Hypocrites have a very hard heart. They convince themselves they are just as good as everyone else. They compare themselves to other believers based on that person's shortcoming.

19. The hypocrite gets much gratification out of the fall of other church members. The fall of others gives them an excuse or justification for their shortcomings.

20. Again, the church is full of hypocrites. They will remain in the church until the return of Christ. Christ must do the separating.

21. You must be discerning of their spirits. Be very aware of who you are dealing with. If not, you could get caught up in the web of deception or hardness.

22. Hypocrites are very aware of certain aspects of the Word. Their own personal lives of compromise are at odds with the Word. They tend to disagree greatly with the Word, but they also know how to use the Word to their defense. Again, be aware of the hypocritical spirit in the church because they are there.

Lesson 10
The Laborer
Matthew 9:37-38; I Corinthians 3:9

1. **(Matthew 9:37-38)** "Then saith he unto His disciples, The harvest truly is plenteous, but the labourers are few; 38 pray ye therefore the Lord of the harvest, that he will send forth labourers."

2. The last person and the most needed person in the church are the laborers. In Greek the word laborer means *"worker."*

3. There is so much work needed for the Kingdom but where are the laborers? Where are those who are willing to get their hands dirty for Jesus Christ? Today everyone in the Kingdom wants a clean job. Everyone wants a job that will not take much energy or time, or that job that appears to get the most prestige.

4. **(Matthew 9:37)** Jesus said, "The harvest is plentiful, but the laborers are few." Jesus wants to send forth laborers but they are so difficult to find in the church. Because our lives are filled with so much other responsibilities, we just don't have time to work for GOD.

5. Every person who is righteous in the body of Christ is needed to fulfill some part in an assignment in God's Kingdom. When Jesus walked here on earth He was trying to change man, but He was also looking for those who would continue His Work once He went back to heaven.

6. **(1 Corinthians 3:9)** "For we are labourers together with GOD: ye are God's husbandry, ye are God's building." We are laborers with Jesus Christ. We are supposed to be doing what He did and what He wants us to do now.

7. There are souls to be saved, demons to be cast out and sick people who need healing. There is plenty of work to be done. Again where are the laborers?

8. Another name for a laborer is minister, which means *'men at work.'* We are supposed to be working for GOD continuously. The ministry of GOD is the work of GOD.

9. The laborers are needed to prepare the body for Christ's return. People are carrying titles and even holding positions, but there is no real work getting done in the body of Christ.

10. The Bible states, *"Many are called but few are chosen."* Few are available to truly be laborers in the Kingdom. Few will lay down their agenda and take on God's assignment.

11. Laborers are needed throughout all areas of the body of Christ. However, everybody is trying to apply for the same job. The church acts as though there is only one job listed. There are many jobs to be carried out.

12. Look around. If the job that you want is filled, then accept another one so that the work of the Kingdom might go on.

13. There are so many jobs left undone because we don't have the laborers. Not all the jobs will make you popular. There are many jobs that no one wants. However, every job in the Kingdom of GOD is very important.

14. **(Philippians 2:16)** "Holding forth the word of life; that I may rejoice in the day of Christ, that I have not run in vain, neither laboured in vain." We cannot let our laboring be in vain. The word vain in the Greek means *empty* or of no value. Your laboring must have purpose and spiritual direction.

15. Many are laboring today with no direction and purpose. Laboring must be effective. Laboring is not just to keep you busy, it is to make you useful in the Kingdom. It is to make the Kingdom of GOD as productive as possible. Jesus did not waste His time with work that had no value. Jesus was not in it to impress; He was in it to bless.

16. You can labor in certain areas and for certain things. We need laborers just for the youth, the prison ministry, and the elderly. We need people to embrace the specific calls of the Kingdom of GOD.

17. Many times, the pastor may appear to be the only laborer; therefore, it weighs down the leader. Sometimes leaders have so much going on that they place themselves in very unhealthy positions. They overwork themselves which eventually makes them ineffective. This makes the church unbalanced because there is someone else who should be fulfilling that assignment instead of that overburdened leader.

18. You must labor according to your manpower, ability, and capability. No one person should be trying to do all the laboring. No one person should attempt to be involved in everything.

19. It has been noted that out of every 25 people, you will get only 1 laborer. It will take time to develop works in the church because it takes time to get laborers.

20. Pastors should be about the work of their ministry. GOD will send laborers as needed. Most of all we must pray for laborers to come. We don't need just membership; we really need laborers to finish His Work.

21. Everyone should ask GOD to make them a laborer so that the work of the Kingdom can be completed. Then Christ can return. Ask GOD to show you your part as a laborer. As a leader, find out the abilities of the people in the church. Do not force people to take on a job in the church. However, if their lives are not up to par, just give them the opportunity to labor. But do not allow laboring to be more important than the life. Their labor can be very ineffective if their life is out of order. Again, pray to be a laborer for Christ and pray for laborers to come.

Works Cited

Brand, C. O., Draper, C. W., & England, A. W. (2003). *Holman illustrated Bible dictionary*. Nashville, Tenn.: Holman Bible Publishers.

Dockery, D. S. (1998). *Holman concise Bible commentary: simple, straightforward commentary on every book of the Bible*. Nashville, Tenn.: Broadman & Holman Publishers.

Henry, Matthew. *Matthew Henry's commentary*. New modern ed. Peabody, Mass.: Hendrickson Publishers, 1991. Print.

Hindson, E. E., & Kroll, W. M. (1994). *The KJV parallel Bible commentary*. Nashville: T. Nelson Publishers.

Life application Bible: New Revised Standard Version. (1990). Iowa Falls, Iowa: World Bible Publishers.

Rapids, M. (2002). *Holy Bible: King James Version*. Grand Rapids, Mich.: Zondervan.

Strong, J., Kohlenberger, J. R., & Swanson, J. A. (2001). *The strongest Strong's exhaustive concordance of the Bible* (Larger print ed.). Grand Rapids, Mich.: Zondervan.

Concise Studies I
(Makeup of the Church)
Workbook

Lesson 1

1. Who or what is a sinner?

2. The ultimate goal of CHRIST concerning the sinner is to_____.

3. What is the purpose of the Word in the church?

4. Many sinners come to the church out of_________________.

5. If he can kill a sinner, Satan has accomplished his what?

Lesson 2

6. What are the saved people in the Body of Christ?

7. What do many people who get saved become?

8. Those who only know Jesus as Savior or rescuer, tend to what? It is as though He is a _______________. They only notice Him when they are_______.

9. Often people, who only have salvation, function on ________. They tend to lean heavily on ____________________,

10. For people to maintain salvation, their salvation or their faith cannot be __________.

Lesson 3

11. What or who is the unbeliever?

12. The unbeliever is a person who lacks________________.

13. When a person is an unbeliever, they make __________________.

14. Many times in the church, miracles and blessings cannot come forth because of unbelievers. They lack the ability to ___________________.

15. Most unbelievers are ____________________. Unbelief is what we call a ______________________.

Lesson 4

16. What does to be born again mean?

17. To truly embrace being born again, you must accept Him as Savior and Lord. What are God's three major roles or personages?

18. When people are truly born again, what do they struggle with?

19. When we are truly born again, we____________. What will be present?

20. When people truly become born again, they have a ____________________.

Lesson 5

21. Who or what is the believer? The believer is one that ________________.

22. Believers position themselves for ____________________.

23. The true believer has nothing to be____________________. They don't have to _________.

24. What do believers create first of all?

25. When there are a multitude of believers, what does it represent? It creates a true working atmosphere for ______________.

Lesson 6

26. What are or who are Christians?

27. Christians are very faithful to _____________________, but not necessarily to _____________________________.

28. What is another name for a Christian? Who are they led by?

29. What does the word harmless mean?

30. Christians draw by ___________________.

Lesson 7

31. Who or what is the disciple? The disciple is one that can be _______.

32. One of the first things a disciple has to be is _________________.

33. What is the difference between a Christian and a disciple?

34. What must disciples be?

35. To be a disciple, your own personal will ______________________.

Lesson 8

36. A saint is one who is_____________________. It is that person who has truly ___________________.

37. Because of their purity, name the three entities that saints shall judge.

38. Every saint has a ministry of __________.

39. When a saint does not know the Will of GOD, what happens?

40. In what two areas will a saint die?

Lesson 9

41. What do the words hypocrisy or hypocrite mean?

42. Hypocrites are workers of _____________. They practice a _________.

43. How do hypocrites justify their sin?

44. The hypocrite gets much gratification out of ___________________.

45. The fall of others gives them an excuse or ____________________.

Lesson 10

46. The word laborer in Greek means ______________________

47. What is another name for a laborer is ____________________ which means _________.

48. What are the laborers needed to prepare?

49. Many are laboring today with no ________.

50. It has been noted that out of every 25 people, you will ______________.

Concise Studies
(Make Up of the Church 1)

Assignments

(All homework, practical, and scripture information, must be on a separate sheet of paper. If it is written on this paper, there is a 50% deduction from your grade automatically.) Homework, practical, and Bible observation must be a paragraph long or more).

Homework

Explain a way of judging a sinner (Lesson 1:11)

Practical

Give an example of dealing with an unbeliever (Lesson 3:21)

FIVEFOLD MINISTRIES

***Accredited by National Bible College Association**

Safe Haven Interdenominational Bible College and Training Institute
PO Box 457
Zebulon, NC

FIVEFOLD MINISTRY
Table of Contents

FIVEFOLD MINISTRIES
Ministry Categories
(Introduction)

1. The Ministry Categories are:
   a. Office Gifts-given by Jesus
   b. Revelation Gifts-given by the Holy Spirit
   c. Motive Gifts -given by GOD.

2. We will study each category and gift in detail. You must understand the different categories in order to understand their operation.

3. **(Ephesians 4:8-11)** "Wherefore he saith, When he ascended up on high, he led captivity captive, and gave gifts unto men.**9** (Now that he ascended, what is it but that he also descended first into the lower parts of the earth?**10** He that descended is the same also that ascended up far above all heavens, that he might fill all things.)**11** And he gave some, apostles; and some, prophets; and some, evangelists; and some, pastors and teachers.

4. The office gifts are given by Jesus Christ. It is Jesus who chooses the five gifts. They are called office gifts because they are true leadership positions and not everyone can walk in them. You cannot covet them or ask for them. Jesus himself must choose to give them to you. That is why the scripture declares "he (Jesus) gave some".

5. One of the most dangerous things is to attempt to walk in one of the office gifts and truly not be called by Christ to do it. When you take on one of these titles without being summoned by Christ, then you are taking on unnecessary suffering. You suffer according to the hat that you are wearing.

6. There are many people in the church suffering unnecessarily because they are wearing a title that does not fit them. There was a young lady in a church who had been in another church previously, and someone had ordained her has an Evangelist. But she was not a true Evangelist. She kept going through sicknesses and financial situations. When the new pastor recognized what was going on, he stripped her of the title. Her life, immediately, began to turn around.

7. When Jesus assigns you a certain position, he equips you for that position and most of all, the suffering that goes along with it. However, the key thing is that you will not go through unnecessary suffering.

8. The fivefold ministry has an order and that is why they are written in a certain order. The order determines their anointing and their position. It also determines what they carry. You will learn this as we go on. The order also determines their judgment.

9. Once the fivefold ministry was introduced to the church, it was the most misunderstood operation, and misused. People began to just jump on the titles without true knowledge and understanding. Thank GOD for the fivefold ministry. But it is very dangerous when used incorrectly. Because of the misunderstanding of the usage of the offices, satan has used it against us. Many houses of GOD or most say churches, are doing much damage to themselves and the people around them.

10. **(Ephesians 4:12)** "For the perfecting of the saints, for the work of the ministry, for the edifying of the body of Christ"

11. There are three purposes of the fivefold ministry and that is:

a. Perfecting of the saints.
b. Work of the ministry.
c. Edifying of the body of Christ.

12. The word *"perfecting"* means the completion of. Before Jesus can come for the bride, the bride must be complete. Everything about the bride of Christ, the saints, must be in order. The bride, which is the saints, must be without spot or wrinkle. They must be holy and righteous.

13. Each of the fivefold ministries plays a part in perfecting the saints. They must know their part. Many people take on the title of the fivefold ministry, but they do not truly know their part in the fivefold ministry or how to help bring completion to the household of faith.

14. The fivefold ministry is for the work of the ministry. Each person in the fivefold ministry has a specific assignment. This is what you will learn. "Ministry" means men at work. That is why the disciples were so effective because they knew their assignments. They truly understood the work of the ministry.

15. Because the body of Christ does not understand the work of the ministry, everyone is trying to do the same jobs, leaving many jobs left undone. Often people pick the most popular one thinking that will increase them, it will not. Only what you have been chosen to do, will you be most effective in.

16. For example, when each level of the fivefold ministry was manifested, people would change their title to the most popular or recent one. Many prophets changed their titles to apostle when the apostleship appeared to be more popular. Thus, causing many of them to be out of order because they were not apostles. By doing this, it affected their anointing, calling and position.

17. **(Romans 12:4)** "For as we have **many members** in one body, and all **members** have not the same office".

18. Lastly, the fivefold ministry is for edifying the body. The word *"edify"* means to birth forth. The fivefold ministry is to bring forth what is in the body of Christ so that we might get the fullness of all offices, gifts, and talents.

19. Each one of the fivefold ministries should be in place to help develop different ones in their rightful place. But because this is not being done, many people do not know their true place in the body.

20. **(Romans 12:5)** "So we, being **many**, are one body in Christ, and every one **members** one of another".

21. **(I Corinthians 12:12)** "For as the body is one, and hath **many members**, and all the **members** of that one body, being **many**, are one body: so also is Christ".

22. When the true fivefold ministry is in operation, it takes every member and helps put it in its rightful place. Again, there are many members, and it is the job of the fivefold ministry to place them properly.

Lesson 1
The Apostle

1. What is an apostle? An apostle is one that is sent by Jesus Christ. Apostle is the last ministry to restore the church/body of Christ, and the House of GOD. The apostle is to set the final order of the house. Apostle is to truly get the bride ready for the return of Jesus Christ.

2. **Matthew 19:30** (The first shall be last and the last shall be first):
   a. The Apostle was the first gift in the Church.
   b. The Apostle is the last gift being restored to the Church.
   c. Apostle will come back to prepare the Church for Christ's return.

3. The apostle is territorial, which means the apostle is assigned to a certain area and a certain people. Apostle must be sent by GOD to an area because there is a certain need for them to be there. It is not just because people are unsaved, that is the Evangelist's job. (You will understand that more later.)

4. The apostle must go to an area because there are a people there who have a special spiritual need. They may already be saved but correction is needed. There could have been a recent failed ministry and people have been left unattended, wounded, or ignorant. Many times, the apostle is prayed to that area by the broken people, and they don't even know it.

5. Many time people will make themselves an apostle if they start a new church. But starting a new church does not make you an apostle. There are two types of anointing that will come on someone for them to start a new ministry, and that is called spiritual anointing or a seasonal anointing. Spiritual means the power to do and seasonal means just for that period of time.

6. GOD will give the power to open a new ministry but that is all they are supposed to do, work with that ministry. The power is seasonal, that means just for that time period. It will not last.

7. It is dangerous when someone makes themselves an apostle and they only have a spiritual or seasonal anointing. They end up placing themselves and their ministry under unnecessary hardship. There have been sicknesses, failed marriages, and

major financial failures, because of operating outside of the willed anointing.

8. One of the first things that apostles do is establish foundation and root. The first foundation that apostles will lay is with an evangelized people or an unlearned people. This will determine what area of apostleship that specific apostle operates in.

9. If that apostle's strength is more toward soul winning, then they will function more toward the evangelical side, like Peter did. If their anointing is more toward teaching, then their focus will be on the unlearned people. The unlearned people may already be saved but yet, ignorant in the word, or operation of the kingdom of GOD.

10. The second way that apostles will deal with foundation is through digging up old foundations where there is:
    a. A very traditional area.
    b. A very denominational area.
    c. People were taught a wrong or a confused doctrine.
    d. A cult.

11. Sometimes an apostle may be assigned to a church in leadership to correct or dig up. The purpose of that is to prepare that ministry or the house of GOD to embrace the fivefold ministry and the fullness of the operation of the gifts.

12. Apostles will also do a lot of adjusting foundations, which are:
    a. People who have learned some truth but not all truth.
    b. Limited learning of the word.
    c. Not totally rooted.

12. Apostles establish new order, such as:
    a. New or old ministries must have spiritual order.
    b. Order must be present for power.
    c. How to work the gifts together.
    d. Take the limitation off the ministry.
    e. Properly direct the ministry as to its type.
    (Example: teaching, healing, deliverance, etc.)
    f. What ministries (ministry gifts) go with order?

13. One of the key things in establishing order is making that ministry aware of the type of ministry it is. Many ministries struggle because they do not know in what true

area is their strength. Are they a teaching ministry, deliverance ministry, healing ministry, or fellowship ministry?

14. The apostle's job is to make them aware of this so that they can function properly in the kingdom of GOD. If not, they will be trying to do things that do not fit their ministry.

15. Apostles are to reveal hidden revelation
    a. Truths in scripture.
    b. Truths in ministry.
    c. Truths about Christ.
    d. Truths about individuals.
    e. Time schedules.

16. The last days apostles will reveal many revelations to the body of Christ, not for show but to the prepare the body for the return of Christ. Most of all, the apostle will reveal the time schedule of the body and individual churches. Timing will be the key in the last days.

17. Apostles have birthing power, which means:
    a. Reveal hidden gifts.
    b. Develop gifts.
    c. Ministries.
    d. Maturity.

18. Many people get frustrated in ministries because they do not know what is in them nor how to bring it forth. One of the main jobs of an apostle is to reveal that gift. Make it evident in that individual and help that person develop that gift.

19. When a person sits with an undeveloped gift, it weakens the body and that individual ministry. That is why you must find it and develop it. One must be brought to spiritual maturity also. That means learning how to handle the gift effectively.

20. There are Four Types of Apostles:
    a. Chief (Jesus, himself).
    b. 12 Disciples (Walk with Jesus).
    c. Paul (New Revelation) (was not with Jesus in flesh).
    d. Today's Apostle (Hidden Revelation).

21. The chief apostle is Jesus Christ, and no one can be him. The second set of apostles were the 12 disciples. The only way that anyone could have been one of them was to have seen Jesus in the flesh. That is why they replaced Judas with Mathis because he had seen Jesus in flesh.

22. Paul is the third type of apostle because he wrote new revelation. Some have tried to say that Paul was a replacement apostle. But he was not, because he never saw Jesus in the flesh.

23. The last apostle is the last day apostle. Today's apostles reveal hidden revelation. The information used to prepare for the return of Christ. They set the last day church in order. Some have said that there are no more apostles, and they went out with Paul, but that is not true. The last apostle is in existence and is well needed for last day revelation.

24. The office of the Apostle:
    a. Requires much prequalification. (Luke 12:48)
    b. Man must be made before ministry. (Ephesians 2:20)
    c. Judgment on a higher standard. (James 3:1)

25. You cannot just walk into the apostle office because you feel as though you are ready. You must be qualified by GOD, not man. The person must be made first. The person must go through deliverance conversion, discipleship, and order first. Your life must be in order before you worry about the gift, calling, and title. The apostle will be judged greatly because of the title and position. That it isn't to be taken lightly in the kingdom of GOD.

26. The characteristics of an apostle are:
    a. Anointed in all five gifts.
    b. Have each gift with measure.
    c. Jesus had the gifts without measure.
    d. Anointed in all five because of their assignment.

27. Apostles are anointed as the prophet, evangelist, pastor, and teacher. But they are anointed with measure. They have a limitation. Jesus is the only one who has all of the gifts in their fullness. Apostles must have all because of their true assignment until a true prophet or evangelist comes along.

28. Apostles will return <u>and</u>
    a. Break traditional barriers.

b. Stir up dead gifts.
c. Perfect the Bride of Christ.
d. Remove manmade order.
e. Remove the one-man show.
f. Start the Acts church again.

Lesson 2
The Prophet

1. **(Exodus 7:1)** "And the LORD said unto Moses, See, I have made thee a god to Pharaoh: and Aaron thy brother shall be thy prophet".

2. The second of the fivefold ministry is the prophet. The true prophet reveals revelation. The true prophet shall reveal all truth to all of mankind. The prophet is the second office gift.

3. Prophets are totally different from the:
    a. Gift of prophecy.
    b. Spiritual prophecy.
    c. Faith prophecy.

4. A prophet deals with:
    a. Foretelling (present).
    b. Forth telling (future).
    c. Confirming (what has already been told).

5. The office of the prophet has the word of knowledge because he/she can tell the present. They have the word of wisdom because they can detail and prophesy. And much of the voice of the prophet is confirming and most of all confirming what GOD has already said.

6. The office of the prophet will carry the anointing of the:
    a. Evangelist.
    b. Pastor.
    c. Teacher.

7. A prophet must be able to:
    a. Teach the Word.
    b. Preach the Word.
    c. Evangelize the Word.

8. The prophet does not walk in the office of the apostle. The prophet can start churches. It is a spiritual anointing or seasonal. When the prophet carries the anointing of the evangelist, pastor, and the teacher, they are with measure. Because the prophets true calling is prophecy not soul winning, pastoring, or teaching.

9. If a person calls themselves a prophet and they cannot teach, evangelize, or pastor, then they are not a prophet. They may very well have the gift of prophecy, but they are not a prophet.

10. Prophets function for the:
a. Local body.
b. Nationwide body.

11. The true prophet should be able to prophesy to their local body of believers as well as give a word to the entire body of Christ. A true prophet's word is clear and well timed. It is not a Logos, *"thus say the Lord,"* word. Their word should be supported with the written word. But it should be beyond the prophetic of just the written word.

12. The prophet strongly functions in the:
a. Gift of prophecy.
b. Word of knowledge.
c. Wisdom.
d. Discernment.

13. Some prophets will have the:
a. Gifts of tongues.
b. Interpretation of tongues.

14. The gift of tongues and interpretation of tongues for a prophet will be used for revelation of prophecy, not just to speak in tongues. Most prophets spend a lot of time praying in the spirit. But public use of tongues is for interpretation for the prophetic.

15. Prophets will function in the following motive gifts:
a. Prophecy.
b. Teaching.
c. Exhortation.

16. Prophets have birthing power:
a. Can discern your specific gifts.
b. Bring you into the fullness of that gift.
c. Help you detail the gift.

17. The prophet can expose what type of gift an individual may have. They can help one point out the specific way an individual should use their gift. They also can help someone mature in their gift.

18. **(I Peter 1:10)** "Of which salvation the prophets have enquired and searched diligently, who prophesied of the grace that should come unto you:

19. The true gift of prophecy will develop, based on one's maturity in the Lord, and how well you handle revelation and the presentation of prophecy.

20. Prophets plant seeds about things that you don't know. There are many who have missed their blessings and opportunities because they did not know that the prophet could know things that they did not know at that time.

21. Prophets prepare you for the future, they talk about what is to come.

22. Prophets talk about the present:
    a. Exactly what is going on in the "now".
    b. This is dealing with the word of knowledge.
    c. They use prophetic preaching.

23. Prophets deal with the future, in:
    a. Individuals.
    b. Ministry.
    c. Nation.

24. Prophets speak with:
    a. Condition (There are certain things that you must do to make the prophecy come to pass).
    b. Unconditional (The prophecy will come to pass with or without your help).

25. Prophets use the word of wisdom:
    a. Giving details for a given a situation.
    b. Mind of GOD (God's Perfect Will for the situation).

26. Prophets confirm:

a. Repeating something you know.
b. It is not new information.
c. One can be confirmed or witnessed up to three times.
d. After three times, it goes from a witness to:
   Warning
   Wrath
   Woe

Lesson 3
Evangelist

1. Evangelist means ***one sent to:***
    a. Win souls.
    b. Establish.
    c. Bring deliverance.
    d. Break up ground.

2. **Evangelist is the <u>third</u> office.**

3. Evangelists must be able to:
    a. Pastor.
    b. Teach.

4. Evangelists function greatly in:
    a. Gifts of healings.
    b. Miracles.
    c. Discernment.
    d. Deliverance.

5. Most Evangelists only prophesy when dealing with the area of deliverance.

6. An Evangelist can establish ministry:
    a. Will not stay usually over two years.
    b. Spend time digging out the roots.
    c. Tearing down barriers.
    d. Spend time preparing a Pastor.

7. Evangelists tend to be on the move constantly.

8. **Evangelists have a heart for winning <u>souls.</u>**

9. Evangelists are not territorial. They are open to any area where there are unsaved people.

10. **Evangelists can pastor, but they do not have a true pastor's <u>heart.</u>**

11.Evangelists function strongly in:

a. Deliverance (devils are cast out).
b. Healing (diseases are healed).
c. Miracles.

12.Biblical examples of Evangelists:

a. Peter – Apostle functioning strongly in evangelism.
b. Philip – (Act 21:8).

13.All can do the work of an Evangelist, but you cannot walk in the Evangelist's office.

14.The work of the Evangelist is:

a. Soul Winning.
b. Healing.
c. Deliverance.
d. Miracles

15. An evangelist's heart is to work in any area where there is soul winning.

16.True evangelists will become frustrated if they:

a. Are confined to one place or;
b. Lack seeing people who need,
    1. Deliverance
    2. Healing,
    3. Miracles.

17.Most true Evangelists do not make good Pastors for a long period of time due to their passion to operate in the deliverance ministry.

18.Evangelists go into local churches to:

a. Expose sin.
b. Dig up bad foundations, but not replace the foundation.
c. Bring revival.
d. Soul winning.
e. Tear up fallow ground.
f. Help a pastor build ministry.
g. To bring healing and deliverance.

Ministry Categories (*Continued)*

Lesson 4 -Pastor

1. Pastor – A Shepherd who:
    a. Tends the flock.
    b. Nurtures the flock.
    c. Loves the flock.
    d. Chastises the flock.
    e. Heals the flock.
    f. Teaches the flock.
    g. Directs the flock.
    h. Allows the gifts to operate.
    i. Meets the needs of the flock.
    j. Brings completeness to the flock.

2. All Pastors should have:
    a. Great teaching abilities.
    b. Word of Knowledge.
    c. Word of Wisdom.
    d. Discernment.
    e. Administrative gifts.

3. Pastors must seek the:
    a. Direction of the ministry.
    b. Type of ministry.
    c. Seasons of the ministry.
    d. Needs of the ministry.
    e. Purpose of the ministry.

4. Pastors will have a Shepherd's heart:
    a. Heart for the people.
    b. To be with the people.
    c. To understand the people.
    d. To love the people.

5. Pastors are stationary.

6. Pastors are focused on their:
    a. Local area.
    b. Local families.
    c. Local community.

7. Pastors *can* function in:
    a. Deliverance.
    b. Healing.
    c. Prophetic.
    d. Miracles.

8. However, if Pastors are focusing on the above areas too much, they are:
    a. Usually not true Pastors.
    b. Out of their calling.
    c. Out of position.

9. Their focus should be teaching, training and development.

10. Pastors should be <u>training</u> others to function in these areas.

11. Pastors can bring others in, when needed.

12. Pastors can do outreach for a time; however, they should be teaching sheep to bring in sheep.

13. An Apostle and an Evangelist can soul win continuously, even while they are pastoring because that is part of their primary anointing.

Lesson 5
(Teacher)

1. Teacher – one who teaches:
    a. Breaks down information.
    b. Details information.
    c. Brings information into clear understanding for others.
    d. Makes information usable.

2. Teachers and Pastors flow together.

3. Teachers operate in the:
    a. Teaching ministry.
    b. Word of Wisdom.
    c. Word of Knowledge.
    d. Administrative gifts.

4. The office of the Teacher is a leadership office. It is totally different from the:
    a. Sunday School Teacher.
    b. Youth Teacher.

5. Most often, the position of the Teacher is a Pastor who has a strong teaching ministry.

6. Their ministry will flow in the teaching.

7. People will be delivered through their teaching.

8. That is why the Pastor and Teacher ministries run together.

9. Someone may be able to teach but the teacher's anointing is on a much greater level.

10. Teachers may operate in other areas:
    a. Healing.
    b. Deliverance.
    c. Prophecy.

11. The Teacher's focal point will be teaching.

12. Teaching others to move in other area s such as:
    a. Healing.
    b. Deliverance.
    c. Prophecy.

13. The Teaching office is a very disciplined office.

14. When Jesus first came on the scene, he came as a Teacher.

15. Teacher's office can move in prophetic teaching.

16. Teachers truly will have a Pastor's heart also.

17. The teacher will flow and feel like the Pastor.

Works Cited

L. Kenneth Hagan, Gifts of the Spirit

Dr. Bill Hamon, Prophets and Personal Prophecy

Brand, C. O., Draper, C. W., & England, A. W. (2003). *Holman illustrated Bible dictionary*. Nashville, Tenn.: Holman Bible Publishers.

Dockery, D. S. (1998). *Holman concise Bible commentary: simple, straightforward commentary on every book of the Bible*. Nashville, Tenn.: Broadman & Holman Publishers.

Henry, Matthew. *Matthew Henry's commentary*. New modern ed. Peabody, Mass.: Hendrickson Publishers, 1991. Print.

Hindson, E. E., & Kroll, W. M. (1994). *The KJV parallel Bible commentary*. Nashville: T. Nelson Publishers.

Life Application Bible: New Revised Standard Version. (1990). Iowa Falls, Iowa: World Bible Publishers.

Rapids, M. (2002). *Holy Bible: King James Version.* Grand Rapids, Mich.: Zondervan.

Strong, J., Kohlenberger, J. R., & Swanson, J. A. (2001). *The strongest Strong's exhaustive concordance of the Bible* (Larger print ed.). Grand Rapids, Mich.: Zondervan.

Fivefold Ministry Workbook

1. What are apostles?

2. What does territorial mean?

3. What does establishing order mean?

4. What does digging up old foundation mean?

5. What is birthing power?

6. What are the four types of apostles? Explain each.

7. Apostles will return and do what?

8. What anointing will the office of the prophet carry?

9. A must be able to do what?

10. The prophet strongly functions in what?

11. What does it mean for a prophet to have birthing power?

12. What is condition and un-condition?

13. What does it mean for a prophet to confirm?

14. What motive gifts do prophets function in?

15. What does evangelist mean?

16. Evangelist functions greatly in what?

17. Why isn't evangelist territorial?

18. What is the work of the evangelist?

19. True evangelist will become frustrated if they?

20. Why it is that true evangelist does not make good pastors?

21. Why does evangelist go into local churches?

22. Pastors must seek for what?

23. What is a pastor?

24. What is a Shepherd's heart?

25. What are pastors focused on?

26. What are four things pastors can function in?

27. What should all pastors have?

28. Teachers flow with whom?

29. What do teachers operate in?

30. A teacher is a pastor who has what?

Five-Fold Ministry
Assignments

(All homework, practical, and scripture information, must be on a separate sheet of paper. If it is written on this paper, there is a 50% deduction from your grade automatically.) Homework, practical, and Bible observation must be a paragraph long or more).

Homework

1. Give an example of birthing power from of an apostle?

Practical

2. Give an example of a prophet foretelling and forth telling?

Please try and type all essays if possible. If you cannot type your essay, please make sure your teacher is aware of it. Your essay and Bible study lessons must be turned in with all of your homework. Your essay must be 100 words. Please be aware that your homework and essays count as 20% each of your total of grades.

100 Word Essay

Write a paper on what you believe your gift is. Explain in detail using information from the book.

Name____________________
Site ______________________
Instructor _________________
Date______________________

Concise Studies I & Five-fold Ministry Test

(Each Question is Worth 10 Points)

1. Who are the save people in the body of Christ?

2. What does it mean to be saved by hope?

3. What happens when people only get saved?

4. When people really get born again, what type of heart do they have?

5. Explain what a believer is.

6. Explain an apostle is territorial.

7. Explain the first shall be last and the last shall be first.

8. What are the motives gift of the prophet?

9. When will an evangelist become frustrated?

10. What does it mean for a pastor to be stationary?

CONCISE STUDIES II

Safe Haven Interdenominational Bible College and Training Institute
PO Box 457
Zebulon, NC 27597

CONCISE STUDIES II
Table of Contents

Lesson 1
The Theology of the House of GOD, The Church, and The Bride of Christ

1. **(1 Peter 4:17)** "For the time is come that judgment must begin at the house of GOD: and if it first begin at us, what shall the end be of them that obey not the gospel of GOD"?

2. **(Ephesians 5:23)** "For the husband is the head of the wife, even as Christ is the head of the church: and he is the savior of the body".

3. It is time now that we come to a clear understanding of who is or what is the house of GOD, the church, and the bride of Christ? Who will be going back with Jesus when he comes?

4. Jesus will come back, but who is he coming back for? What should we be doing here on earth while we are waiting? What will he be looking for in the church? Who and what will please GOD? What will anger GOD?

5. There are many questions to be answered and we must answer all of them correctly to be ready for the return of Christ. Many will miss His return because the church is not being prepared for His return. The question everyone must ask themselves as well as each pastor is, am I prepared, and have I prepared the people?

6. First, the House of GOD is not the church, it is a place. It is the dwelling place of the saints. It should be the gathering place for all believers.

7. It is the place that should inhabit the presence of the Lord. That is why it is called the House of GOD. It is the place where God's glory shall appear. It is His house, and he should be totally welcome in His house.

8. **(Ecclesiastes 5:1)** "Keep thy foot when thou goest to the house of GOD, and be more ready to hear, than to give the sacrifice of fools: for they consider not that they do evil".

9. The House of GOD is a place where all should come to hear the word of GOD. It is place where the truth should be taught and preached. People should leave the house

of GOD convicted, saved, delivered, healed, changed, encouraged, and free. If truth is being taught properly, it is the House of GOD.

10. *"Keep thy foot"* means to guard your steps when you enter the house of GOD because the house of GOD is holy. People should not be allowed to come into the house of GOD any kind of way. There should be reverence and respect for the House of GOD above any other place.

11. People will treat their own house, houses of others, and even the White House, with such honor and respect. There are people who will not allow you to come into their home with your shoes on because they have expensive floors. Yet we will walk into God's house any kind of way.

12. We want sinners to come to be saved. However, when a sinner is invited to the house of GOD, they must be conscious of the holiness and sacredness of His house. We are not to reject them, but they must understand it is His house.

13. **(Matthew 27:51)** "And, behold, the veil of the temple was rent in twain from the top to the bottom; and the earth did quake, and the rocks rent".

14. When the veil was ripped in the temple, it gave all access back to the Father through the name and the blood of Jesus. But it does excuse the proper respect and usage of the House of GOD.

15. You see, if the fivefold ministry were operating properly, the evangelist would get the sinner saved before even bringing them to the House of GOD. They would prepare them and then bring them. The disciples won them in the street and then they went into home churches to be taught. Then they were sent to the House of GOD.

16. That is why the Jehovah Witnesses do house to house visits before they bring you to the Kingdom Hall. They train you to be a witness before they bring you into their dwelling place, so that you will know how to reverence and respect the it.

17. Because many Houses of GOD are so contaminated with the world, sin and unrighteousness, the presence of GOD is not there. God's glory left a long time ago, or it never came to that specific house because it was not of Him.

18. **(I Samuel 4:21a)** "And she named the child Ichabod, saying, The glory is departed from Israel:

19. Because Eli's son brought so much sin, dishonor, and disrespect to the house of GOD, God's glory left. They went through the rituals of sacrifice, but His glory was nowhere to be found.

20. It is only because of the mercy and grace of GOD that many have not dropped dead, because of the way they have handled the house of GOD. Pastors will be held accountable for not making people aware of the sacredness of His God's house.

21. Older people did not understand a lot of about scripture, but they took the holiness and the sacredness of the house of GOD profoundly serious. That is why they would not allow anyone to just walk up into the pulpit, touch the communion table, or even dress a certain way when they came to the House of GOD.

22. Sometimes people would say they were making a GOD out of the communion table or the pulpit, but they were not. They understood honor and respect. They feared the wrath of GOD.

23. **(I Samuel 3:12-14)** "In that day I will perform against Eli all things which I have spoken concerning his house: when I begin, I will also make an end. **13** For I have told him that I will judge his house for ever for the iniquity which he knoweth; because his sons made themselves vile, and he restrained them not. **14** And therefore I have sworn unto the house of Eli, that the iniquity of Eli's house shall not be purged with sacrifice nor offering forever".

24. We are now trying to appease a new generation, not making them aware of the consequences of crossing the line of holiness. Eli did not deal with his sons who were contaminating the House of GOD. Therefore, GOD dealt harshly with Eli by taking his life, and removing His glory.

25. Many people are not being raised in the House of GOD; therefore, we feel as though we must lower our standards to draw them. Jesus did not lower His holiness or righteousness to influence anyone.

26. No, we are not talking about going out purchasing expensive suits that people cannot afford simply trying to impress people. We must teach people to come into to true reverence and respect as they grow in the Kingdom of GOD.

27. **(Matthew 21:12-13)** " [12] Jesus entered the temple courts and drove out all who were buying and selling there. He overturned the tables of the money changers and the benches of those selling doves. [13] "It is written," he said to them, "'My house will be called a house of prayer,'[a] but you are making it 'a den of robbers.

28. Jesus became incredibly angry when he walked into the temple (House of GOD) and saw that it was being defiled by people selling and buying things. Jesus said the "the House of GOD is a house of prayer.

29. What have we done to the House of GOD today? Have we made it a den of robbers? Have we made it a place just for raising money, having programs, spending more time honoring man than honoring GOD? GOD is not pleased, with what we have done to His house. We must examine our Houses of GOD. Has the glory of GOD left your temple, sanctuary and you can't even recognize it?

30. If you notice, this is the one time that GOD became so angry. It was when they were defiling the temple of His Father. He became angry at their dishonor. Is he angry at us today because of our dishonor? We eat and do anything in this sacred place. We would NEVER do that in the queen's palace. We would NEVER do that in the white house.

31. There was no such thing as even drinking water in the sanctuary. But because water bottles have become available, we feel as though we must pass out water around the sanctuary. People can wait. We have started unnecessary habits.

32. We chew gum and eat candy because we have lost reverence. The house is a sacred place. Imagine that you are going before the king; you would not go with a piece of candy in your mouth, nor would you go chewing on gum.

Lesson 2
Spiritual Behavior

1. **(1 Timothy 3:15)** "But if I tarry long, that thou mayest know how thou oughtest to behave thyself in the house of GOD, which is the church of the living GOD, the pillar and ground of the truth".

2. There is a certain way that all should behave in the House of GOD. The word *"behave"* means to have conversation or live out. When you are in the House of GOD, there are only certain things that you should say or even act out.

3. There was a time when people would not even walk on the grounds of the House of GOD if they had alcohol in their system. They would not dare smoke on the grounds. Now people behave themselves any kind of way in the House of GOD and on the grounds.

4. You may at any time see a group of people just sitting around saying anything, gossiping. There may be those standing right at the door smoking a cigarette, with no shame or remorse.

5. People have made the House of GOD the same as a coffee shop. People are comfortable eating, drinking, and chewing gum in the House of GOD as though it is just a hangout place. The house of GOD is a very sacred place. It is not a hang out place.

6. **(1 Timothy 3:5)** "For if a man know not how to rule his own house, how shall he take care of the church of GOD"?

7. As a parent, it must start with teaching the children how to behave themselves. We must not take this lightly. We have developed all kinds of programs to compensate for children not being in the actual sanctuary. But that does not give them an excuse not to know how to behave and have respect for God's house.

8. Respect for the House of GOD starts with rulership at home. It must be taught in your own house. If there is no respect at home, there will not be respect at the House of GOD.

9. As pastors, when children come to church, if the parents are not aware then you must make them aware. You do not want curses and punishment to come because of disrespect and dishonor of the House of GOD.

10. Often, we are afraid to say anything to parents and children now, because of the way people act. We are afraid of losing members. But the blood will be on those leaders' hands if they do not deal with the situation. That is no different than when a father does not discipline his child at home, causing premature death to come upon them because of disrespect.

11. The presence of GOD or the anointing will not flow in a house that is out of order. When people do not behave themselves properly in the House of GOD, it brings disorder.

12. **(Matthew 21:14)** "And the blind and the lame came to him in the temple; and he healed them".

13. Another name for the House of GOD is *"Temple"*. When the temple is handled properly, there should be an anointing there that will cause the lame and blind to come to be healed. When the temple is handled properly, there will be anointing in the temple from prayer and worship that bring healing and deliverance.

14. That is why many people come in and go out of the temple the same way they came in; because there is no anointing there for healing and deliverance.

15. **(Haggai 1:3-7)** "His reply to them is this: "Is it then the right time for you to live in luxurious homes, when the Temple lies in ruins? **5** Look at the result: **6** You plant much but harvest little. You have scarcely enough to eat or drink and not enough clothes to keep you warm. Your income disappears, as though you were putting it into pockets filled with holes! **7** "Think it over," says the Lord Almighty. "Consider how you have acted and what has happened as a result! **8** Then go up into the mountains, bring down timber, and rebuild my Temple, and I will be pleased with it and appear there in my glory," says the Lord.

16. GOD said *"Consider your ways"* look at how you treat my temple. GOD told the people that they live in fine homes, yet the temple of GOD laid in ruin, what a disgrace. Again, the House of GOD has become just a hang out place. We often leave the temple in ruins. Leaving it dirty from day to day and week to week.

17. We go home to clean and nice homes. We rush out of service because it is time to go, leaving the temple any kind of way. There are people that when having a meal at you house, they would not dare go to bed and leave dirty dishes in the sink, because of the way they feel about your home.

18. Yet the housekeeper only comes and cleans once a week, as though they are doing GOD a favor or because they are getting paid. But God's house should be treated with honor. The temple should always be kept clean. We should never leave a service without first addressing the house of GOD. What if GOD wants to come before the next service or before the housekeeper gets a chance to come?

19. Often when people do not keep their own houses clean, they do not recognize the importance of keeping the House of GOD clean. They treat it with disrespect and dishonor, because that is how they treat their own. We must force people to recognize the need of respecting the house of GOD.

20. In the Book of Haggai, GOD let them know that once they built the temple properly, he would be pleased with it, and he would bring His glory to it. We must know that GOD's glory comes when He is pleased with the spiritual temple and natural temple.

21. The temple of GOD is not for impressing people. It is for blessing GOD and then the people. Many people attempt to purchase buildings trying to impress people. They purchase buildings that they cannot afford. Then the temple becomes a place of struggle instead of a place of blessings.

22. **(Matthew 21:23a)** "And when He was come into the temple, the chief priests and the elders of the people came unto Him as He was teaching".

23. God's temple should truly be a place of teaching the word of God. That is exactly what Jesus did. He brought forth truth in the temple. He would have NEVER abused or dishonored His Father's temple.

24. We must teach people about the temple. One of the first classes that new converts should have is behavior in the temple of GOD. We start out teaching gifts and positions. They don't need to know about that in the beginning. They are not ready.

25. They need to know how to respect and honor what belongs to GOD. If they can't handle the natural blessing, how do you think they will be able to handle the supernatural blessings. People should know the difference between what the house of GOD is , and the church.

26. Even though we say arbitrarily that *"we are going to church,"* we are not going to church. We are going to the house of GOD. The house of GOD is the place. The church is the people.

27. **(Acts 5:25)** " Then came one and told them, saying, Behold, the men whom ye put in prison are standing in the **temple**, and teaching the people".

28. The disciples followed the same thing, they went into the temple to teach the word of GOD. There is always an external teaching and an internal teaching.

29. **(Luke 5:3)** "He got into one of the boats, the one belonging to Simon, and asked him to put out a little from shore. Then he sat down and taught the people from the boat".

30. Jesus would teach external and internal. Jesus taught outside of the temple to a lost people. He taught those who did not understand the laws of GOD. He taught those who followed him and lacked understanding. He did not take the sinner to the temple. He knew they did not understand the value of the temple.

31. **(Matthew 21:23**) When Jesus returned to the temple and began teaching, the leading priests and elders came up to him. They demanded, *"By what authority are you doing all these things? Who gave you the right?"*

32. The priest and the elders confronted Jesus about His teaching in the temple. But they did not know that he knew all the laws of the temple as well as they did. Jesus knew exactly what to teach in the temple and how to teach it. He understood the sacredness of the temple. He knew who could understand His teaching in the temple.

33. That is why the disciples did the very same thing. They would teach in the temple and out of the temple. When the disciples would teach outside of the temple, they would turn those people over to the pastor of the temples. They were ready then to handle the sacredness of the temple of GOD.

34. **(Acts 2:46)** "And they, continuing daily with one accord in the **temple**, and breaking bread from house to house, did eat their meat with gladness and singleness of heart.

35. Again, this can very well be our principles of today. People should teach internally and externally concerning the temple of GOD. If ministers would be willing to teach from house to house, they would never go lacking work, for the kingdom of GOD.

36. It is sad because most ministers are just sitting around waiting on a chance to preach in the pulpit, instead of using their bible knowledge on individuals right there in their own homes.

37. When people first come to church, why not set up time to go to their houses and do some individual teaching with them about salvation and the house of GOD. People will then understand the process of honor and reverence.

Lesson 3
God's Judgment

1. **(I Peter 4:17)** "For the time is come that judgment must begin at the house of GOD: and if it first begin at us, what shall the end be of them that obey not the gospel of GOD"?

2. GOD will judge the House of GOD. The word *"judge"* means to sentence for what has or has not been done. GOD will bless the righteous in the house and curse or reject the unrighteous.

3. And if it first begins at us, the "us" are the righteous, the true believer, the saints, those that are truly walking in holiness. GOD will truly evaluate the lives of the people who come to the House of GOD, that call themselves the children of GOD.

4. The true children of GOD are those obeying the gospel. They make it their business to do whatever the Bible declares that they do. But for those who don't obey, woe unto them.

5. GOD will judge every earthly saint for their:
   a. Obedience.
   b. Righteousness.
   c. Holiness.
   d. Sanctification.

6. Our earthly judgment in the House of GOD will determine if we make it to heaven or to hell. GOD will judge His house for those who are prepared for the rapture and prepared to be His son's bride.

7. The word *"scarcely"* means only a short time before. The "only a short time before" means before GOD begins true punishment and deforestation. We will leave this earth just in time.

8. GOD characterized three major people who are a part of the House of GOD, but two will not make it in, and that is the sinner and the ungodly.

9. The sinner is that person who is coming to church, but they have never accepted Jesus Christ as their personal Savior. They may be doing good works, yet have

never confessed salvation. It does not matter how morally good they are, if they have never accepted Jesus as Savior, they are sinners.

10. Many will set up in a traditional church and be faithful members but never understand true salvation. Many people at one time thought joining the church or just getting baptized, and receiving the *"right hand of fellowship"* was enough.

11. When one joined the church, it was called *"giving the right hand of fellowship"*. All someone had to do was join the church through water baptism and they assumed this made them a valid Christian. They were, literally, welcomed by a handshake.

12. There are actually pastors that are not saved. They went to schools of theology, received a degree in ministry, and assumed that was enough. There are many who pastor churches, preach to congregations every Sunday, and yet don't know Christ for themselves.

13. There was a pastor of a church in the 80s who was on his death bed. He had pastored the church for over 30 years. While on his death bed, a group of young people went to visit him.

14. While visiting him and praying for him, one of them asked him, was he assured in his salvation. He responded back by saying *"what is that?"* He said that he had been baptized and been preaching for years.

15. The young person asked him, *"but have you truly accepted Jesus by confession and received the baptism of the Holy Spirit?"* He responded that he did not know anything about that. He said that he had been a *"faithful worker and he thought that was enough."*

16. They led him to Christ on his death bed. What a shame that he had preached and led people all those years, yet he did not know Christ as his Savior. Can you imagine how many people came through that church without ever receiving salvation?

17. **(1 Timothy 1:9)** "Knowing this, that the law is not made for a righteous man, but for the lawless and disobedient, for the **ungodly** and for sinners, for unholy and profane, for murderers of fathers and murderers of mothers, for manslayers."

18.**(2 Peter 2:5)** "And spared not the old world, but saved Noah the eighth person, a preacher of righteousness, bringing in the flood upon the world of the ungodly.

19.The ungodly are those who have accepted Jesus Christ and go through the motion of salvation, but they are just what the word say, *"ungodly."*

20.They live a life that does not represent the kingdom of GOD. They are used by the enemy. They refuse to be delivered and set free. They have a hypocritical spirit. They are wicked and evil and are members in many churches.

21.These are those that will be judge in the house of GOD. GOD will expose them and deal with them because of their lack of Christianity. GOD will make a clear distinction between those who really belong to him and those who belong to the devil.

Lesson 4
The Bride of Christ

1. **(Ephesians 5:25-27)** "Husbands, love your wives, as Christ loved the church and gave himself up for her, that he might sanctify her, having cleansed her by the washing of water with the word, so that he might present the church to himself in splendor, without spot or wrinkle or any such thing, that she might be holy and without blemish".

2. Who is the bride of Christ? It is literally the wife of Jesus Christ. They are the people that Jesus is coming back for in the rapture. It is the group of people lumped in one, whom Christ will wed in the air.

3. They are called *"her"* because they are considered a bride. It is a sanctified people that have set themselves aside from the world, preparing themselves totally for His return. They are people being instructed by the word of GOD to get ready for His return.

4. Yes, the bride is the church. Even though they are one in the same, the focus must be on His return. Because no matter what the church is doing, the true church understands that they are daily preparing for His return.

5. **(2 Corinthians 11:2)** "For I feel a divine jealousy for you, since I betrothed you to one husband, to present you as a pure virgin to Christ".

6. Jesus waits for His pure virgin. One who has not been touched anymore by sin or the world; one who has called itself out from among them. Most of all, He waits for her to get ready by the approval of the Father. The bride approval is not based on Jesus, it is based on the Father.

7. **(Matthew 25:13)** "Watch therefore, for ye know neither the day nor the hour wherein the Son of man cometh".

8. **(Matthew 24:36)** "But about that day or hour no one knows, not even the angels in heaven, nor the Son, but only the Father".

9. Jesus does not even know when he is coming, the angels, nor any man. The sky will open when the Father declares that the bride is ready to be married to the Son. He will then allow His only begotten Son to stand and meet His bride,

10. **(Esther 2:12)** " Now when every maid's turn was come to go into king Ahasuerus, after that she had been twelve months, according to the manner of the women, (for so were the days of their purifications accomplished, to wit, six months with oil of myrrh, and six months with sweet odours, and with other things for the purifying of the women;)

11. The bride must go through purification before she can meet the bridegroom, before she can stand before the king of kings and Lord of Lords. Every level of washing is necessary before GOD can allow her to fully connect His Son.

12. **(Ephesians 5:25)** "Husbands, love your wives, as Christ loved the church and gave himself up for her,

13. Understand sinlessness and sin will never be allowed to connect again. It was that one time that the Father allowed all of the sins of the world to rest upon His almighty Son. But He will never allow that again. The bride must be pure and holy.

14. Jesus gave himself totally for His bride because He loved her. Because of the Father, He would do anything for His bride. But now the bride must do their part by getting ready for His return. The bride must waste no more time preparing because He will only come one time for This bride.

15. **(Ephesians 5:27)** "So that he might present the church to himself in splendor, without spot or wrinkle or any such thing, that she might be holy and without blemish."

16. **(John 14:1-3)** "Let not your hearts be troubled. Believe in GOD; believe also in me. In my Father's house are many rooms. If it were not so, would I have told you that I go to prepare a place for you? And if I go and prepare a place for you, I will come again and will take you to myself, that where I am you may be also."

17. Jesus is preparing a place for His bride. Heaven was not designed for man. It was designed for Trinity and the angels. Because of the sins of this world, man must now go to heaven. But it has to be prepared. Jesus will equip heaven for His bride.

18. Think of a man making sure that he has a place to take His bride after he marries her. He does not take her back to His mother's house. He as the groom, should have a place for her. Jesus is assured to have a place to take His bride.

19. **(Matthew 25:1-13)** "Then the kingdom of heaven will be like ten virgins who took their lamps and went to meet the bridegroom. Five of them were foolish, and five were wise. For when the foolish took their lamps, they took no oil with them, but the wise took flasks of oil with their lamps. As the bridegroom was delayed, they all became drowsy and slept".

20. The bride cannot be foolish and not be ready when the groom returns for her. The Father knows exactly how much time to give to the bride before he will return. Once the Father declares that enough time has been given, he will send His Son.

21. It does matter if they think they are ready or not. They must not be foolish. The bride lives in a marriage mode. The bride is always dressed for the wedding. The bride is constantly careful not to be stained by anything.

22. **(Ephesians 5:1-33)** "Therefore be imitators of GOD, as beloved children. And walk in love, as Christ loved us and gave himself up for us, a fragrant offering and sacrifice to GOD. But sexual immorality and all impurity or covetousness must not even be named among you, as is proper among saints. Let there be no filthiness nor foolish talk nor crude joking, which are out of place, but instead let there be thanksgiving. For you may be sure of this, that everyone who is sexually immoral or impure, or who is covetous (that is, an idolater), has no inheritance in the kingdom of Christ and GOD.

Lesson 5
The Body of Christ

1. **(Ephesians 4:11-12)** "And he gave some, apostles; and some, prophets; and some, evangelists; and some, pastors and teachers;[12] For the perfecting of the saints, for the work of the ministry, for the edifying of the body of Christ".

2. **(Romans 12:4)** "For just as each of us has one body with many members, and these members do not all have the same function".

3. **(1 Corinthians 12:14-20)** "For the body does not consist of one member but of
many. **15** If the foot should say, "Because I am not a hand, I do not belong to the
body," that would not make it any less a part of the body. **16** And if the ear should say,
"Because I am not an eye, I do not belong to the body," that would not make it any
less a part of the body. **17** If the whole body were an eye, where would be the sense of
hearing? If the whole body were an ear, where would be the sense of smell? **18** But as
it is, GOD arranged the members in the body, each one of them, as he chose. **19** If all
were a single member, where would the body be? **20** As it is, there are many
parts,[b] yet one body".

4. Who is the body of Christ? The body of Christ is the laborers in the kingdom of GOD. GOD, Jesus, and the Holy Spirit, gave each member of the body of Christ a purpose for the work to be done. Each person in the body of Christ should have a specific assignment.

5. Again, joining a church does not make you a part of the body of Christ. It makes you a member of a local congregation or people. To be a member of the body of Christ, you must be a born-again believer, with laboring abilities.

6. **(Romans 12:5)** "So we, being many, are one **body** in **Christ**, and every one member one **of** another".

7. The body of Christ is about joining together laborers for the kingdom of GOD. For the body of Christ to be affective, there must be unity. They must know their place and know how to walk together.

8. The reason that there is so much work left undone is that we as a body of believers do not know how to work together as a group of believers. So, we get very little done. If the hand is fighting against the arm and the fingers are fighting against the hand, nothing gets done.

9. There are three types of assignments:
    a. Motive gifts.
    b. Revelation gifts.
    c. Office gifts.

10. GOD gives the motives gifts. Those are the gifts that everyone is created and born with. They are general and they are usually called talents. These may appear to be your fingers or fingernails, but they are important to the body of Christ.

11. How could Jesus have made it without the Martha who cooked the meals when the disciples came to town. How would the prophets of old have made it without the widow woman being in place, or the Shulamite woman? How would an organization be maintained without a good secretary in the church?

12. **(1 Corinthians 12:28)** "And GOD has appointed in the church first apostles, second prophets, third teachers, then miracles, then gifts of healing, ***helping, administrating***, and various kinds of tongues".

13. There are many members. Everyone is born with a **motive gift**. Some people have more than one motive gift, but you must find it. Your motive gifts or talents will usually come out in your day to day living. It may come out in a job or when you go to college.

14. Again, in the body of Christ, the motive gift is so necessary. It is not popular, so it is seldom recognized. Motive gifts are a part of perfecting the saint. They bring discipline and organization to the body. They don't appear to be the real spiritual gifts, but they are yet the most important gifts.

15. For example, it is difficult to have a hand with no fingers. Those fingers make up the motive gifts. They make up the simple but most crucial things in the body of

Christ. The hand cannot truly be effective without the fingers. That shows the importance of motive gifts.

16. **(1 Corinthians 12:8-10)** "For to one is given through the Spirit the utterance of wisdom, and to another the utterance of knowledge according to the same Spirit, [9] to another faith by the same Spirit, to another gifts of healing by the one Spirit, [10] to another the working of miracles, to another prophecy, to another the ability to distinguish between spirits, to another various kinds of tongues, to another the interpretation of tongues".

17. There are the **Revelation gifts**, given by the Holy Spirit. These gifts are to reveal truth to the body of Christ. They are to uncover what is needed for the body to grow and mature. They help to give the body direction.

18. As a person is filled with the Holy Spirit, these gifts will sooner or later reveal themselves to the body or the individual. The pastor must not rush these gifts. They must allow the Lord to reveal them.

19. These gifts can be very dangerous in immature believers. If these gifts manifest without maturity it could be damaging. It is like Tabitha in the sitcom Bewitched. Powers manifested when she was a child. She did not know how to control them. She would be touching her nose and moving things around in front of the wrong people. She did not know the danger of her power.

20. **(Ephesians 4:11-12)** "And he gave some, apostles; and some, prophets; and some, evangelists; and some, pastors and teachers;[12] For the perfecting of the saints, for the work of the ministry, for the edifying of the body of Christ".

21. The **office gifts** are given by Jesus Christ himself. These are called positions. They are the generals of the kingdom. They bring forth the order of the church. The key word to this scripture is *"SOME"*.

22. The office positions cannot be just taken on in the body of Christ, Jesus must give them to each individual. He must be the one to pick them. These gifts or positions you cannot just desire, they must be given.

23. The office positions concerning the body is the headship positions. They make sure that all other gifts align properly. These gifts can do much damage. They can destroy many lives if not handled properly. These office positions are the brain of the body. (You will learn much about each gift in the book of Gift Matching).

Lesson 6
The Laborers are Few

1. **(Matthew 9:37-38 NIV)** "[37] Then he said to His disciples, "The harvest is plentiful, but the workers are few. [38] Ask the Lord of the harvest, therefore, to send out workers into His harvest field."

2. The word *"harvest"* means the production that should be brought in from seed that has been planted. It is the work that needs to be done. It is the souls that need to be won. The word "plentiful" means not lacking, in overflow.

3. There is much work to be done. Therefore, the body of Christ is to be the workers for the kingdom. There is so much work left undone because GOD cannot find laborers in the body. Jesus started out with many, but He only ended up with twelve.

4. Out of every twenty-five people sitting in the church, there will only be one true worker. Therefore, in a church of a hundred people, you only have four laborers. Isn't that sad. The rest of people may be faithful Christians, but they will not be workers. Again, you may have many Christians in the church, but they will not necessarily be the body of Christ.

5. The word *"few"* means limited. The body of Christ is limited because of laborers. That is why Jesus said, "pray for laborers, workers to come." The longer that it takes for workers to come the longer it will take for Jesus to return.

6. Often the harvest is ready. What does that mean? It is like a garden of vegetables that are ready to be picked but nobody is there to pick them. Therefore, the vegetables simply rot on the vine. How many people are ready to come in to be witnessed to and no one is available to pick the harvest. The harvest is left to rot on the vine.

7. Thank GOD for ministering angels. If it were not for angels doing the work, many souls would have been left unreached or dealt with. Many lives would have been left unattended due to the lack of laborers in the vineyard.

8. **(Ephesians 4:11-12)** "And he gave some, apostles; and some, prophets; and some, evangelists; and some, pastors and teachers;[12] For the perfecting of the saints, for the work of the ministry, for the edifying of the body of Christ".

9. The key thing to the body of Christ is *"the perfecting of the saints"*. The word perfecting means the completion of. Laborers are needed to complete each child of GOD, from salvation to the day that Jesus Christ returns for bride.

10. The bride is incomplete because so much of the body of Christ is out of place. That is why you have so many people in the body of Christ left undelivered, unhealed, lacking total freedom, because the laborers, the workers are out of place.

11. Where is the true evangelist that should be helping that person get the foundation of salvation, helping that individual be delivered of evil spirits? Because the laborer is out of place, people are simply left incomplete, not knowing what they are truly looking for in life.

12. When Jesus came to earth, that's the reason that he had to play each role of the fivefold ministry and also each role of sixteen gifts. He had to take those twelve men and complete them before he left the earth.

13. The body of Christ, the laborers, are lacking because people are more interested in a title and position, versus the job itself. They like being called by the title but don't want the work that goes along with it.

14. Many times, with the children of GOD, they want to be in a headship position. They want to be the head, but not the eyes or ears, because those roles do not seem to be important roles. But the eyes and the ears are the true discerners. They are the most important role a person can play.

15. **(Luke 13:27)** "But he shall say, I tell you, I know you not whence ye are; depart from me, all ye **workers** of iniquity".

16. It is sad because many workers in the kingdom of GOD are workers of iniquity. They are only working for themselves, the money, or their own glory. That is why they are called "workers of iniquity." Their motives are all wrong. They really don't care anything about the people of GOD nor the kingdom of GOD. That is why GOD is going to tell them *"to depart."*

17. So much of the work of GOD has become contaminated by the world. It is not pure sanctified work. It is mixed in with unclean suggestions directly from Satan himself, making the world think that our work is the same as theirs, but it is not. As laborers, workers in the kingdom of GOD, we must not compromise for any reason.

18.**(2 Corinthians 11:13)** "For such are false apostles, deceitful **workers**, transforming themselves into the apostles of Christ.

19.The word *"deceitful"* means liars. There are many who are deceitful workers in the kingdom of GOD. They are often lying to the children of GOD to get what they want. They will act the part and look the part, but they are not the part.

20.They have turned themselves into false laborers. They are pretending that it is about Jesus when it is actually just about deceiving the children of GOD for the sake of the kingdom of satan. They work for the devil directly. They come to simply bring down the kingdom of GOD. They are outright deceivers.

21.**(Philippians 3:2)** "Beware of dogs, beware of evil workers, beware of the concision".

22.The word *"evil"* means of no value of benefit. There will be workers in the kingdom of GOD that have no value or benefit to anyone.

23.We are not to become sinners to win sinners. We do not become unclean to win unclean people. Jesus walked among the sinners but yet remained holy and righteous. As laborers in the vineyard, we must do the same.

Lesson 7
The Revelation Gifts

1. **Revelation gifts reveal or uncover hidden truth.**

2. Revelation gifts reveal:
    a. The reason behind the problem.
    b. Details concerning the problem.

3. Revelation gifts:
    a. Help direct the body.
    b. Help bring true understanding.

4. There are nine revelation gifts (I Corinthians 12:6-11)
    a. Word of wisdom.
    b. Word of knowledge.
    c. Gifts of healings.
    d. Working of miracles.
    e. Prophecy.
    f. Faith.
    g. Discerning of Spirits.
    h. Different kinds of tongues.
    i. Interpretation of tongues.

5. **All of the gifts are important.**

6. Word of Wisdom
    a. It is the mind of GOD.
    b. Knowing how to activate something in the right way.
    c. Knowing how to apply something right.
    d. Giving you details as to how to walk something out.
    Examples:
        (a) Joshua – wall – 7 times.
        (b) Gideon – 300 men.
    e. Giving someone detailed information as to how to carry out things for:
        (a) Ministry
        (b) Business

7. Word of Knowledge
    a. It is direct information about the present.
    b. Word of knowledge deals with the now.
    c. Word of knowledge deals with a present problem or situation.
    d. A word of knowledge does not tell you how to deal with situations.
    e. For example: The woman at the well **(John 4:18)** having 5 husbands.
    f. The Word of Knowledge will help you face your situation at present time.

8. Gifts of Healings
    a. It is a way of getting people free of an infirmity or sickness.
    b. It states gifts of healings.
    c. There are many different ways to get people healed.
    d. There are many different reasons as to why people are sick.
    e. There are approximately seven different areas of healing:
        1) Laying on of hands.
        2) Casting out a demon.
        3) Prophetic healing.
        4) Bitter roots.
        5) Generational curses.
        6) Mental deliverance.
        7) Fear.

9. **Gifts of <u>healing</u> are part of the signs and wonders.**

10. When you have one of the fivefold ministry gifts, you may have one of the specific areas of healing.

11. You must seek GOD as to which one to use in each give situation.

12. Many people use the wrong one, therefore, healing does not occur.

13. **(Mark 16:17-18)** "And these signs shall follow them that believe; In my name shall they cast out devils; they shall speak with new tongues; They shall take up serpents; and if they drink any deadly thing, it shall not hurt them; they shall lay hands on the sick, and they shall recover".

14. The first type of healing is the ***laying on of hands.*** There are two major things that come with the laying on of hands:
   a. You must believe.
   b. It must be done in the name of JESUS.

15. **There are <u>two</u> people who must believe:**
   a. The person laying on the hands.
   b. The person receiving healing.

16. The person laying on the hands:
   a. Must believe in laying on of hands.
   b. Must believe in miracles.
   c. Must believe the person truly can be healed.
   d. Must believe GOD that has commissioned you to do it.

17. The person receiving the healing:
   a. Must believe in healing.
   b. Must believe the healing belongs to them.
   c. Must believe in the power of GOD.
   d. Must believe that GOD is using the individual laying on the hands.

18. There are two types of laying on of hands:
   a. Laying on of hands by faith.
   b. Laying on of hands by the anointing.

19. **(Mark 1:40-42)** A man with leprosy came and knelt in front of Jesus, begging to be healed. "If you are willing, you can heal me and make me clean," he said. Moved with compassion, Jesus reached out and touched him. "I am willing," he said. "Be healed!" Instantly the leprosy disappeared, and the man was healed.

20. **Whenever the power of GOD is present, the healing will come strictly by the <u>anointing.</u>** Everyone who is available to the anointing can be set free.

21. Even if faith is not present, healing can still come forth. The anointing will override the limited or weak faith.

22. There are people who have the gift of healing and when the anointing comes upon them, they can quickly lay hands and get results.

23. **(Mark 5:32-34**) "But he kept on looking around to see who had done it. Then the frightened woman, trembling at the realization of what had happened to her, came, and fell at His feet and told him what she had done. And he said to her, "Daughter***, your faith has made you well.*** Go in peace. Your suffering is over."

24. Healing comes through faith. This can be done anywhere. Faith of healing operates in two formats:
    a. Faith to faith.
    b. Faith to the anointing.

25. **Faith to faith is when <u>two people</u> with faith touch and agree.** Therefore, healing is manifested.

26. Faith to the anointing is when there is an anointed vessel or item that someone connects to. When the woman with the issue of blood connected to anointing of the hem of JESUS' garment, she was healed.

27. Whenever a person lacks faith, you must stop and minster to them or healing may not come forth.

28. Sometimes one person's faith is enough if it is strong enough.

29. **(Mark 1:31)" So** he went to her bedside, ***took her by the hand,*** and helped her sit up. Then the fever left her, and she prepared a meal for them".

30. Laying on of hands can be on any place on the body. Sometimes you may have to touch a second time in a different place. Most of all just believe in the touch.

31. **(Mark 16:18)** "They shall take up serpents; and if they drink any deadly thing, it shall not hurt them; they shall lay hands on the sick, ***and they shall recover".***

32. When you lay on of hands, you must expect recovery, even if you do not see immediate results. ***Healing is all in the expectancy.*** You must get caught up in the recovery, not the sickness.

33. As people are leaving the altar you must encourage them to become consumed with their healing, not their situation.

34. To lay hands, we are qualified by our faith and experience. You must have the faith to believe that it can happen. However, if you are not wise when laying on the hands, it can be ineffective and detrimental.

Lesson 8
Prophetic Healing

1. **(Psalm 107:20)** "He sent His word, and healed them, and delivered them from their destructions". The second type of healing we will deal with is ***prophetic healing.***

2. **Prophetic healing is when <u>one speaks</u> a Rhema word (a word directly from the Holy Spirit) over a sick person and they are healed.**

3. Prophetic healing can be used in three ways:
    a. Speaking a certain scripture
    b. Speaking certain powerful words
    c. Calling out the disease itself

4. **(Matthew 8:8)** "The centurion answered and said, Lord, I am not worthy that thou shouldest come under my roof: but speak the word only, and my servant shall be healed."

5. With prophetic healing, you do not have to touch the person at all. The healing is in:
    a. Words
    b. The anointing in the air
    c. The anointing carrying the healing to the person through the words

6. **(Mark 11:22-23)** "And Jesus answering saith unto them, Have faith in GOD. 23 For verily I say unto you, that whoever shall say unto this mountain, Be removed, and be thou cast into the sea; and shall not doubt in his heart, but shall believe that those things which he saith shall come to pass; he shall have whatsoever he saith."

7. **Prophetic healing can be done through <u>faith</u>.** A person can speak over themselves or someone else. Therefore, through the power of faith, the mountain of sickness can be removed.

8. In prophetic healing through faith, there are three things one needs:
    a. Faith – believe what you say
    b. Your words – say the right words
    c. Repetition – repeat it until it is believed

9. If you hear someone begging, then they do not believe. They are saying the wrong words, and their repetition is in vain. You must stop them and do some teaching to get them on the right track.

10. **There is nothing wrong with <u>repetition,</u> as long as it is in order.** The right repetition develops the right mindset concerning healing.

11. From a service, you may have to send people home with prophetic healing to develop their faith. Prophetic healing will also be used to rid the person of doubt and fear.

12. The person may also need to go home with prophetic healing because the healing was not complete the first time it was spoken.

13. Understand that when you pray, you are asking, but when you speak you are putting a command on the anointing. You are commanding that problem, or the devil himself, to go.

14. You must command the mountain directly. Do not be too general or it will appear that:

    a. **You are afraid.**
    b. **You are inexperienced.**

15. Prophetic healings are designed for you to be very specific.

16. Many true prophets who operate in deliverance ministry will use prophetic healing because their foundation gift is prophecy.

17. When the strength of their anointing is prophecy, prophetic healing will flow very easily.

Lesson 9
Faith Plans of God

1. **(2 King 5:10)** "And Elisha sent a messenger unto him, saying, Go and wash in Jordan seven times, and thy flesh shall come again to thee, and thou shalt be clean".

2. Now we will deal with the ***specific faith plans of GOD*** for receiving healing. What are specific faith plans? They are certain details given by GOD to a person to receive their healing.

3. For example, GOD gave Naaman specific details from Elisha to go and wash in a pool seven times and he would be healed. This is what you call a ***faith plan.*** All Naaman had to do was follow them.

4. Many times, GOD will give a minster a specific faith plan for a person in church to receive their healing such as:
    a. Say a certain thing a certain amount of times.
    b. Run.
    c. Walk around a certain amount of times.
    d. Bend.

c. Whatever the plan may be, all the person has to do is follow it. Many will not follow because they are:
    a. Embarrassed.
    b. Afraid.
    c. Prideful.
    d. Doubtful.

d. **(John 9:6-7)** "Then he spit on the ground, made mud with the saliva, and spread the mud over the blind man's eyes. [7] He told him, "Go wash yourself in the pool of Siloam" (Siloam means "sent"). So, the man went and washed and came back seeing"!

e. This man had to go to a specific place to receive his healing. Even though Christ had put mud on his eyes from His power, the total healing could not come forth without going to that certain place.

f. **(1 King 17:21)** "And he stretched himself out over the child three times and cried out to the Lord, "O Lord my GOD, please let this child's life return to him."

g. There are many things that may appear crazy, but if GOD gives the plan, it will work every time. Elijah stretching his body over the child's body appeared foolish, but it was the plan of GOD. Therefore, it worked.

h. **Every plan of GOD is used to bring glory to Himself, not man.** The plan is for the world to see the true power of GOD.

i. Some details can be very specific but preferred such as:
    a. Rise up.
    b. Stretch forth.
    c. Take up.

j. If people respond in faith, they will get their results. But they must respond with faith. Obedience and faith will bring results.

k. **You cannot alter any of the plans just because you do not like certain portions.** Naaman did not want to go and wash in Jordan. He wanted to go to a different river. It would not have worked if he didn't go to Jordan.

l. **You cannot copycat plans for your own usage.** You must ask GOD for a specific plan for that specific situation. There have been many who tried it and did not work. They got no results.

m. You must link yourself to the Spirit so that he can reveal His plans to you. Specific plans make kingdom work so much easier. Also, you will get quicker results.

Lesson 10
Repentance-Forgiveness of Sin

1. **(Matthew 9:2)** "And, behold, they brought to him a man sick of the palsy, lying on a bed: and Jesus seeing their faith said unto the sick of the palsy; Son, be of good cheer; thy sins be forgiven thee".

2. Now we will deal with healing through the ***repentance or the forgiveness of sin.*** Many people today are sick because of sin or the lack of forgiveness of sin.

3. The man in the above scripture was sick with palsy. JESUS did not touch him, but he forgave His sins which brought forth the healing. Again, it was the sin in his life that brought on the sickness.

4. **Sin is a spiritual <u>blockage</u> to healing.** Many people remain sick all of their lives because the sin is not exposed. There are those who know that it was an act of sin, but they are embarrassed about the sin, so they attempt everything else, except true repentance.

5. **(John 1:29)** "The next day John seeth Jesus coming unto him, and saith, Behold the Lamb of GOD, which taketh away the sin of the world".

6. There are those who need true salvation. They need to be saved from sin, which is the world, not just sins or their personal strongholds.

7. Salvation is spiritual healing which in turn can produce physical healing. This is why you must not be afraid to ask sick people, "Are you saved?"

8. **Lack of <u>salvation</u> can be holding up healing.** The person can have faith for their healing, but the bondage of sin is blocking the process of healing.

9. **(John 5:14)** "Afterward Jesus findeth him in the temple, and said unto him, Behold, thou art made whole: sin no more, lest a worse thing come unto thee."

10. There are those who are sick from repeating sins. When people repeat sins, the sickness can come back, and it can get worse. That is why it is important to minister to people about sin concerning their healing.

11. **(Mark 11:25-26)** "And when ye stand praying, forgive, if ye have ought against any: that your Father also which is in heaven may forgive you your trespasses. 26 But if ye do not forgive, neither will your Father which is in heaven forgive your trespasses."

12. Many people are sick because they have unforgiveness in their heart against someone. They lack forgiveness toward:
   a. Parent.
   b. Child.
   c. Mate.
   d. Co-worker.

13. Many people who have chronic stomach problems, severe headache, and chronic pain syndromes can have unforgiveness in their hearts.

14. There was a woman in a church who always had chronic leg pain. It was due to a lack of forgiveness toward her son.

15. There are four types of forgiveness:
   a. Forgiveness from GOD.
   b. Forgiveness from others.
   c. Forgiveness others.
   d. Forgiving oneself.

16. If a person has a lack of forgiveness, there is unusually a lot of anger, bitterness, and condemnation, which also brings a great deal of sickness. When a minister picks up anger and bitterness, you must continue getting to the root of the issue. You will probably find unforgiveness.

17. You must discern the spirit of the person. You must not be afraid to confront a person about their sin/sins if you are expecting healing.

18. You can't bypass sin and unforgiveness with prophecy and the laying on of hands. It is constantly tried in the church, and it will not work.

Lesson 11
Generational Curses

1. There are many who are sick because of generational curses. What is a generational curse? *It is something that is passed from generations or family members to another.*

2. Generational curses are throughout **the world**. There are many sick from certain illnesses that have been passed from parents, grandparents, or great grandparents.

3. When people go to the doctor, the doctor will ask for a family history. The reason why they ask for the history is because they are usually trying to find out if the sickness you have possibly came from another family member.

4. Many people have generational curses through blood transmitted diseases such as sickle cell anemia. These are generational diseases that are transferred through the parent having the disease or two parents carrying the trait.

5. In this case, you must curse the curse and you must come up against the curse of the parents and rebuke the disease.

6. Then there are those who are cursed by genetic transfers such as cancer. Many doctors do genetic studies on people to see if they will have a certain disease. Again, you must rebuke the curse. It is a generational disease.

7. There are people who are totally content by using genetic studies. They have already accepted certain diseases upon themselves from genetic studies.

8. Doctors have convinced people they are going to have certain diseases from genetic studies. They have convinced them they are going to have certain kinds of cancers. You must rebuke that curse so that the person can be free.

9. Sometimes there may be no sign of the disease yet. But because of the study, the person will become mentally sick. Fear will dominate their mind. You must rebuke the curse for freedom to come.

10. There are those who have curses through bad habits developed from others. There are people who are sick with obesity, high blood pressure, and diabetes because of bad habits.

11. You must rebuke the curse and begin to help them understand the curse. They must also be involved in the healing process. It will require more than that just rebuking the curse. They will have to change their lifestyle as a part of the healing process.

12. There are curses of sickness through witchcraft. Many people have certain types of sicknesses through witchcraft brought on by themselves or others.

13. There are many who have gotten involved with worshipping idol gods. There are those that have been to witches and warlocks. Because of being involved with that kind of activity, they actually have physical illnesses.

14. There are those who have eaten food that people have tainted with witchcraft substance.

15. Witchcraft is a type of demonic spirit that has been placed on or eaten by the person that can bring on physical sickness.

16. There were two young men playing with a Ouija board. They were constantly playing with it. One of the young men lost total usage of his legs. Once the spirit of witchcraft was exposed, the spirit was rebuked, and the person's legs began to move again.

17. There was a young lady who drank from a can that someone had put something in. She became very ill. But with time, it was discovered that someone had put something in her drink. This person was trying to hurt a Christian young woman. She came and the spirit was rebuked, and she was healed.

18. Witchcraft is a very dangerous thing. People have been known to have boils and other illnesses because of witchcraft curses. You must not play in the devil's territory. The devil *is* real.

19. Then there is the witchcraft of medication. Pharmaceutical medications can be under the influence of witchcraft. *Witchcraft is the power to control something or someone.* When someone is on certain medications, they can be under the spirit of witchcraft or a curse. They are being controlled by a substance.

Lesson 12
Spirits of Sickness

1. **(Mark 9:25)** "When Jesus saw that the people came running together, He rebuked the foul spirit, saying unto him, Thou dumb and deaf spirit, I charge thee, come out of him, and enter no more into him".

2. **Sometimes a sickness can be a <u>demon</u>.** There are people who are possessed, and that is why they are sick. When a person is possessed, that person must be delivered. The spirit must be cast out to bring total healing.

3. **When a person has a demon, their body is <u>controlled</u> by a spirit.** The spirit itself brings on the sickness to the flesh. There are people who cannot walk or talk because of the spirit.

4. This man's son had a dumb spirit; he could not talk. His life was controlled by the spirit. His healing was to come by casting out a demon.

5. **(Mark 5:6-8)** "But when he saw Jesus afar off, he ran and worshipped him, and cried with a loud voice, and said, what have I to do with thee, Jesus, thou Son of the Most High GOD? I adjure thee by GOD, that thou torment me not. For he said unto him, Come out of the man, thou unclean spirit. And he asked him, What is thy name? And he answered, saying, My name is Legion: for we are many."

6. There are those who have *<u>mental illnesses</u>* because of spirits. Some cannot even function in society. These are people who need total deliverance.

7. There may be legions of demons in the person, which means many. They may not all come out at one time. You may have to expose them one at a time.

8. If a person will get total deliverance, they usually can go back and function normally in society.

9. Many people have growths and boils on them because of spirits. Satan loves ugliness because it brings so much attention to him. There are people who are disfigured because of the ugliness of Satan. The devil also likes drawing attention to himself.

10. There are those whose speech can be controlled by spirits. Some have stuttering problems. Once they receive the Holy Spirit, the demonic spirit leaves, and their language becomes clear.

11. **(Luke 4:38-39)** "And He arose out of the synagogue and entered into Simon's house. And Simon's wife's mother was taken with a great fever; and they besought him for her. [39] And He stood over her, and rebuked the fever; and it left her: and immediately she arose and ministered unto them."

12. There are spirits of sickness that are not terminal or long term. There can be spirits of sickness that are short term such as headaches or fevers.

13. There was someone doing a service one night they had been warned not to touch anyone unless at the altar for prayer. There was a man who came up the aisle of the church suddenly. He grabbed the minister's hand on purpose to transfer a spirit. The spirit attacked her head.

14. The next day they had a headache. They could not figure out what was going on until hours later. They began to pray, and the Holy Spirit brought it to their attention that they were not to touch anyone. They rebuked the spirit, and the headache went away immediately.

15. There are those who have the spirit of pain. Their bodies hurt them in a certain area. No medication seems to help. There was a situation where a woman had a pain in her stomach for 6 years. She came to service, deliverance came, and the pain went away.

16. Many people are walking around with chronic pain, and they cannot get rid of it. They are hooked on all kinds of medications. The real problem is that they have a spirit of pain.

17. Most incurable diseases are spirits. Because Satan comes to steal, kill, and destroy, his ultimate goal is to destroy everyone he can.

18. He knows that if you do not recognize he is a spirit, he will just move from one part of the body to another part. Sometimes you can hear people say, *"The cancer is now gone from the lungs to their liver."* He will plant his seed everywhere he can.

19. Many people continue to turn to natural drugs trying to control the spirit when the spirit must be cast out. The incurable or terminal illness usually leads to death because there is also a death spirit.

20. To cast him out, you must first bind him up. You take his authority and then you must cast him out. You must stop his working power.

21. You must let him know you recognize that the condition is a spirit. You must declare the spirit to go immediately.

22. The person must reject the spirit also. Some people have become comfortable living with a spirit of infirmity. They must desire to have a clean house.

Lesson 13
Healing

1. **(1 Corinthians 1:27)"** But GOD hath chosen the foolish things of the world to confound the wise; and GOD hath chosen the weak things of the world to confound the things which are mighty."

2. There are four major items that can be used for healing:
    a. Anointing oil.
    b. Water.
    c. Handkerchief.
    d. Communion.
    e. Slain in the Spirit.

3. ***The anointing oil is <u>symbolic</u> of the Holy Ghost.*** It is a representation of power. However, the true power is in the Holy Ghost and faith. The oil is an outward sign of GOD's power.

4. Also, GOD will use water. *Jesus called Himself "the Living Water."* When He was at the well, He told the woman to *"drink of Him"* because He was the Living Water. The water represents the power which He was and is.

5. When JESUS died on the cross, water and blood came out of His side. Water came out because it is a form of *<u>judgment.</u>*

6. There are people who can be healed during baptism because of the water. The water will judge the sickness. It will sentence the sickness to death. Naaman was healed in the river of Jordan.

7. There are those who can drink the water and it will bring healing to the body. Again, because water means judgment, it can judge anything in the body.

8. People have been healed of constipation, aid, ulcers, and other things because of drinking the water.

9. There are those who bathe in the water because of the anointing. You can use water in regular church services and revivals. People can bring water at all times for deliverances.

10. Water can be used in the hospital for someone who is sick and cannot go to the baptism pool. Water can be sprinkled over the vessel for healing. GOD can bring divine healing just like that.

11. **(Act 9, 10, and 11)** Many use cloths or handkerchiefs. It is not the handkerchief or the cloth, it is the anointing. The anointing can be on objects. Demons can be cast out by the cloth.

12. If you understand the healing ministry, you can wear a handkerchief on your body to release the anointing for healing and deliverance. It is a wonderful thing to see the anointing GOD released through the cloth.

13. The cloth can have hands placed on them during intercessory prayer. Also, handkerchiefs can be placed at the altar.

14. When people are using the cloth, you must encourage them to keep using it. It can be placed on the sickness or placed on the bed, but they are to keep using it until they see results.

15. Cloth can be cut up and placed all over your body or house for victory. There are times when people can put names on the cloth for relatives and through this, salvation and healing can come.

16. Healing can come forth in communion because the wine and bread is Holy. People can receive healing right there.

17. It has happened several times in different church services. During communion, the power of faith in the communion brought forth healing.

18. When a person sees themselves taking on the blood of JESUS and the Body of Christ, they can see themselves taking on the wholeness of Christ.

19. People also can be healed by being slain in the Spirit. There are many who truly go under the Power of GOD, and being under the total influence of the Spirit, healing will come.

20. Never rush being slain in the Spirit because the Holy Spirit is very well working on that person or the situation.

Lesson 14
Types of Sicknesses

1. There are some sicknesses that are there to bring Glory to GOD. You must be able to recognize that. This type of sickness will not be a demon or a generational curse.

2. There are times when the world must see the healing and then magnify GOD because of the healing. GOD uses that person to bring salvation, deliverance, and most of all, Glory to His Kingdom.

3. The disciples wanted to know who had sinned. JESUS said *"no one."* It allowed GOD to manifest His power to man.

4. When Lazarus died, JESUS could have gotten there much earlier, but His timing was about the Glory of GOD.

5. Sometimes you may be praying for someone to get healed and it seems as though it may never happen. But many times, the timing is based on GOD's Glory. The timing will happen when all eyes are on the Power of GOD.

6. Sometimes when people get discouraged with timing, they begin to <u>blame</u> people. When you are discouraged with timing, you will only discourage the person trying to get healed and can cause that person to give up.

7. **(Luke 17:11-14)** "As He entered a village there, ten lepers stood at a distance, 13 crying out, "Jesus, Master, have mercy on us!" 14 He looked at them and said, "Go show yourselves to the priests." And as they went, they were cleansed of their leprosy."

8. There are those who may not get healed <u>immediately.</u> It will happen as time goes on. This can happen with the laying on of hands, the water, the oil, and the cloth.

9. Again, this will happen based on the timing of GOD. We must keep our focus on the healing, not the time. If you get caught up on the time more than the healing, you may easily miss the blessing.

10. The ten lepers got their healing as they went. They did not get it while they were standing in front of Jesus. Sometimes the person will not get their healing standing directly in front of the preacher; it may happen in the car, in their bed, or even on their job. *You must just believe.*

11. Healing does not have to be understood, it has to be received. One of the main things that will mess up the timing of healing is people trying to understand the process instead of just believing. Many people have left the altar defeated because of the lack of belief.

12. You must pay close attention as to whether or not the person is receiving the healing or analyzing the healing. If they are trying to understand the process, you are just wasting your time.

13. The blind man did not try to comprehend his breakthrough. All he said was *"I once was blind, but now I see."* This was a person ready to receive.

14. You may have to pray for mercy. There are those that you must ask GOD to have mercy on them. *You are asking GOD to have compassion on that person. This kind of healing is based on your faith, their desire, and GOD's compassion.*

15. This is a person who may not have a fighting spirit anymore. Sometimes it is a child, or it can be a sinner. You must ask GOD to show you if this is how you should pray. It can be done, and healing can come.

16. There was a lady in her home that a pastor visited. She was very sick. As they continued to pray the situation was not changing. The Lord spoke to the pastor and told him *"to pray a mercy healing on the person*" because the person was worn out.

17. When they prayed this type of prayer the person was healed immediately. There are many times in the Bible when GOD moved with compassion. He moves based on mercy. He had compassion for the individual and healing came. You must be able to discern this in the Spirit.

18. There are some healings that are going to come through intercessory prayer. The saint's prayers can produce much. Sometimes saints must come together and travail for one individual. They must be willing to labor in prayer until they get the necessary results.

19. **(James 5:14-15)** "Are any of you sick? You should call for the elders of the church to come and pray over you, anointing you with oil in the name of the Lord. [15] Such a prayer offered in faith will heal the sick, and the Lord will make you well." Intercessory prayer for a sickness can bring healing.

20. This can be done by one individual or a multitude of individuals. You must know when to call on the Body of Christ for help.

21. You must also know when to pray in the Holy Spirit concerning sickness. *The Holy Ghost knows how to pray a perfect prayer.* You must do this when you don't know exactly how to pray.

22. Intercessory prayer can get you results. It is a great way to bring healing to an individual. You must pray until GOD tells you to stop. We sometimes give up too soon.

Lesson 15
The Healing Ministry

1. The healing ministry is a wonderful thing. But if you are more concerned about your looks and your reputation, you will not be able to function in healing and deliverance.

2. When you are dealing with the healing ministry, you cannot be afraid. You cannot be afraid of:

a. The person getting healed.
b. The people in the congregation.
c. The devil.

3. *One of the greatest hindrances in healing is fear.* It is either the person getting healed or the person being used. ***Fear will block healing every time.*** If you are afraid, just leave the person or the situation alone until you can get past fear.

4. You cannot be afraid of failure. Everybody may not get healed, but act like it and believe like everybody will. If you are afraid of failure, you will not pursue true healing.

5. You may pray for 50 and only 1 get healed, but you must keep on praying. Don't be discouraged by the 49. You must tell yourself, "There is one more person that is not sick anymore."

6. You must not allow yourself to get discouraged as a leader or a person being in the healing ministry because the healing ministry is not about you, it is about the Glory of GOD.

7. ***Doubt will stop healing.*** If you doubt the power of GOD or GOD using you, the healing will not come. You must get all of the doubt from yourself, the person getting healed, and the congregation.

8. JESUS put the doubters out of the room. He would not allow them around him when he was working miracles. You can sense in your spirit when doubters are around.

9. **When you sense doubt, stop praying and minister.** You must get the atmosphere up to a healing atmosphere. If that is not possible, you may have to wait or take the person out of the room.

10. Some healings can come in an atmosphere of worship. Sometimes you may have to stop ministering or praying and go into a spirit of worship so that the anointing can have free course.

11. The healing anointing is very sensitive. ***The Holy Spirit is a still, small voice.*** You cannot treat the anointing just any kind of way.

12. If a person begins to beg GOD, that is usually a sign of doubt. You don't have to beg GOD; you just ask or just receive. If they start to beg, you must stop them and minister to them.

13. If a person will not listen to you while you are ministering or praying, stop them. This is usually doubt because of fleshly desperation.

14. You must get their attention so that they can be ministered to. There are times when people are crying uncontrollably. You must stop them and get them back in control.

15. Sometimes to bring healing, you must take the time to minister to a person about healing so that you can bring them into a place of faith.

16. Ministering will not always bring understanding, but it can bring belief, faith, and the ability for the person to obey specific instructions.

17. You must recognize when there is little faith. Another name for little faith is weak or limited faith.

18. In this situation, you may have to minister to the person or you will have to use your faith. Sometimes you must include the congregation to pull on their faith. You need a balance of faith. You need as much faith as possible.

19. Do not be afraid to dismiss the service, if necessary, for a person needing healing. You must surround yourself with the right people and atmosphere for healing.

Lesson 16
The Healing Ministry *(Continued)*

1. You must prepare yourself for the healing ministry. You cannot take it lightly.

2. We often think that just because we have the Holy Ghost, that is all it takes. The Holy Spirit is the power source, but your part is killing the flesh.

3. When the disciples tried to cast out a devil, they could not because there was too much flesh. JESUS said the power came by fasting and praying.

4. **You must remove <u>flesh</u> by praying, fasting, the Word, righteousness, and holiness.**

5. **You must keep your vessel clean and pure, as much as possible. You must remain in a spiritual healing place at all times.**

6. *You cannot walk around with sin and unforgiveness in your heart and work in a healing ministry. You must stay in constant self- examination.*

7. You must be in constant preparation by the Word and pray. You must not take the gift for granted.

8. *You must pray in the Holy Spirit. Be sensitive to the Spirit. You must always be open to the voice of the Holy Spirit.*

9. **Don't be <u>anxious</u> but be wise in the healing ministry.** You can easily hurt someone by being overly zealous. You must be mature about every situation.

10. You must know how to be discreet, yet bold enough to deal with the situation. The healing ministry again is very sensitive.

11. Again, you must be willing to meet the requirements. If not, you will not be effective in the healing ministry.

12. The healing ministry is not a show. Build your faith for the work of the ministry. You cannot be lazy when it comes to healing and deliverance.

13. *You must be trainable and willing to learn. You must be open to the plans of GOD. This ministry is not about popularity, but it is about victory in JESUS Christ.*

14. ***You must study the Word in <u>depth</u>.*** *You must get knowledge, wisdom, and understanding in the healing ministry.*

15. *GOD desires people healed, and He desires to use many, but you must be willing to meet the requirements.*

Lesson 17
Working Miracles

1. Working Miracles
    a. Doing the supernatural concerning:
        (a) Individual.
        (b) Nature.
        (c) Financial
        (d) Life/Death.
        (e) Physical structures.
    b. We always need miracles in every area of our lives.
    c. Miracles can be used by any fivefold ministry, but mainly used by the Apostle and especially the Evangelist.
    d. Miracles are needed for the unbeliever; that is why the Evangelist operates greatly in the working of miracles.
    e. **No believer should live on miracles.** Eventually believers should be walking in the promises of GOD.

2. Prophecy
    a. Prophecy is used for:
        (a) Foretelling.
        (b) Forth telling.
        (c) Confirming.
    b. Gift of prophecy is not the office of the prophet.
    c. The gift of prophecy does not function in the fivefold office area.
    d. Gift of prophecy does not:
        (a) Preach.
        (b) Teach.
        (c) Evangelize.
    e. Gift of prophecy is localized.
    f. Gift of prophecy can operate in the:
        (a) Word of Wisdom
        (b) Word of Knowledge
    g. Gift of prophecy will or can have the:
        a) Discerning of Spirits.
        (b) Prophetic healing.
    h. The gift of prophecy is excellent for the local church because it:
        (a) Helps to birth gifts in the body.

(b) Helps to keep the vision focused in the local church.
(c) Expose falseness in the local church.

3. Gift of Faith
   a. **Gift of Faith is a supernatural plan from GOD;** therefore, having supernatural ability to carry things out.
   b. 3 Types of Faith
      (a) Saving Faith: Faith to receive Christ.
      (b) Fruit of Faith: Daily living Faith.
      (c) Gift of Faith: Supernatural Faith.
   c. The Gift of Faith is needed for:
      (a) Healing.
      (b) Miracles.
      (c) Moving mountains.
      (d) Financial miracles.
   d. A person with the Gift of Faith will:
      (a) Believe the impossible.
      (b) See the impossible.
      (c) Expect the impossible.
      (d) Move in the impossible.
   e. People with the Gift of Faith can operate in the:
      (a) Healing ministry.
      (b) Miracle ministry.
      (c) Prophetic healing.
   f. A person with the Gift of Faith, again, will move greatly in the supernatural

Lesson 18
Spirit of Discernment

Discernment

a. To see the internal purpose, motive, and intent behind why a person does a certain thing.
b. Discernment is one of the most important gifts one can have.
c. **Discernment is needed for your <u>everyday</u> life.**
d. The gift of discernment can be used with every office gift and motive gift.
e. Discernment is needed for the deliverance ministry especially.
f. Discernment exposes the root of the issue.
g. In dealing with the gift of healing, one must discern the cause of the sickness.
h. Many do not get delivered because they do not know the cause.
i. Again, the causes of sickness:
    - (a) A demon.
    - (b) An infirmity.
    - (c) Sin.
    - (d) General curse.
    - (e) Bitter roots
    - (f) Others.
j. **Discernment will expose the <u>causes.</u>**
k. Discernment exposes the intent of the heart.
l. Discernment exposes the thought pattern.
m. Discernment exposes spirits of the flesh.
n. Discernment can give one word for prophecy to bring a breakthrough.
o. Discernment exposes exact dates and times.
p. Discernment exposes details and direction.
q. Again, the gift of discernment can be and should be a part of all revelation gifts.
r. Discernment is vital for:
    - (a) Business deals.
    - (b) Young employees.
    - (c) Developing friendships.
    - (d) Working in ministry.
    - (e) Dating/developing relationships.

(f) Many other things in life.

s. Embrace the gift of discernment; it can keep you out of much trouble.

Lesson 19
Divers Kinds of Tongues

a. Divers kinds of tongues is:

1. The ability to speak in many different languages.
2. You are not naturally trained, but it is given by the Holy Ghost.
3. It is wonderful gift for:
   - (a) Intercessors.
   - (b) In the presence, other nationalities.
   - (c) With the interpretation gift.

4. The gift is sensitive, and it must be led by the Holy Ghost in a public setting.
5. It can be used generally in praise and worship setting.
6. One should ask for the gift of interpretation if they have divers kinds of tongues.
7. It is wonderful to see someone speak in tongues and then interpret it.

b. Interpretation of Tongues

a. To be able to understand the language and speak it.
b. It is a matching gift with divers kinds of tongues.
c. It is wonderful to have for a public setting of speaking in tongues.
d. Interpretation of tongues will:
   - (a) Produce great prophetic messages.
   - (b) Edify the body.
   - (c) Bring understanding to the body.
   - (d) Bring glory to GOD.

e. **(Interpretation of tongues stops <u>confusion</u> in the Body of Christ.)**

Lesson 20
The Motive Gifts

1. Everyone has a motive gift

2. Usually you are born with a motive gift

3. They are given by GOD

4. These gifts are neglected or overlooked, because they *appear* less important

5. They are really the most important gifts because they are:
   (a) The foundation gifts.
   (b) The functioning gifts.
   (c) The balancing gifts.
   (d) The backbone gifts.

6. We really need these gifts for the church to function properly.

7. Again, motive gifts are not noticed but are the true backbone of the whole spiritual operation.

8. **There <u>are 7</u> Motive Gifts**
   (a) Prophecy
   (b) Ministry
   (c) Teaching
   (d) Exhorter
   (e) Giving
   (f) Ruler (leader)
   (g) Mercy

A. Prophecy
   a. This is neither a prophet nor a person with gift of prophecy.
   b. This is a person who prophesies according to their proportion of faith.
   c. They speak according to the level of faith they have.

1. This prophecy is not a:
   (a) Specific Rhema (Word from Heaven)
   (b) Specific Logos (word from the writer)

2. With this prophetic gift, the prophets just speak what they truly believe in their hearts.

3. They speak:
   (a) Encouragement.
   (b) Healing.
   (c) Scripture.
   (d) Strength.

4. Their prophetic word comes from their faith.

5. A person who prophesies from their faith can have the gift of faith.

6. It can be a person who has built up their faith from the Word.

7. It can be a person speaking from their own experience.

8. Ministry
   a. **Ministry is men at *work.***
   b. These are people who do all different kinds of work in the ministry without a specific title of calling.
   c. However, it can be a specific assignment.
   d. Ministry to:

1. Youth	8. Death and Dying
2. Elderly	9. Administrative
3. Battered Women	10. Finances
4. Armor Bearers	11. Deacons
5. Music	12. Mother's Board
6. Janitorial	13. Visitation Ministry
7. Prison	14. Missions

   e. Those are some of the greatest ministries.
   f. No church could run properly without these ministries.
   g. Many churches never really develop because people do not want these ministries.

9. Teaching
   a. This is not the office of the teacher or the revelation gift of teaching.
   b. This is a person who has an internal ability to train and develop others in specific areas.

c. This is a person who has an external ability to train and develop other in specific areas:
d. These people are on your training and development team.
e. They can be on the educational team.
f. They can teach in areas of:
    1. Schools.
    2. Bible College with structure materials.
    3. Other training areas.

10. Exhorter/Exhortation
    a. Exhorters possess:
        (1) Birthing power.
        (2) Excitement power.
        (3) Motivational power.
    b. People with this gift make excellent motivational speakers.
    c. These are people who can excite you to try the impossible.
    d. Birthing power.
        (1) Use a gift you did not know you had.
        (2) Look for hidden talents.

    e. Exciting Power/Motivating Power
        (a) Help you move toward the impossible.
        (b) Causes one to become stirred up about something.
        (c) Causes one to focus on and at something specific.

    f. People with the ability to exhort, uplift life and restore hope.
    g.
    h. A person who releases.

11. Giving much with no reservation:
    1. Has a heart for giving with right motives.
    2. Releases out supernatural amounts.
    3. Normally will help those others will not help.
    4. A giver never complains about giving.
    5. A real giver is not prejudiced as to who they give to
    6. Givers give by:
        (a) Free will.
        (b) Direction of the Holy Spirit.
    7. Givers are filled with:
        (a) Compassion.

(b) Passion

8. Givers give with simplicity:
   (a) Looking for nothing in return.
   (b) Plentifully.
   (c) Pure heart.
   (d) Open opportunity.
   (e) With no regret.

F. Ruler

1. A Ruler is a <u>leader.</u>
2. We need strong leaders in the church.
3. There are many born with leadership qualities.
4. These leaders are not part of the office gifts.
5. They can lead on:
   (a) Jobs.
   (b) Military
   (c) In their homes.

6. Every man is born a ruler because he must be head of his home.
7. He must be able to properly direct his family, not as a dictator but as a leader.
8. Leaders are needed desperately in the Body.
9. This leader might or might not be a minister.
10. The leader may have a specific call or ministry.
11. This leader is one who can lead groups such as:
    (a) Single Women
    b) Battered Women
12. This leader is:
    (a) Diligent.
    (b) Focused.
    (c) Rules well.

G. Mercy

1. A person who shows compassion.
2. Compassion is a quality in someone who is willing to suffer for causes, people and situations.
3. Passion is how much you are willing to suffer.
4. A person who is merciful will suffer through anything for the Kingdom of GOD.

5. The merciful will:
    (a) Go without food.
    (b) Stay up all night.
    (c) Sleep on the street.
    (d) Go to jail.
    (e) Lose limbs.
6. All of the disciples walked in mercy.
7. We need more people who have the spirit of mercy.
8. We need people who will:
    (a) Pray all night.
    (b) Feed the hungry.
    (c) Witness to the loss at any cost.
    (d) Go to foreign countries
9. What happened to the gift of mercy?

9. You may have more than one motive gift.

10. Most motive gifts work together.

11. If you are a ruler, you should have mercy.

12. **If you are a minister, you should be a <u>ruler.</u>**

13. Just as the Fruit of the Spirit are the foundation of all the other gifts and offices, Motive gifts are the foundation of all other gifts and offices.

G. If you are a Pastor and cannot rule well, then you will have a disaster.

Works Cited

M. Kenneth Hagan, Gifts of the Spirit

N. Dr. Bill Hamon, Prophets and Personal Prophecy

O. Brand, C. O., Draper, C. W., & England, A. W. (2003). *Holman illustrated Bible dictionary*. Nashville, Tenn.: Holman Bible Publishers.

P. Dockery, D. S. (1998). *Holman concise Bible commentary: simple, straightforward commentary on every book of the Bible*. Nashville, Tenn.: Broadman & Holman Publishers.

Q. Henry, Matthew. *Matthew Henry's commentary*. New modern ed. Peabody, Mass.: Hendrickson Publishers, 1991. Print.

R. Hindson, E. E., & Kroll, W. M. (1994). *The KJV parallel Bible commentary*. Nashville: T. Nelson Publishers.

S. *Life application Bible: New Revised Standard Version*. (1990). Iowa Falls, Iowa: World Bible Publishers.

T. Rapids, M. (2002). *Holy Bible: King James Version*. Grand Rapids, Mich.: Zondervan.

U. Strong, J., Kohlenberger, J. R., & Swanson, J. A. (2001). *The strongest Strong's exhaustive concordance of the Bible* (Larger print ed.). Grand Rapids, Mich.: Zondervan.

Concise Studies II
WORKBOOK

1. How many revelation gifts are there?

2. What is the word of wisdom?

3. What is the word of knowledge?

4. Why does it state, “The gifts of healing”?

5. Name the seven different areas of healing?

6. Gifts of healing are parts of what?

7. What are working of miracles?

8. Why is that miracles are needed for unbelievers?

9. Why is that believers should not live on miracles?

10. The gift of prophecy does not?

11. The gift of prophecy can operate in what?

12. Why is the gift of prophecy good for the local church?

13. Name the three types of faith?

14. A person with the gift of faith will do what?

15. People with the gift of faith can operate in what?

16. What is discernment?

17. Name three things discernment will expose?

18. What is discernment vital for?

19. What can discernment keep you out of?

20. What are divers of tongues?

21. What should one ask for if they have divers of tongue?

22. What is interpretation of tongues?

23. What does interpretation of tongues stop in the church?

24. Who has a motive gift?

25. Where do motive gifts come from?

26. Why are motive gifts being over looked?

27. Why are motive gifts the most important gifts?

28. What is prophecy in the motive gifts?

29. Name some specific motive gifts in ministry?

30. What do exhorters possess?

31. Exciting power and motivating power will help you move toward what?

32. What is the motive for gift giving?

33. Givers give by what?

34. What are givers filled with?

35. What is a ruler?

36. Why is every man born a leader?

37. The merciful will do what?

38. What is the foundation of all gifts and office?

39. If you are a ruler you should have what?

40. What do givers give with?

41. If you are a pastor and you can't rule well then what will happen?

Concise Studies II
Assignments

(All homework, practical, and scripture information, must be on a separate sheet of paper. If it is written on this paper, there is a 50% deduction from your grade automatically.) Homework, practical, and Bible observation must be a paragraph long or more).

Homework
Explain what you think your revelation gift is.

Practical
Explain what you think your motive gift is.

Essay

Please write a 100-word essay on how you would keep the house of GOD in order spiritually, physically, and naturally.

Name___________________________________

Site ___________________________________

Instructor ______________________________

Date____________________________________

Concise Studies II
Test
(Each Question is Worth 10 points Each)

1. Explain the house of GOD.

2. Explain the church.

3. Explain the body of Christ.

4. Explain the difference between prophecy and faith prophecy.

5. Explain a labor.

6. Explain the gift of wisdom.

7. Explain prophetic healing.

8. Explain discernment.

9. Explain spiritual prophecy.

10. Explain interpretation of tongues.

THE THEOLOGY OF THE MIND

Safe Haven Interdenominational Bible College and Training Institute

PO Box 457

Zebulon, NC 27597

The Theology of the Mind
Table of Contents

Lesson 1
Waste Not Want Not

1. One of the most significant statements ever written is *"The Mind is a terrible thing to waste."* This statement was written for several reasons. One was because so many people lack education. Lack of having the ability to prosper because they are not using their minds.

2. Yet the mind is wasted every day, not because of a lack of education, but because **the mind is Satan's playground.** It is Satan's actual working territory. More people are losing their minds than ever before.

3. **Over 40% of all kindergartners are in some form of depression.** The teenage suicidal rate is now higher than it has ever been. More Christians will kill themselves than ever, but yet they are "supposed" to be Christians.

4. Countless books have been written on the mind during the last 20 years concerning the church. Yet people are more depressed in the church than ever before.

5. **(1 Peter 4:19)** "Wherefore let them that suffer according to the will of GOD commit the keeping of their souls to him in well doing, as unto a faithful Creator."

6. That is why Peter said, *"you are going to suffer, and while suffering or going through, your mind must be kept."* Satan's ultimate goal is to run you crazy if he can. He declared that we are to commit the keeping of our minds to GOD. Another name for the word soul is mind.

7. We must understand Satan does not want anything we have except our minds, and to send us to hell. Material things mean nothing to Satan, he will just use the loss of material things to drive you crazy. If he can take your car or your house, then many are apt to lose their mind, even possibly take their lives.
8. The mind is made up of three major parts:
   a. Mind (thought process).
   b. Will (desires).
   c. Emotions (feelings).

9. **Satan really wants us as believers, to get caught up in our thought process, making <u>decisions for ourselves</u>.** He wants us wrapped up in our own desires. And he wants us to be consumed with our feelings and emotions, which in turn will make us absent of faith.

10. **(Romans 1:17)** "For therein is the righteousness of GOD revealed from faith to faith: as it is written, The just shall live by faith."

11. We do not live by feelings or our thought patterns. We do live by what we can think out or figure out, we live by what our little finite mind cannot comprehend, and that is FAITH.

12. GOD creates everyone as a threefold being:
    a. Spirit.
    b. Soul.
    c. Body.

13. The soulish part of everyone consists of:
    a. Mind (thinking).
    b. Will (choice).
    c. Emotions (feelings).

14. **(Genesis 2:25)** "And they were both naked, the man and his wife, and were not ashamed."

15. In the Garden of Eden, Adam and Eve had innocent, pure minds. Their minds had never been contaminated by anything filthy, that is why they were naked. They did not see each other as anything but pure because their minds were pure. The word *"innocent"* in Hebrew means absent of guilt.

16. Because their minds were pure, they had nothing to be guilty about. When your mind is pure, you will not look at anything or anyone in the wrong way.

17. **(Genesis 3:7)** "And the eyes of them both were opened, and they knew that they were naked, and they sewed fig leaves together and made themselves aprons."

18. Once they sinned, their minds became contaminated. Immediately Adam and Eve looked at each other in a whole different way. They looked at each other through the eyes of sin and impurity, no longer through the eyes of innocence.

19. **(Genesis 3:10-11)** "And he said, I heard thy voice in the garden, and I was afraid because I was naked, and I hid myself. And he said, Who told thee that thou wast naked? Hast thou eaten of the tree, whereof I commanded thee that thou shouldest not eat"?

20. The reason why GOD asked Adam and Eve *"who told you that you were naked"?* Because he knew their thought pattern had changed. They were no longer seeing through innocent eyes, they were seeing through the thought pattern of good and evil.

21. Consider when putting a one-year-old boy and girl into the bathtub together. They can remain innocent because their thought patterns have not been contaminated. But once they are at the age of 18, the same things cannot be done, because their thought patterns are no longer innocent.

22. There was a group of people who lived overseas. When the first Tsunami came, they interviewed them as to why they knew to go to high land, and everyone else was killed. They said that they knew when the feeling and the flow of the water had changed. But the significance of these people was that they all walked around naked. They lived in an innocent state because they had never seen TV. They had never read magazines. They had nothing to do with regular civilization. Therefore, they maintained an innocent mindset.

23. The development of the mindset is brought on by what you see, hear, touch, taste, and smell. It is brought on by the five senses. That is why it is so vital to guard your mind, especially your children.

24. Every day we lose our innocence by what we feed into the mind. Children watch TV shows too early in life; therefore, developing sexual desires or abnormal desires, creating unnecessary problems in their lives.

Lesson 2
Mind of the Perfect Will

1. **(Genesis 1:28)** "And GOD blessed them, and GOD said unto them, Be fruitful, and multiply, and replenish the earth, and subdue it: and have dominion over the fish of the sea, and over the fowl of the air, and over every living thing that moveth upon the earth."

2. Adam and Eve, from the beginning of time, had a mind that was totally subject to the perfect will of GOD. They knew the voice of GOD, they knew the will of GOD. Their minds only receive what the Father said.

3. **(Genesis 3:8)** "And they heard the voice of the Lord GOD walking in the garden in the cool of the day: and Adam and his wife hid themselves from the presence of the Lord GOD amongst the trees of the garden."

4. **(Genesis 2:18-20)** "And the Lord GOD said, It is not good that the man should be alone; I will make him a help meet for him. And out of the ground, the Lord GOD formed every beast of the field and every fowl of the air; and brought them unto Adam to see what he would call them: and whatsoever Adam called every living creature, that was the name thereof. And Adam gave names to all cattle, and to the fowl of the air, and to every beast of the field, but for Adam, there was not found a help meet for him."

5. Adam's mind was so in-tune with the mind of GOD, the perfect will of GOD, that he knew exactly what to name every animal. Adam was not GOD, but he was created to think just like GOD until sin came.

6. **(Philippians 2:5)** "Let this mind be in you, which was also in Christ Jesus."

7. Adam and Eve lost the mind of GOD because of their sin. So when Jesus came and walked the earth, he declares "that we are to have the mind of Christ." There is a difference.

8. When Adam and Eve were created, their minds were so innocent they could think just like GOD or just as the Father wanted them. But because our thoughts are so contaminated with sin, we must have the mind of Christ.

9. **The mind of Christ is a mind of <u>total obedience</u>.** While Jesus was on earth, he never thought for himself, he simply went to His Father, and His father told him what to do. He just obeyed. He had a total mind of obedience.

10. **(John 4:34)** "Jesus saith unto them, My meat is to do the will of him that sent me, and to finish His work."

11. All Jesus did was find out what His Father wanted, and he carried it out. That is precisely what we are to do today. We are not supposed to think for ourselves. We are to allow the Father to think for us. It does not mean we do not have common sense, but because of the contamination of the mind and sin, GOD now wants to control our thinking.

12. Make sure you understand being educated and thinking the Will of GOD are two different things. **Our education is to allow us to function on a <u>day to day basis</u>.** But it will in no way give us the ability to figure out the will of the Father.

13. **(Luke 9:14-17)** "For they were about five thousand men. And he said to His disciples, Make them sit down by fifties in a company. And they did so and made them all sit down. Then he took the five loaves and the two fishes, and looking up to heaven, he blessed them, and brake, and gave to the disciples to set before the multitude. And they did eat, and were all filled: and there was taken up of fragments that remained to them twelve baskets."

14. Our minds will never figure out how the will of the father could be to take two fish and five loaves of bread and feed five thousand people. Again, all Jesus done was hold the substance up to the father, receive His will, bless it, and it multiplied.

15. **(Psalm 37:23)** "The steps of a good man are ordered by the Lord: and he delighteth in his way."

16. **Because of sin, we now must allow GOD to <u>demand our steps</u>**. The word order means to demand. Once you understand how to have the mind of Christ, you will realize you do not have to figure out anything. All you have to do is sit back and let GOD demand things to happen, we just obey.

17. **(Luke 22:42)** "Saying, Father, if thou be willing, remove this cup from me: nevertheless not my will, but thine, be done."

18. You must also understand when Adam and Eve sinned, their own will came alive. When they ate of the tree, their personal will overpowered the will of the Father. That is why when we take on the mind of Christ, we denounce our will allowing the will of the Father to become dominant.

19. When Jesus said, *"not my will, but thou will be done,"* he immediately denounced His will. He denounced His own thought pattern and made himself totally subjected to the will of His father.

20. **(Psalms 37:23)** "The steps of a good man are ordered by the Lord: and he delighteth in his way."

21. When we have the mind of Christ, GOD can order our steps. He can direct our coming and goings, all we have to do is surrender to the Father, like Jesus.

22. Our battle will always be our mindset concerning our will. Because with our own mindset, we have planned our lives for ourselves. Once we get saved, it is tough to give up our will to the will of the father. Most often, the will of the Father will go against our will, which is our desires of the flesh.

23. **(Matthew 19:20-24)** "The young man saith unto him, All these things have I kept from my youth up: what lack I yet? Jesus said unto him, If thou wilt be perfect, go and sell that thou hast, and give to the poor, and thou shalt have treasure in heaven: and come and follow me. But when the young man heard that saying, he went away sorrowful: for he had great possessions. Then said Jesus unto His disciples, Verily I say unto you, That a rich man shall hardly enter into the kingdom of heaven. And again, I say unto you, It is easier for a camel to go through the eye of a needle than for a rich man to enter into the kingdom of GOD."

24. The rich young man had already planned out his life. He was good, but yet he was not in the perfect will of GOD. When Jesus told him to go sell all that he had and give the money to the poor, he could not take on the mind of Christ. He could not give up his will and totally obey the Father.

25. Again, to do the mind of Christ is to be willing to totally obey the will of the Father. You don't think it out, you just simply DO it out. GOD knows His plans; therefore, you do not have to figure them out, you just have to carry them out.

26. **(Numbers 16:28)** "And Moses said, Hereby ye shall know that the Lord hath sent me to do all these works; for I have not done them of mine own mind."

27. Moses let them know, "all I am here to do is obey the will of the Father." You must see when you have the mind of Christ when you willing to simply obey. You are doing GOD's work, not your own. That is exactly what Jesus said, "He was here on earth to finish the Father's work."

28. You don't have to worry about anything because GOD takes care of His own work. You are just the vessel he is using to carry it out. If we could quickly take on the mind of Christ, this walk could be just that simple.

29. **(Number 24:13)** "If Balak would give me his house full of silver and gold, I cannot go beyond the commandment of the Lord, to do either good or bad of mine own mind; but what the Lord saith, that will I speak"?

30. When you develop the mind of Christ, it does not matter what the world may offer you, you will ONLY do the will of the Father.

Lesson 3
My Mind has Deceived Me

1. There is hardly a day that goes by that we don't see or hear of another minister falling for one reason or another. As you read their disheartening reports, you will notice that each one was preventable.

2. And as we move forward in our ministries, we must be wary of the common downfalls that destroy ministries.

3. **One of the first downfalls of ministry simply is the <u>spirit of deception.</u>** It is the minister being deceived by someone or they deceive themselves as a leader, minister, or pastor.

4. **(Genesis 3:13)** "13 Then the Lord GOD asked the woman, "What have you done?" "The serpent deceived me," she replied. "That's why I ate it."

5. The word deception or to be deceived means to be lied to. It simply means an *"OPEN FACED LIE."* Eve declared, "The serpent lied to me. He made me believe something that just simply was not true." That one lie brought Adam's and Eve's kingdom totally down.

6. **A ministry will never succeed if it is <u>built on a lie</u>.** Many pastors and ministers lay their foundations on lies, making false promises that they simply cannot keep.

7. GOD never calls heroes. He calls servants. Too many pastors want to be heroes and supermen. Too many leaders want to present an image instead of a faithful ministry.

8. Many leaders lie to themselves concerning their own gifts and shortcomings. Because they lie to themselves, the devil can so easily set them up for downfalls. You must be willing to see who you are and where you are at all times.

9. As we studied in the Associate class, there are four stages to ministry, you are:
   a. The people.
   b. With the people.
   c. In front of the people.
   d. Beyond the people.

10. ***"ARE THE PEOPLE"* means that you have the <u>same shortcomings</u> that the people have.** You have some of the same issues that the people you are trying to lead have. They are broken, and so are you. However, that does not mean you are not called to lead. You just have to recognize where you are.

11. ***"WITH THE PEOPLE"* means that you are now showing signs of how the Word is genuinely working for you**. You begin to show the actual evidence of the Word that you are preaching. The people themselves can start to see real proof of the power and promises of GOD.

12. ***"IN FRONT OF THE PEOPLE"* means that you become the true leader.** The people recognize that you are the one to follow. They do not follow because of a title; they develop, follow, and support because of the evidence and authentic leadership. You now possess the ability to take the people into true victory.

13. ***"BEYOND THE PEOPLE"* means that you can now develop other leaders, not just followers.** You begin to connect to leadership more than the congregation as a whole.

14. If you are trying to operate in the wrong stage, you will set yourself up for a major fall. You cannot operate at "beyond the people" when you are still "the people." You must be "SO" willing to see your own shortcomings.

15. Many leaders are deceived by other people. The devil will send others to deceive you and your congregation. Many people will come into your congregation and lie to you has a leader trying to get to you or your congregation.

16. We all want to trust, but we must be aware of bringing people on board too quickly, no matter who they say they are. Many ministries have lost considerable amounts of money and even their congregation by being deceived in this way. Many wolves will come in sheep's clothing, proclaiming that the Lord sent them to you. Beware and be discerning of the spirit.

17. **(Joshua 9:22)** "And Joshua called for them, and he spake unto them, saying, "Wherefore have ye beguiled us, saying, We are very far from you; when ye dwell among us?"

18. Joshua was deceived by a people he made a commitment to. Once he did, he could not get out of the situation/vow.

19. **(Deuteronomy11:16)** "Take heed to yourselves, that your heart be not deceived, and ye turn aside, and serve other gods, and worship them;"

20. Deception is rampant in the church because of what is in the heart of many leaders. As a leader, you must check your heart because you will be deceived many times, based on what is in the heart.

21. Don't lie to yourself concerning what you are really feeling and seeing about things concerning your own heart. Believe your heart. It is telling you the truth, whether good or bad.

Lesson 4
Mind of Transgression

1. **(Exodus 23:21)** "Beware of him, and obey His voice, provoke him not; for he will not pardon your transgressions: for my name is in him."

2. **(Isaiah 53:5)** "But he was wounded for our transgressions, he was bruised for our iniquities: the chastisement of our peace was upon him, and with His stripes, we are healed."

3. Transgression is the first thing that entered the mind of Eve to start the act of wrongdoing. It was the first thing that caused Eve to act out or carry out her process to sin.

4. Transgression is the key thing that affects the mind. **Transgression literally means when the thought pattern is controlled by planning out wrongdoing.** It is when man plans out sin, disobedience, wrongdoing, and negative choices. Transgression literally means "the process to."

5. Eve started the mind of transgression. Because she saw the tree was good to her. She planned out to eat, even though she knew it was wrong. Then gave it to her husband. She thought it out, and then she planned it out.

6. **The process of transgression is when the mind is deceived by wrong choices or a self willful choice.** That leads to disobedience or sin. Thoughts get planted in one's mind through the bloodline or by a person's surroundings.

7. Because Eve kept being surrounded by the serpent, then her thought pattern began to be controlled by her surroundings. She kept listening to the same thing.

8. Transgression is transferred in the blood because it is transferred from a parent. Children grow up thinking just like their parents because of the transfer. That is why the Israelite children grew up thinking just like them because of the bloodline. Even though they were not in Egypt, they did not grow up in Egypt; they had an Egyptian mentality, because of transgression. It had been transferred to them from their parent that came out of Egypt.

9. **(Genesis 4:8)** "And Cain talked with Abel, his brother: and it came to pass, when they were in the field, that Cain rose up against Abel his brother, and slew him."

10. **Transgression was immediately passed down the bloodline with Adam and Eve's child, Cain.** Cain planned to kill his brother because of jealousy.

11. Often children that grow up in poverty or growing up in the projects (low-income surrounding) they tend to have a mind of transgression. The poverty mentality was transferred to them. Without knowing, their thought pattern is already planned out for them.

12. That is with everyone, without knowing because of transgression, our thought patterns can already be planned out for us. That is why we grow up thinking as we do.

13. **(Psalm 25:7)** "Remember not the sins of my youth, nor my transgressions: according to thy mercy remember thou me for thy goodness' sake, O Lord."

14. When a mother has a child out of wedlock, and then her daughter comes along and does the very same thing, yes, it is a generational curse. But it is FIRST transgression. The thought pattern is already planted there, even though she does not know it.

15. She may even say she is going to do something different and end up falling into that same trap, because of transgression. When she is put in that same position, the familiar thought pattern will take over, if there has not been deliverance.

16. **(Psalm 51:3)** "For I acknowledge my transgressions: and my sin is ever before me."

17. David recognized that his thought pattern was developed by what he had grown up in. He understood that transgression was transferred to him from his father. That is why David acknowledged it.

18. **(Psalms 51:13)** "Then will I teach transgressors thy ways, and sinners shall be converted unto thee."

19. Everyone is born a transgressor. Everyone is born with the mindset to plan out to do wrong. That is why when you tell a baby not to touch something, and they do anyway, it is because they are already a transgressor.

20. **(Proverbs 22:6)** "Train up a child in the way he should go: and when he is old, he will not depart from it."

21. Every parent can STOP the destruction of transgression by properly training a child. The word train in Hebrew means to discipline. It means to set proper order.

22. You must train or set proper order according to the word of GOD, not according to what you want or even what your parents did. It must be according to the word of GOD. When you are training or discipline a child, you are setting proper order in their mindset. The mind is being developed while also being trained to think the right way, GOD's way.

23. Israel did not train their children according to the laws of GOD, they taught them according to what they had learned in Egypt. They also passed a lot of things from their bloodline. That is why the next generation of the Israelites was so full of transgression.

24. Because today's generations are NOT being adequately trained, they have become full of transgression; proper biblical order isn't getting set in their lives. They are being taught from the internet, from negative music, and negative surroundings. They have no set order in their lives.

Lesson 5
Spare the Rod, Spoil the Child

1. **(Proverbs 13:15)** "Good understanding giveth favour: but the way of transgressors is hard."

2. When a person is properly trained, when a person is given good understanding, then favor will come. But when a person is led by transgression, they are planning out their lives by their own mind, then their way will eventually be hard. The word "hard" in Hebrew means grievous.

3. Many parents have cried tears over a specific child because that child has been in and out of trouble. They have fallen in many areas, because they are being led by transgression, planned out wrongdoing. The child's ways are hard or grievous.

4. **(Isaiah 53:5)** "But he was wounded for our transgressions, he was bruised for our iniquities: the chastisement of our peace was upon him; and with His stripes we are healed."

5. **When Jesus said, "he was wounded for our transgression," he was saying, "he took on an actual <u>discipline for the mind</u>.** The word "wounded" literally means to beat or spank away.

6. **(Proverbs 13:24)** "He that spareth his rod hateth his son: but he that loveth him chasteneth him betimes."

7. The reason a parent spanks a child is to discipline them or change their mindset about what they did or what they were planning to do. It means to beat away the wrong choices.

8. **Jesus was <u>wounded or spanked</u> for our mindset.** He was wounded so that we would have the ability to change our minds without us having to be punished. He took the spanking for us. So all we have to do is receive the word and simply change our mindset. But if we don't, then we must take the beating for ourselves.

9. The prison system is full of people who must be chastened or beaten for their transgression. They are there because of their mindset. They are taking their own beating because they are literally saying, "Jesus' beating was not enough for them."

10. **(Psalms 51:13)** "Then will I teach transgressors thy ways, and sinners shall be converted unto thee."

11. The minute that Jesus gathered His 12 disciples, he began to teach them. He knew their thought pattern was all wrong. He started the process of delivering them from transgression. That is why he set them down and began to teach them "The Beatitude." Because Jesus knew attitude comes from the thought pattern.

12. That is why you must understand why both Peter and Judas fell. Even though they walk with Jesus for three years, they were still struggling with transgression. Their minds still need deliverance. Jesus knew what their thought patterns were. Judas had "planned" to do Jesus wrong because of transgression. (Paul fell but did not plan to do wrong).

13. **(Matthew 26:32-35)** "But after I am risen again, I will go before you into Galilee. Peter answered and said unto him, Though all men shall be offended because of thee, yet will I never be offended. Jesus said unto him, Verily I say unto thee, That this night, before the cock crow, thou shalt deny me thrice. Peter said unto him, Though I should die with thee, yet will I not deny thee. Likewise also said all the disciples."

14. Jesus knew what was in the mind of Peter. Peter did not understand transgression, and most of us, do not either. Our thought pattern has been well developed by so many things, we just don't know it.

15. **(Romans 7:19-25)** "For the good that I would I do not: but the evil which I would not, that I do."

16. Paul truly understood transgression. Paul understood the process of the mind. Paul recognized because of his past, there were things planned out for him already in his thought pattern.

17. Paul understood he had to work on his thought pattern continually. He had to be disciplined in his mind. He had to be taught all over again, in the meantime, be delivered of the mind.

18. That is why as soon as someone gets saved, they need to be set down to be taught and trained so that they can be delivered from transgression, their wrong thought pattern. **New converts struggle so hard because of transgression.** Their thought pattern is totally contrary to the word of GOD. (we will deal with the curse of transgression in another book)

19. **(Hebrews 12:6-7)** "For whom the Lord loveth he chasteneth, and scourgeth every son whom he receiveth. If ye endure chastening, GOD dealeth with you as with sons; for what son is he whom the father chasteneth not?"

20. Whom GOD loves he spanks or discipline, because of the mindset. As Christians, GOD will still punish us because often, we still have a mind of transgression. We always carry out the process of wrong, because of the way we still think.

21. **(2 Corinthians 12:7-8)** "And lest I should be exalted above measure through the abundance of the revelations, there was given to me a thorn in the flesh, the messenger of Satan to buffet me, lest I should be exalted above measure. For this thing, I besought the Lord thrice, that it might depart from me".

22. GOD understood the mindset of Paul. He knew where Paul had come from, so GOD had to keep Paul in a humble state. Because of Paul's abundance of Revelation and knowledge, it would have been easy for Paul to exalt himself, because of the mind of transgression.

23. This is why so many ministers end up falling because of the mind of transgression. They do not realize they have that kind of thought process. They end up getting in high positions or having a whole lot. Then they end up exalting themselves above measure, because of their mindsets.

24. **(Psalm 37:38)** "But the transgressors shall be destroyed together: the end of the wicked shall be cut off."

25. Your mind can lead you into some very destructive places because of transgression. We must recognize transgression before it is too late.

26. **(Isaiah 46:8)** "Remember this, and shew yourselves men: bring it again to mind, O ye transgressors."

Lesson 6
A Sound Mind

1. **(2 Timothy 1:7)** "For GOD hath not given us the spirit of fear; but of power, and of love, and of a sound mind."

2. The very first thing that Adam and Eve had before sin was a sound mind. **The word "sound" means balance, discipline, or orderly**. Adam and Eve both had a very balanced thought pattern, nothing was out of order.

3. **Your life will only be as balanced, disciplined, and orderly, as your thought pattern.** Whatever area of your life is off-balance, out of order, or undisciplined, that is the area your thinking is off.

4. When you see someone has committed suicide, it was because their thought pattern was all off-balance, completely out of order. The person could not see life in an orderly way. These are people who see life through a stain glass window, through a mirror of life-ending before it's time.

5. **When seeing someone addicted to a particular thing, their thought pattern is off-balance.** That person that is addicted to alcohol or drugs their every thought is figuring out to get their next fix. They may have hungry children at home. They still have not balanced their thought pattern.

6. Again wherever in your life, your thought pattern is disorderly, that will be the part of your life that is off-balanced. When people are going through a financial problem if you listen to them long enough, you will know that they do not rightly think of money. When they receive their paycheck, saving or not overspending will not be a priority in their lives. Because they do not think correctly.

7. If people are having marital problems, it initially started with their thought patterns. They lack thinking sound when it comes to marriage. Their thought pattern is disorderly and off-balance when it comes to their relationship. They must be willing to bring their thought pattern under subjection first to correct their marital situation.

8. The thought pattern is controlled by five things:
   a. Ignorance.
   b. Wrong information.

c. Deception.
d. Chemical imbalance.
e. Demonic sources.

9. When a person has a thought pattern of ignorance, it merely means they are unlearned in that specific area of their lives. Therefore, they cannot change what they do not know. They cannot think correctly in that particular area because of their lack of knowledge. That is why the devil never wants us to know the truth.

10. **(John 4:16-18)** "Jesus saith unto her, Go, call thy husband, and come hither. The woman answered and said, I have no husband. Jesus said unto her, Thou hast well said, I have no husband: For thou hast had five husbands; and he whom thou now hast is not thy husband: in that saidst thou truly."

11. This woman's thought pattern was all off-balance when it came to relationship and marriage. She had been through five different men, yet there was no true relationship. She did not know how to think according to the word.

12. When the thought pattern is orderly and balance, that area of your life will be balanced and orderly. Studying and receiving the Word of GOD is what will give you the balance.

13. Many people in the church have a life off-balanced because they have received the wrong information. Therefore, they continue to walk out a chaotic life because false information causing a wrong way of thinking.

14. **(Genesis 3:4)** "And the serpent said unto the woman, Ye shall not surely die."

15. Eve became subject to the enemy because she received and accepted wrong information, ending in defeated results. False information will get you the wrong results. You may not know it right away, but it will manifest over time.

16. As we talked earlier, deception is one of the keys to thinking incorrectly, it comes because someone hears a lie, receive the lie, and then act on the lie.

17. Because of deception, the mind is not hungry for the right thing. We are too preoccupied for righteousness. But because of the nature of sin, we hunger after wrong or sinful thoughts of unrighteousness.

18. Many movies come out about vampires. In these films, even though they may have food right in front of them, all their hunger is blood. They hunger like that because their nature has changed. Their complete thought pattern is about their next kill for blood. The vampire's thought pattern is no longer sound, discipline, or orderly.

19. When you do not have a sound mind, you are subject to do anything. When you hear of someone being pushed over the edge, or simply just losing it for that moment. It has happened because there was yet a place in their mind that was not sound.

20. You can never say what you won't do , because balance and order all come from having a sound mind. There have been people who have killed someone, yet they cannot explain why they did it. It is because, at that very moment, one lost the soundness of mind.

21. Some people do have chemical imbalances concerning their minds. This may be a person who suffers from some form of depression, Dementia, and Alhemizers. This person may have to be on medication to maintain balance, discipline, and order in their lives. Chemical imbalances can cause a person's mindset not to be sound.

22. Many cannot be sound-minded because of demonic activity in their minds. In the Bible, the young boy that was throwing himself in the fire, and the man who began to live in the graveyard, these were people whose minds were controlled by demonic sources.

23. When sin entered the world, the first thing it threw off was the thought pattern of man. That is why the first thing Adam said to GOD was, "I WAS AFRAID." That is why GOD said, "I did not give you the spirit of fear."The word "fear" here means disorder. Suddenly, everything in Adam and Eve's life was out of order, undisciplined, and unbalanced.

24. **(1 Corinthians 14:33)** "For GOD is not the author of confusion, but of peace, as in all churches of the saints."

25. The author of confusion represents the thought pattern. GOD was letting man know he did not teach them to think out of order, undisciplined or unbalanced. The confusion comes based on how an individual thinks, originated strictly by the devil.

26. If you want too much or too little of something, and if you are too far to the extreme in something, it's because your thought pattern is off-balanced. It is undisciplined, entirely out of order in that area.

27. We are made up of three things, we are a spirit, we have a soul, and we live in a body. The soulish part of you consists of three things: mind, will, and emotions. Before sin, the spirit man was totally in control. But once sinned came, the soulish man took over. Paul said, "I die daily." *Dying daily"* means bringing the soulish part back subject to the Spirit of GOD.

28. **(James 1:21)** "Wherefore lay apart all filthiness and superfluity of naughtiness, and receive with meekness the engrafted word, which is able to save your souls."

29. The word *"Engrafted"* means to implant. The word save means to rescue, and the word soul means mind. The first key, or purpose, of studying the Word is to put the Word so deep into your heart that it rescues your mind or your thought pattern from:
    a. Yourself.
    b. Devil.
    c. World.

30. **(James 1:21)** "Wherefore lay apart all filthiness and superfluity of naughtiness, and receive with meekness the engrafted word, which is able to save your souls."

31. The word *"Meekness"* means to have an open attitude to receive and accept. The word availability to truth. If your mind is not available to the truth in that area, then you will remain in bondage. Balance, order, and disciplined thinking brings continuous victory and increase victory.

Lesson 7
A Steadfast Mind

1. **(Ruth 1:18)** "When she saw that she was stedfastly minded to go with her, then she left speaking unto her."

2. The word *"steadfast"* in Hebrew means a consistent mindset. A mind that it is not wavering from one belief to next. There are many believers who lack consistency, walk in a state of confusion.

3. Satan knows if he can cause a person to waver in mind, they will never be consistent in their spiritual walk. Many believers are committed today, yet they will mentally change tomorrow.

4. Thank GOD for choices; however, the more options one has, the more one is apt to struggle with stability. You must remove as many choices as possible concerning any given situation.

5. **(Joshua 24:15)** "And if it seem evil unto you to serve the Lord, choose you this day whom ye will serve; whether the gods which your fathers served that were on the other side of the flood or the gods of the Amorites, in whose land ye dwell: but as for me and my house, we will serve the Lord."

6. Joshua removed all choices except one for his family. He completely chose to serve GOD. Joshua was not distracted by his surroundings because of his steadfast mindset.

7. You must also understand how steadfast Joshua's mindset had to be. Forty years, Joshua had to wait in the wilderness. As all of the others who came out of Egypt with him died off.

8. He was promised to go into the promised land. He could let nothing shift his mindset concerning the promised land. Even though much time went by, a forty-day journey turned into a forty-year journey. Yet his mindset remains steadfast.

9. **Timing is one of the main effects on the body of Christ. Satan uses time against them because of the lack of understanding concerning the timing of GOD.**

10. It was the timing that tormented Job the most in his situation, not the situation itself. It is the timing that torments most believers, not the situation.

11. Israel got in trouble because they had gotten involved with so many idols GOD in Egypt. Therefore, they kept giving themselves to many choices, bring on mental deception. Again, dealing with choices, you must eliminate as many as possible to keep the mind stable.

12. **(1 Corinthians 15:58)** "Therefore, my beloved brethren, be ye steadfast, unmoveable, always abounding in the work of the Lord, forasmuch as ye know that your labor is not in vain in the Lord."

13. When a person has a consistent mindset, their work will be focused according to the perfect will of GOD. If their mindset is not constant, their work will be all over the place. There will be no balance in their kingdom assignments. This is why the body of Christ, the church, is so unstable.

14. The word *"unmovable"* means positioned with consistency. Such as Nehemiah had a steadfast mind; he was positioned with consistency.

15. That is why the people could not throw him off track with his work because he had such a steadfast mindset.

16. **(John 11:4-6)** "When Jesus heard that, he said, This sickness is not unto death, but for the glory of GOD, that the Son of GOD might be glorified thereby. Now Jesus loved Martha, and her sister, and Lazarus. When he had heard therefore that he was sick, he abode two days still in the same place where he was."

17. Jesus was unmovable. Jesus was fixed in position based on what His father wanted from him. He did not come just because Mary and Martha called him. His mind was steadfast on what he was to do for His father. He was not moved by their emotions or their tears.

18. Because of the world n which we live, there are so many distractions thrown at the body of Christ. Day to day survival has become a distraction for many Christians. Therefore, their mental status is inconsistent, lacking focus.

19. **(Matthew 6:25)** "Therefore I say unto you, Take no thought for your life, what ye shall eat, or what ye shall drink; nor yet for your body, what ye shall put on. Is not the life more than meat, and the body than raiment."

20. Jesus told the disciples to *"take no thought."* The word *"thought"* in the scripture means consideration. It literally means give no time to. They were not to waste their thoughts on how they were going to survive. GOD had already figured that out for them. All they had to do was to obey.

21. Because the church is consumed in their own survival, they continue wasting their thoughts on things that do not benefit them at all. Many Christians are killing themselves because of the lack of natural things. Their minds cannot figure out how they are going to pay bills, maintain a particular lifestyle. Therefore, they are becoming self-destructive.

22. **(Philippians 4:19)** "But my GOD shall supply all your need according to His riches in glory by Christ Jesus."

23. Our natural source does not come from the earth; it comes from the heavenly realm. No GOD does not rain down manna from heaven, but it is GOD who figures out how each need is to be met. He uses whom he pleases. All we have to do is stay obedient.

24. Once we attempt to figure out our own source, then we become our personal god. This how many people nearly lose their minds. Because our finite minds will never comprehend how GOD wants to bless us. Our thoughts are to stay consistent on pleasing GOD.

25. If pastors could recognize that one of the main reasons why church members shift around so , is because they lack steadfastness of mind.

26. **(Deuteronomy 4:39)** "So remember this and keep it firmly in mind: The Lord is GOD both in heaven and on earth, and there is no other."

Lesson 8
A Mind to Work

1. **(Nehemiah 4:6)** "So built we the wall, and all the wall was joined together unto the half thereof: for the people had a mind to work."

2. What is *"a mind to work"?* It is a mind that is available to obedience. The men that were working with Nehemiah were available to obedience. Even though they were being attacked by the enemy, they remained focus on obedience to the plan of GOD.

3. One of the areas that the church will be weak in, especially in the last days, is having people who will have a pure mind to work. They will lack being available to total obedience.

4. **(Matthew 4:18-20)** "And Jesus, walking by the sea of Galilee, saw two brethren, Simon called Peter, and Andrew his brother, casting a net into the sea: for they were fishers. And he saith unto them, Follow me, and I will make you fishers of men. And they straightway left their nets and followed him".

5. Jesus picked men who he could develop their minds into the mindset of total obedience. He did not just pick religious people, he chooses men with the right mindset.

6. **As a saved person, your mind <u>must be examined</u>**. You must determine where your mindset is. If your mind is not to become obedient in the kingdom of GOD, you very well need some form of deliverance. You must ask yourself, "why am I not available to do kingdom work?

7. A multitude followed Jesus, but when he asked them to "eat His body and drink His blood," many turned and walked away. They found this saying was too hard because of their mindset.

8. **(Isaiah 1:19)** "If ye be willing and obedient, ye shall eat the good of the land."

9. **The word <u>"willing"</u> means to have an available mindset to the work of the kingdom of GOD.**

10. There will be little work getting done in the last days in the kingdom because the people will lack a mindset for kingdom work.

11. The harvest is plentiful, but the laborers are few. There will be a lot of work that needs to be done, but the question is, who will do it?

12. The body is now so preoccupied with so many things. Getting people to have a mindset for kingdom work will be quite difficult. It will cost too much for this generation. It will appear that they have too much to give up.

13. To have a mind to work, one must be willing to give up something. You will have to guard your mind while working. Satan will give you every opportunity not to do kingdom work. That is why it will be so imperative to safeguard your thought pattern.

14. **(Isaiah 38:3)** "Remember, O Lord, how I have always been faithful to you and have served you single-mindedly, always doing what pleases you." Then he broke down and wept bitterly".

15. To do the work of the kingdom of GOD, one must be single-minded. To be single-minded, your focus must be directed on pleasing GOD, not man. Your focus is doing work for GOD, not man.

16. **It is difficult being single-minded in such a time as this because of <u>distractions</u>.** Distractions hampers the ability to focus on the kingdom work.

17. In the society we are in today, the focus is to keep man so busy with other things, that being focused prevents being effective in anything. The goal of the enemy is to keep the mind of the believer's thought pattern completely outside of kingdom work.

18. Paul was single-minded. Paul declares, "In him do I live, move and have my being." Paul wanted to work only for the kingdom of GOD. Paul wanted man to be like him, having the mind totally focused on the work of the kingdom.

19. When Gideon got ready to fight, he started out with 25,000 men, but he took only 300 men to war with him because of their mindset. He could not take anyone with him who did not have a mind to work.

20. There was a divine separation; those who had a fearful mind, those who had their minds on their families, those who could not focus. There will be a divine separation in the body of Christ in the very same way.

Lesson 9
The Discerning Mind

1. **(Psalms 119:169)** " O Lord, listen to my cry; give me the discerning mind you promised."

2. The next thing we need to understand is the discerning mind. What is a discerning mind? **A discerning mind is a spiritual mind that is in tune with <u>the actual spiritual world</u>.** A mind that can unscramble what is of GOD and what is not.

3. Again many Christian people will be caught up in the wrong thing because they will not be able to see through the power of the enemy. Their thought patterns will be consumed with matters of the world.

4. You must be able to distinguish between what thoughts are of the enemy vs. those that are of GOD. There will be things placed in your mind that may not seem wrong, but yet they will not be of GOD. This is Satan's working ground.

5. There are times when Satan can make you think things appear to be right. And if you do not have a discerning mind, you will easily accept them and not even know it.

6. Christians are being deceived every day because Satan is placing thought in their minds that appear to be right, but they are not righteous. Righteous literally means they are in the perfect will of GOD. Right thoughts are things that do not necessarily break laws.

7. **Satan will place many thoughts in the head of Christians that will <u>appeal to the flesh</u>.** They will seem right to man, but yet they are out of His will. They will cost the person everything, like it did Adam and Eve.

8. Sometimes Satan can have a man thoughts about a certain woman. She may not be married, but she is not necessarily supposed to be his wife. If he cannot discern that thought, he will be drawn into the wrong thing, the improper relationship, without even knowing it.

9. **(Genesis 18:12-15)** "Therefore Sarah laughed within herself, saying, After I am waxed old shall I have pleasure, my lord being old also? And the Lord said unto Abraham, Wherefore did Sarah laugh, saying, Shall I of a surety bear a child, which am old? Is anything too hard for the Lord? At the time appointed, I will return unto thee, according to the time of life, and Sarah shall have a son. Then Sarah denied, saying, I laughed not; for she was afraid. And he said, Nay; but thou didst laugh."

10. The Lord discerned the thought of Sarah. She had a mind of doubt when the Lord declared that "she would have a baby at her old age." He did read her mind. He spiritually discerned her thought pattern through the spirit.

11. Do not get mind reading and discerning of thought mixed up. **Mind reading is <u>of the enemy</u>.** Those are satanic tricks to control people. Discerning of thoughts is GOD showing the spiritual place that a person's mind is at that time.

12. Discerning of thought is really about one's own self. It is making sure your own thought pattern is not being used by the enemy. One must be careful that the devil is not setting you up before it is too late.

13. **(Genesis 3:6)** "And when the woman saw that the tree was good for food and that it was pleasant to the eyes, and a tree to be desired to make one wise, she took of the fruit thereof, and did eat, and also gave unto her husband with her; and he did eat."

14. Had Eve discerned her thought pattern, she would not have fallen into sin. She would have recognized she was not thinking rightly, according to the words that

GOD had given her. She would have realized she was thinking outside of the true Will of GOD.

15. This is what each one of us should be doing; we should be discerning our thoughts, making sure we are not thinking outside of the spiritual realms that GOD would have us to think.

16. **(Philippians 4:8)** "Finally, brethren, whatsoever things are true, whatsoever things are honest, whatsoever things are just, whatsoever things are pure, whatsoever things are lovely, whatsoever things are of good report; if there be any virtue, and if there be any praise, think on these things."

17. When we have a discerning of mind, we measure our thought patterns against the word of GOD. There is no way anyone could commit suicide with a discerning of mind because they would measure their thought patterns against the truth.

18. But, once the enemy has taken over the mind, it is difficult to measure the spirit against the word. That is why you must continue to discern your thought pattern. If not, the enemy can begin to take it over.

19. That is what happened to Job, the enemy began to mess with his mind. He began to lose the discerning spirit; that is why he started saying foolish things about his situation.

20. You must discern your thought patterns continually. If not, you can so easily and quickly get set up by the enemy.

Lesson 10
Peace of Mind

1. **(Proverbs 29:17)** "Discipline your children, and they will give you peace of mind and will make your heart glad."

2. We must understand to overcome the enemy; there must be a peace of mind. **The word "peace" in Hebrew means silence of the mind.**

3. There must be a silence of mind to overcome the devil. The devil will torment the mind because man does not know how to silence the mind. This is why man can not be totally in tune with GOD because he is always in turmoil.

4. When the mind can be silent, the heart can be glad. The word "glad" means satisfied. When the heart is satisfied, it means it is being controlled by the Holy Spirit.

5. **(2 Samuel 14:17)** "Yes, my lord, the king, will give us peace of mind again.' I know that you are like an angel of GOD in discerning good from evil. May the Lord your GOD be with you."

6. When there is the silence of mind, it means the mind is at rest. The mind is not worried about anything. It is when the mind accepts that GOD is totally in control.

7. It is when the mind operates on the total belief system. If GOD said it, that truly does settle it. When the body of Christ lacks peace of mind, many in the body of Christ are tormented by constant worrying.

8. It is sad to see how many people in the church worry all of the time. Their minds are controlled by the systems of the world instead of the word of GOD. They lack having true peace of mind.

9. **(John 14:27)** "I am leaving you with a gift—peace of mind and heart. And the peace I give is a gift the world cannot give. So don't be troubled or afraid."

10. **Peace of mind is a gift from GOD. The word "gift" means divine influence.** When GOD releases the gift of peace of mind upon someone, he gives them divine control of the mind.

11. When you receive the divine mental influence of the mind, it means that GOD can take control of the thought pattern, giving Satan no more control of the mind.

12. Peace of mind is something you cannot get from the world. You can only get peace of mind from and through GOD. People are trying every kind of worldly system trying to get peace of mind.

13. That is why there are so many Christians with mental illness because they are saved still trying to use the worldly system to bring peace to their minds. It will never work. It will only be a temporary fix.

14. Here is a fact the devil wants us to remain ignorant of. Peace of mind is a complete gift from GOD, and he gives it freely. We must be available to it and are open to receive it. He will freely release it to us.

15. **In the last days, if the people of GOD do not understand the peace of mind, you will see many Christians operating in severe mental illness.** You will see many pastors losing their minds.

16. Counseling will become one of the main areas of ministry because of mental illness in the church. We will believe we can talk people into their personal victory when people truly need deliverance of mind.

17. We, as believers, are not supposed to be troubled or afraid. Yet more Christians lived troubled and in fear of people in the world because they do not understand the peace of mind.

18. When Adam and Eve sinned, the first thing that entered in man was fear. After fear entered, the trouble of mind immediately began. When Eve allowed Satan to penetrate her mind, she became subject to all the troubles and sorrows of this world.

19. Every time we open ourselves to the mental operation of the world, we will become troubled and tormented by the things of the world. We will worry about what we should not. We will be afraid of things that have no meaning to our lives.

20. **(John 14:1)** "Let not your heart be troubled: ye believe in GOD, also believe in me."

21. We will be troubled of heart if we allow wrong thoughts into our minds. Our hearts will be overwhelmed by the cares of this world. This is what happened to Adam and Eve. This is what happened to Cain. We must release our minds to the Holy Spirit entirely, or the devil will destroy us through the mind.

Works Cited

Brand, C. O., Draper, C. W., & England, A. W. (2003). *Holman illustrated Bible dictionary*. Nashville, Tenn.: Holman Bible Publishers.

Dockery, D. S. (1998). *Holman concise Bible commentary: simple, straightforward commentary on every book of the Bible*. Nashville, Tenn.: Broadman & Holman Publishers.

Henry, Matthew. *Matthew Henry's commentary*. New modern ed. Peabody, Mass.: Hendrickson Publishers, 1991. Print.

Rapids, M. (2002). *Holy Bible: King James Version.* Grand Rapids, Mich.: Zondervan.

Strong, J., Kohlenberger, J. R., & Swanson, J. A. (2001). *The strongest Strong's exhaustive concordance of the Bible* (Larger print ed.). Grand Rapids, Mich.: Zondervan.

Theology of the Mind Workbook

Lesson 1

1. One of the most significant statements ever written is ____________________________

2. Over_____________ of all kindergartners are in some form of depression.
3.
4. Satan's ultimate goal is to ___________________________ if he can.

5. Satan really wants us as believers, to get caught up in our thought process, making ____.

6. Their minds had never been contaminated by anything filthy, that is why they_________________________________.

Lesson 2

7. Adam and Eve, from the beginning of time, had a mind that was totally subject to the ____________________________________.
8.
9. Adam and Eve lost the mind of GOD because _________________________.

10. Our education is to allow us to function on a _________________________. But it will in no way give us the ability to ____________________ the will of the Father.

11. Because of sin, we now must allow GOD to _________________________. The word order means to ____________________________.

12. Once you understand how to have the mind of Christ, you will realize you do not have to _________________________________.

Lesson 3

13. ____________________________ is the minister being deceived by someone or they deceive themselves as a leader, minister, or pastor.

14. A ministry will never succeed if it is ______________________. Many pastors and ministers lay their foundations on lies, making ______________________ that they simply cannot keep.

15. That one lie brought Adam's and Eve's kingdom _________________.

16. "ARE THE PEOPLE" means that you have the same _______________ that the people have.

17. "_______________________________" means that you can now develop other leaders, not just followers.

Lesson 4

18. Transgression is the first thing that entered the mind of Eve to start the act of _________________________________.

19. Transgression literally means when the thought pattern is controlled by ______________________________________.

20. Transgression is transferred in the blood is because it is transferred _________________________. Children grow up thinking just like their _______________________ because of the ________________________.

21. Everyone is born a ___________________________. Everyone is born with the mindset to plan out __________________________.

22. Every parent can STOP the destruction of transgression by properly ______________________________.

Lesson 5

23. When a person is _________________________, when a person is given good understanding, then favor _________________.

24. Jesus was ____________________________ for our mindset. He was _________________________ so that we would have the ability to change our minds without us having to ___________________________.

25. The prison system is full of people who must be ________________________ for their transgression.

26. Our thought pattern has been _________________________ by so many things, we just don't know it.

27. New ________________________ struggle so hard because of transgression. Their thought pattern is totally ______________________ of GOD.

Lesson 6

28. The word _______________________ means balance, discipline, or orderly.

29. Your life will only be as balanced, disciplined, and orderly, as your ______________________________.

30. If people are having ___________________ problems, it initially started with their ____________________________.

31. Many people in the church have a ________________________ because they have
received the wrong information.

32. Because of deception, the mind is __________________________ for the right thing.

Lesson 7

33. The word ___________________________ in Hebrew means a consistent mindset. A mind that it is not wavering from one belief to next.

34. ____________________________ is one of the main effects on the body of Christ. Satan ____________________________ against them because of the lack of understanding concerning the timing of GOD.

35. Satan ___________________________ against them because of the lack of understanding concerning __________________________ of GOD.

36. The word ____________________________means positioned with consistency.

37. The word __________________________ in the scripture means consideration.

Lesson 8

38. What is "a mind to work"? It is a mind that is _____________________.

39. One of the areas that the church ___________________________, especially in the last days, is having people who will have a pure mind to work.

40. If your mind is not to obedience in the kingdom of GOD, you very well need some ___________________________________.

41. The word ____________________________- means to have an available mindset to the work of the kingdom of GOD.

42. It is difficult being______________________________ in such a time as this because of distractions.

Lesson 9

43. A discerning mind is a spiritual mind that ____________________ with the actual __________________________ world.

44. The mind is Satan's _________________________ ground. You must be able to distinguish between what thoughts are of the enemy vs. those that are of GOD.

45. Satan will place many thoughts in the head of Christians that will _________________________________.

46. Mind reading is of the ___________________________. Those are satanic tricks to _____________________________ people.

47. Discerning of thoughts is GOD showing the _____________________ that a person's mind is at _____________________________-.

Lesson 10

48. The word ____________________________ in Hebrew means silence of the mind.

49. There must be a _____________________________ to overcome the devil.

50. The word __________________________means satisfied.

51. The word ________________________- means divine influence.

52. In the last days, if the people of GOD do not understand the peace of mind, you will see many Christians operating in severe ________________.

The Theology of the Mind
Assignments

(All homework, practical, and scripture information, must be on a separate sheet of paper. If it is written on this paper, there is a 50% deduction from your grade automatically. (Homework, practical, and Bible observation must be a paragraph long or more).

Homework
How would you make a difference in discernment as to whether Satan is speaking to your mind versus GOD speaking to you?

Practical
How would you recognize if someone is operating in a mind of deception?

100 Word Essay
Please try and type all essays if possible. If you cannot type your essay, please make sure your teacher is aware of it. Your essay and Bible study lessons must be turned in with all of your homework. Your essay must be 100 words. Please be aware that your homework and essays count 20% each of your total of grades.

Please describe how you would know someone in the church is dealing with mental illness.

Name ________________
Site_________________ __________________
Instructor_____________
Date _________________

The Theology of the Mind
Test
(Each Question is Worth 10 Points)

1. Explain how the mind is Satan's working ground.

2. Explain how Adam knew exactly what to the name the anminals.

3. Explain how a minister can lay their foundation on a lie.

4. What is the "process of transgression"?

5. Why was Jesus spank for our mindset?

6. What is a “sound mind”?

7. Explain a “steadfast mind”.

8. Explain a “mind to work”.

9. Explain a “discerning mind”.

10. Explain a “peace of mind” .

THE THEOLOGY OF THE TRINITY

Safe Haven Interdenominational Bible College and Training Institute

PO Box 457

Zebulon, NC 27597

The Theology of the Trinity
Table of Contents

Lesson 1
The Word Became Flesh

1. **(John 1:1-3)** "In the beginning was the Word and the Word was with GOD, and the Word was GOD. The same was in the beginning with GOD. All things were made by Him; and without Him was not anything made that was made".

2. **(John 3:16)** "For GOD so loved the world, that He gave His only begotten Son, that whosoever believeth in Him should not perish, but have everlasting life".

3. **(Philippians 3:10)** "That I may know Him, and the power of His resurrection, and the fellowship of His sufferings, being made conformable unto His death".

4. It is time that we know who Jesus is in our lives, and who He is, when it comes to the world. To get victory over the enemy and in this world, we need to know and understand, who Jesus is. The totality of who Jesus is, must now be understood regarding getting victory in this world.

5. **(John 1:1-3)** "In the beginning was the **Word** and the **Word** was with GOD, and the **Word** was GOD. The same was in the beginning with GOD".

6. Now the word *"Word"* is capitalized because it is talking about a person, and that person is Jesus. But now what does that word, *"Word"* mean?

7. That word, *"Word"* literally means *"Will"*. So, if you read the scripture with the translated meaning in it, it will read as: "In the beginning was the **"Will" of GOD** and the **"Will"** was with GOD, and the **"Will"** was GOD. The same was in the beginning with GOD. All things were made by Him; and without Him was not anything made that was made".

8. So, who is Jesus? Jesus is the *"Will"* of the Father. What does the word *"Will"* mean? *"Will"* means exactly what one desires or wants. *"Will"* is everything that the Father wants done, how He wants it done, and when He wants it done. Jesus is the Father's total desires.

9. So how do we know this? **(John 1:3)** "All things were **made** by Him; and without Him was not anything **made** that was **made"**.

10. **(Genesis 1:1)** "In the Beginning GOD **created** the heaven and the earth".

11. There is a difference between **"made"** and **"created".** GOD "created". "Created" means something from nothing. Jesus "made". What does that mean?

12. Whatever GOD *"created",* which would be His "Will", it would be done in the spirit. Jesus would simply manifest what the Father "created" in the spirit or bring it to existence, in the natural. "

13. That is where the word *"made"* comes from. Because the word *"made"* literally means to *"manifest into".*

14. To *"make"* or *"manifest"* means to use something that already exist. When a seamstress makes a dress, she uses material that already exist. She does not *"create",* she makes.

15. Jesus did not just make anything. Jesus simply made or manifested everything that the Father *"Willed"* or had created in the Spirit. *(He obeyed).*

16. When GOD said, *"let there be",* Jesus would *"let there be".* Jesus *"manifested"* whatever GOD spoke in the spirit realm again, into the natural realm. Jesus would make it seen with the natural eyes.

17. You must know who Jesus is. When the Father would speak, the Son would "manifest" it. When the Father would speak, Jesus did not create, Jesus made. The Father *"created"* again; Jesus *"made".*

18. Jesus would *"manifest"* it. That is why the Bible said, *"Everything was "**made"*** by Him". Everything was not *"created"* by Jesus everything was *"made"* by him. It was shaped and formed just the way the Father wanted it done.

19. Jesus is the perfect *"Will"* of the Father. Again, he is the total desire of the Father. As we learn the fullness of who he is and the fullness of the Godhead, then you will understand Jesus' fullness within a Christian.

20. Because anyone who is saved, who has Jesus living on the inside of them, they have the total *"Will"* of the Father living in them. Because Jesus is the complete *"Will"* of the Father. For us, for us as individuals.

The Word Became Flesh
Questionnaire

1. Why is "Word" capitalized?

2. What is the difference between "created" and "made"?

3. When the Father would speak, what would the Son do?

4. Because anyone who is saved, who has Jesus living on the inside of them, they have the _____________________ of the Father living in them.

5. Because Jesus is the __________________________ of the Father.

Lesson 2
The Creation

1. **(Genesis 1:26)** "And GOD said, let Us make man in our **Image**, after Our likeness":

2. Again, what is *"image"?* Image means he made man a threefold being, just like himself:
   a. Man is a spirit.
   b. Man will have a soul (mind).
   c. Man would live in body.

3. What is the "likeness" that we have like them? Man would have the "Will" of the Father in him, which is Jesus. Adam and Eve had Jesus in them. Man would be empowered by the Holy Spirit. Man would have GOD's abilities.

4. In understanding who Jesus is, you then must understand why the Father sent His Son. He did not out of nowhere, send His Son.

5. GOD sent His Son, because Adam and Eve originally had Jesus in them, and that is who they lost, Jesus and the Holy Spirit. Therefore, man needed to get in a position where they could get Jesus, (the will of the Father) back on the inside of them.

6. When man was created, man would know exactly what the Father wanted. How did man know exactly what the Father wanted? Because they had the Will of the Father in them, which was Jesus.

7. That is how man (Adam) knew how to do exactly what the Father wanted. Because man originally had Jesus in him, and he was empowered by the Holy Ghost.

8. People always want to know; how did Adam know what to name the animals? Because Adam had the perfect "Will" of the Father in him, which was Jesus. So, Jesus manifested exactly what the Father wanted through Adam.

9. So, when Adam looked at the animals, guess what? Jesus knew what the Father wanted. Adam knew to call a cow, a cow; because the perfect "Will" of GOD was on the inside, which was Jesus.

10. When Adam and Eve were created, there was only one *"Will"* in the garden; that was the "Will" of the Father. Jesus manifested through Adam and Eve. They did exactly what the Father wanted because Jesus was living in them.

11. The Father's ultimate goal NOW is for every one of us to RECEIVE Jesus back in our lives.

12. When you get Jesus back inside of you, you will know how to do what the Father wants done. All we have to do is yield to the Son and the Holy Spirit, that is within us.

13. Because we do not understand who Jesus is, we do not understand His purpose in our lives. We are just simply saying, "I got Jesus on the inside, I am saved".

14. But if I do not know who I have on the inside, then I do not know who He is on the outside. I am just walking around claiming salvation with a defeated life

15. One of Satan's goals was to wake up Adam and Eve's will and desires; therefore, putting his will and desires in them. His ultimate goal was to wake up a will to do wrong. Once their will and Satan's will came alive, the "Will" of the Father which was Jesus, left. Now man was left with his own will and the will of Satan, in operation.

16. There was only one *"Will"* in the garden from the get-go; that was the *Will of GOD.* Jesus was in Adam; Adam had the *"Will"* of the Father.

17. All Adam had to do was subject himself to that *"Will"* which was Jesus Christ. The *"Will"* of the Father was empowered through and by the Holy Spirit.

18. Again, Adam could receive the *"Will"* and he could do the *"Will"* of the Father, because he had Jesus living on the inside of him. He had Jesus and the Holy Spirit to empower the *"Will"*.

19. Adam did not have to figure out anything. He did not have to second guess himself because the "Will" of the Father was in control in his life.

20. Once we have Jesus in the inside, we do not have to figure out anything. The total *"Will"* of the Father is inside of all believers. The Bible declares, *"We are the*

righteousness of GOD". That means we are the *"Will"* of GOD because Jesus Christ is living in us.

Lesson 3
The Fall of Man

1. **(Genesis 3:5)** "For GOD doth know that in the day ye eat thereof, then your eyes shall be opened, and ye shall be as GOD, knowing good and evil".

2. Satan was saying to them, *"when you disobey, your "will" and my "will"* is going to take over". All Satan wanted Eve to do was to disobey.

3. Once Eve disobeyed, GOD's *"Will"* left, which was Jesus. Her will came alive, and Satan's will came alive. That was Satan's ultimate goal to get the Father's "Will" out of man and get man's will to take over.

4. That is why we act like we act, say what we say, and we do what we do. Once Adam and Eve sinned, Satan's will took over, man's will took over; therefore, man no longer had the "Will" of GOD on the inside.

5. Man no longer had Jesus, the *"Will"* of the Father living in him. Man had nothing to be subject to concerning the Father. Man is only subject to the Father through Jesus Christ, which is His own "Will".

6. Some of us cannot figure out why *"we act like we act", "why we do what we do", "why we go through changes that we go through"*. It is Satan's ultimate goal. When man sinned, he lost the *"Will"* of the Father.

7. **(Genesis 3:9)** "And the LORD GOD called unto Adam, and said unto him, Where art thou"? "Was GOD blind"? If GOD was not blind, why did he ask Adam, where are you?

8. GOD asked Adam, *"where are you"?* Understand that the Father connected with the earthly Adam as His spiritual son. Remember, the way He connected with the earthly Adam as a spiritual son in the earthly realm, was through Jesus Christ.

9. So, when Jesus Christ left, the *"Will"* of the Father left, and GOD had no other connection with man. Adam was the earthly *"Will"* of the Father, because of Jesus being in him. The Father only connects with His perfect *"Will"*. Jesus is His perfect *"Will"*. That is why he wants everyone to have Jesus on the inside, so that he can connect to His perfect "Will".

10. Until Jesus is on the inside, GOD does not have connection with you. The Father connects only to His *"Will"*. Jesus, His Son is His *"Will"*.

11. The Father does not connect to our will. That is why there was a total disconnect between GOD and Adam once Jesus left.

12. You must understand why GOD sent His Son. Jesus did not just come out of nowhere. GOD did not just decide to send Jesus for no reason. Jesus being the "Will of the Father", was the divine purpose.

13. Jesus was first here in Adam, and that's how GOD connected with Adam. The only way GOD could reconnect with man on earth, was to send Jesus a second time, to live on the inside of man.

14. People really do not understand that when Jesus was born into the world, that really was His second time coming. He had once lived in the earthly realm, but it was in a spiritual form, inside of Adam.

15. When Jesus was in Adam, it was GOD's *"Will"* that connected *"Will"* to *"Will"*. When Adam and Eve were here on earth, Jesus was in Adam, the perfect *"Will"* of the Father was in Adam and Eve. Jesus is the perfect "Will" of GOD. He took His Son and put Him inside of Adam and Eve, which was the perfect "Will" of GOD.

16. So, guess what GOD did? He connected *"Will"* to *"Will"*. There was no division. There was *"Will"* to *"Will"*. Whatever GOD wanted; Adam wanted. Whatever Adam wanted; GOD wanted. The perfect *"Will"* was in Adam. That is why the minute Adam and Eve sinned, the "Will" being Jesus, and the Holy Spirit stepped out.

17. **(Genesis 3:9)** "And the LORD GOD called unto Adam, and said unto him, Where art thou"?

18. That is why GOD said, *"Adam where are you"? " I don't see my Son anymore*". The Father was asking, *"where is my Son"?* He was asking *"where is my "Will"?* My *"Will"* has left you. The Father was declaring, "You don't want what I want any more". Therefore, we are disconnected from one another. We are no longer *"Will"* to *"Will"*.

19. It is like a son being born in a home, to a natural Father. The little boy follows his Father around wanting whatever Dad wants. Doing whatever Dad does. They appear to be *"will to will"*. They may be watching TV together, and if Dad crosses his leg, the little boy will cross his legs. He just wants to be like Dad.

20. But one day, the son becomes twenty-one. He does not want anything Dad wants anymore. The son develops his own desires. He does not come home, when Dad says come home. He does not do what Dad says anymore. Therefore, Dad decides it is time for you to leave because our wills no longer connect.

21. **(Genesis 3:23)** "Therefore the LORD GOD sent him forth from the garden of Eden, to till the ground from whence he was taken.

22. For this reason, GOD had to put Adam out of the garden. Their wills were no longer connected. Therefore, GOD knew Adam would completely start to rely on himself instead of Him. No longer was the Father's "Will" in him, which was Jesus.

Lesson 4
One of Us

1. The Father has no connection with us if Jesus is not on the inside. The Father looks down; He does not see anything but the need for redemption. When GOD looks at earth, He only see His Son, which is His "Will" on earth, AND in earth.

2. The Father only connects with His own *"Will"* and His own *"Will"* is Jesus. You must know who Jesus is. You must know who He is. He is the *"Will"* of the Father, that connects *"Will"* to *"Will"*.

3. **(Genesis 3:5)** "For GOD doth know that in the day ye eat thereof, then your eyes shall be opened, and ye shall be as gods, knowing good and evil".

4. **(Genesis 3:22)** "And the LORD GOD said, Behold, the man is become as one of us, to know good and evil: and now, lest he put forth his hand, and take also of the tree of life, and eat, and live forever".

5. Man had become a god. Just like Satan said. That is why GOD said, "man has become one of us, he is now a god". What is it to become a god?

6. To become a god, means you can have your own will, manifest your own will, empower your own will. You do not need or desire the "Will" of the Father anymore. You are now operating independently of the Father.

7. When a child is considered grown, it is literally saying *"that child is operating independently of the will of the parent"*.

8. When GOD put Adam and Eve out of the garden He literally was saying, "they are grown now they are gods on their own, they don't need me anymore".
9. **(Matthew 18:3)** "And said, Verily I say unto you, Except ye be converted, and become as little children, ye shall not enter into the kingdom of heaven".

10. The reason why Jesus told the disciples they had to go back to being little children, was because they had to be able to give up their will and embrace the *"Will"* of the Father, again. For GOD to use them, they had to become dependent on Him, again. Jesus was ***totally*** dependent on His Father.

11. **(Genesis 3:22)** "And the LORD GOD said, Behold, the man is become as one of us.

12. Man had become a god on earth, he was living by his own will and choices. Jesus wanted man to go back to the *"Will"* of the Father. They could only do that by becoming spiritual children. The word *"child"* or *"children"* means to depend upon or to become a dependent of. Man is to become a dependent of the Father.

13. Unless you are willing to become a total dependent of GOD the Father again, He cannot use you. The only way you can become a dependent of GOD, you must receive Jesus as your Savior, which is the *"Will"* of the Father, and then give up your will.

14. Again, Satan's goal was to be as one of them (Trinity). That is why he attempted to exert his will over the *"Will"* of the Father. Angels have free will and they have *"A "heavenly "Will"* of the Father in them. They did not and do not have "THE" will of the Father in them, which is Jesus.

15. **(Isaiah 14:13)** " For thou hast said in thine heart, I will ascend into heaven, I will exalt my throne above the stars of GOD: I will sit also upon the mount of the congregation, in the sides of the north:

16. Satan was saying *"he will place his will above the "Will" of the Father"*. You must understand who Satan wanted to be, he wanted to be the *"Will"* of the Father. But he could not be, because he was a created being.

17. Jesus was not a created being, he derived from the Father himself. We cannot explain His beginning, we cannot explain His end.

18. Satan is not anti-GOD, he is antichrist. He hates Jesus because he is the Son of the Father, He is the *"Will"* of the Father. Satan can only be "A" *"Will"* of the Father. Again, he can never be *"THE"* will of the Father, and he can never be the Son of the Father.

19. **(Revelation 12:9)** "So the great dragon was cast out, that serpent of old, called the Devil and Satan, who deceives the whole world; he was cast to the earth, and his angels were cast out with him".

20. If you notice the same pattern once Satan attempted to exalt his will above GOD's *"Will",* he had to be kicked out of heaven. Satan picked the same pattern for Adam and Eve once their will was exposed and exalted. They were thrown out of the garden.

21. Satan had accomplished his second goal, which was to get them kicked out of the Garden of Eden. His first goal was to get them to sin, which was to go against the "Will" of the Father.

One of Us
Questionnaire

1. The Father only connects with what?

2. What does it mean to become "a god"?

3. What was Satan in "Isaiah 14:13"?

4. Satan is not anti-GOD, he is ___________________________.

5. What was Satan's first and second goal?

Lesson 5
The Person, The Spirit

1. In truly learning about the totality of the Trinity and the world, we must understand there is the person of GOD, Jesus, and the Holy Spirit. There is the spirit of GOD, Jesus, and the Holy Spirit.

2. The *"Person"* of the Trinity was never supposed to enter the earthly realm. The earth was created for man. Adam was to be ruler of this world through and by the power of the Trinity. Adam and Eve were to be the persons on earth. The Trinity was to be the persons of heaven.

3. Just like heaven was not created for man, it was created for Trinity and the angels. Man was always to remain here on earth. But once man fell, then the earth became wicked. Therefore, heaven had to become man's home. Heaven had to be redesigned to accommodate man.

4. **(John 14:2-3) "**In my Father's house are many mansions: if it were not so, I would have told you. I go to prepare a place for you.[3] And if I go and prepare a place for you, I will come again, and receive you unto myself; that where I am, there ye may be also".

5. That is why Jesus said, *"I must go and prepare a place for you"*. When that place is finished, I will come back and get you". Again, because heaven was design for the heavenly organization, not the earthly creation.

6. Hell was not designed for man, it was designed only for Satan, fallen angels, and demons. But because of the wickedness of man, hell is enlarging itself every day, because of the sinful nature of man.

7. **(Exodus 33:20-23) "[20]** And he said, Thou canst not see my face: for there shall no man see me, and live.[21] And the LORD said, Behold, there is a place by me, and thou shalt stand upon a rock:[22] And it shall come to pass, while my glory passeth by, that I will put thee in a clift of the rock, and will cover thee with my hand while I pass

by:[23] And I will take away mine hand, and thou shalt see my back parts: but my face shall not be seen".

8. There is the *"Person"* of GOD who sits on the throne in heaven. No, HE is not human, but He is in an immortal state. We know this because Moses saw the person of GOD.

9. GOD told Moses: *"You can see my back parts, but you cannot see my face"*. Because of whom GOD is, no "***MAN***" has seen GOD. GOD literally took His hand and put it over Moses' face. That is how we know there is a "Person" of GOD.

10. **(Genesis 3:8)** "And they heard the voice of the LORD GOD walking in the garden in the cool of the day: and Adam and his wife hid themselves from the presence of the LORD GOD amongst the trees of the garden".

11. It is noted that GOD would visit Adam here on earth. He would walk and commune with Adam. You must understand before Adam's fell, he was immortal, he was completely pure.

12. You must understand three major words in this scripture, voice, walking, and presence. This means that GOD would come to Adam in His *"Person" state and "spirit" state.*

13. **(Genesis 6:3)** "And the LORD said, My *"spirit"* shall not always strive with man, for that he also is flesh: yet his days shall be an hundred and twenty years".

14. The word *"strive"* means to attend or go after. It means to correspond with. Once man sinned and became totally flesh, GOD could not attend with.

15. After the fall of man, only the "spirit" of GOD moved here on earth with man. Even then, GOD's "spirit" could not strive with man, again, which mean there could be no more divine connection because of sin.

16. **(Leviticus 16:2)** "And the LORD said unto Moses, speak unto Aaron thy brother, that he come not at all times into the holy place within the vail before the mercy seat, which is upon the ark; that he die not: for I will appear in the cloud upon the mercy seat".

17. That is where the Ark of the Covenant came in. Because the spirit of GOD could no longer be in man nor truly with man. His "spirit" literally had to be carried around in a sacred box for man's divine protection.

18. GOD spoke to certain people in the Old Testament all the time. But, His "spirit" could not dwell within man, because of sin. But GOD always had a way of getting to man or being WITH him. That is where the Ark of the Covenant came in.

19. **(Numbers 10:33-36)** "And they departed from the mount of the LORD three days' journey: and the ark of the covenant of the LORD went before them in the three days' journey, to search out a resting place for them.[34] And the cloud of the LORD was upon them by day, when they went out of the camp.[35] And it came to pass, when the ark set forward, that Moses said, Rise up, LORD, and let thine enemies be scattered; and let them that hate thee flee before thee.[36] And when it rested, he said, Return, O LORD, unto the many thousands of Israel.

20. GOD allowed His "spirit" to be in place, so that he could still lead and direct them and have power here on earth for man. GOD yet loved His creation, even though they had fallen.

21. **(Isaiah 6:1)** "In the year that king Uzziah died I saw also the LORD sitting upon a throne, high and lifted up, and His train filled the temple".

22. GOD is sitting on the throne. His position totally is on His throne in heaven. Yet His *"Spirit"* is omnipresent. But again, the "Person" GOD has a total position, that can never be taken away.

23. **(Matthew 23:22)** "And whoever swears by heaven, swears both by the throne of GOD and by Him who sits upon it"

24. **(Revelation 3:21)** "He who overcomes, I will grant to him to sit down with Me on My throne, as I also overcame and sat down with My Father on His throne".

25. The *"Person"* GOD is sitting on His throne. He is not human, He is supernatural, immortal, He is all things to all people; He is GOD, properly positioned on His throne.

26. **(Isaiah 14:13)** "For thou hast said in thine heart, I will ascend into heaven, I will exalt my throne above the stars of GOD: I will sit also upon the mount of the congregation, in the sides of the north".

27. That is why Satan set up his kingdom in the second heaven, to be just like GOD. The stars in heaven are angels that Satan set his kingdom upon, looking to try and steal worship from GOD.

28. We must understand, Satan has been in the presence of GOD. He knows the "spirit" of GOD, he has seen the "Person" GOD, Satan knows the power of GOD, and knows the voice of GOD. The Bible declares "NO MAN HAS SEEN GOD" but, Satan has, because he is not a man.

29. **(Psalm 51:11)** "Cast me not away from thy presence; and take not thy holy spirit from me".

30. In this scripture, David is talking about the "spirit" of GOD not the Holy Spirit. Again, David is referring to his relationship with GOD, and his conversations with GOD.

31. David had to say this, because when David committed an adultery, there was a season that the voice of GOD left David, which was the "spirit" of GOD. The external "Will" of GOD left David, for a season.

32. In the Old Testament, GOD always talk directly to certain people. His voice would be heard by certain people audibly, but His "spirit" could not be with man, because of sin.

33. His "spirit" would appear in places for man and on objects for man, to keep from killing man. When He appeared in the burning bush for Moses, His "spirit" appeared in the bush, yet His voice came directly from the throne of heaven.

The Person, The Spirit Questionnaire

1. The Person of the ______________________ was never supposed to enter the earthly realm.

2. Why did Jesus have to go and prepare a place for man?

3. Who saw the person of GOD? But is it that he did not, see?

4. Why did Satan set up his kingdom in the second heaven?

5. How did GOD talk to most people in the Old Testament?

Lesson 6
The Person, The Spirit
(Continued)

34. **(Isaiah 63:10)** "But they rebelled, and vexed *His Holy Spirit*: therefore, He was turned to be their enemy, and He fought against them".

35. In the Old Testament here, it is not talking about the Holy Spirit it is talking about GOD's "spirit". The statement says", His (GOD) holy (small letter is a character not a person) Spirit.

36. **(Isaiah 63:11)** "Then he remembered the days of old, Moses, and his people, saying, where is he that brought them up out of the sea with the shepherd of his flock? Where is he that put *His Holy Spirit* within him"?

37. Again, it is not talking about the holy spirit, it is talking about the "spirit" of GOD. The *"spirit"* of GOD is holy. But it is the *"spirit"* of GOD not the *"Person"* of GOD or the *"Person"* or *"Spirit"* of the Holy Ghost.

38. In every man there is:
    a. The spirit of GOD
    b. The spirit of Jesus
    c. The spirit of the Holy Ghost

39. **(1 Corinthians 12:3)** "Wherefore I give you to understand, that no man speaking by the Spirit of GOD calleth Jesus accursed: and that no man can say that Jesus is the Lord, but by the Holy Ghost".

40. When noticed in the scripture, GOD talks about His "spirit" and He talks about the Holy Ghost.

41. We have the *"spirit"* of GOD. Because it is through the *"spirit"* of GOD, that we developed our will, and our ability to think. Understand that Adam received his ability to have his own will, from the "spirit" of GOD.

42. He received the *"Will"* of the GOD from Jesus Christ. Also He received power to enforce GOD's *"Will"* from the Holy Spirit.

43. Man received his ability to think on his own, by having a mind from the *"spirit"* of GOD. (We will talk more about this later.)

44. GOD had to give everyone a mind (a will) because GOD did not make us as robots. His desire is that everyman freely choose to be led by him.

45. **(Genesis 2:16-17)** "But of the tree of the knowledge of good and evil, thou shalt not eat of it: for in the day that thou eatest thereof thou shalt surely die".

46. This command is the reason why GOD had to put the tree in the garden. Man could not be in a robotic position in order to have the ability to choose.

47. **(Proverbs 3:5-6)** "Trust in the LORD with all thine heart; and lean not unto thine own understanding.**6** In all thy ways acknowledge him, and he shall direct thy paths".

48. GOD put His "spirit" in us again, giving all of us the ability to think for ourselves. But he wanted everyone to rely on the Jesus, the "Will" of the Father in us. That is why He does not want us to "lean (depend) on our own understanding".

49. To understand the "spirit" of GOD means to have the ability to think, and the ability to have our own will. When man sinned, the "spirit" of GOD left him, the "Will" of GOD left him (which was Jesus), and power left him, (which was the Holy Spirit.)

50. Man began to be subject to his own will, and the will of Satan. That is why GOD said, "His *"spirit"* would not always dwell with man". We must understand that GOD was functioning externally with man. Having a few that were not leaning to their own understanding indicates they were operating in their own personal will.

51. **(Isaiah 63:10)** "But they rebelled, and vexed *His holy Spirit*: therefore, he was turned to be their enemy, and he fought against them".

52. **(Ephesians 4:30)** "And grieve not the holy Spirit of GOD, whereby ye are sealed unto the day of redemption".

53. In this scripture, most people teach that this is talking about the Holy Spirit. The scripture declares "the holy Spirit of GOD. The "holy" is with a small "h". The reason why it has a small "h" is because it is talking about the Spirit of GOD.

54. The words *"grieve"* and *"vexed"* means to torment or in total disappointment. The way that you grieve the "spirit" of GOD is by going against His "Will", choosing your will over His "Will". Do not get "grieve" and "blaspheme" mixed up. They do not mean the same thing.

55. GOD was constantly *"grieved" and "vexed"* because Israel was constantly going against His "Will". This is why, as GOD sits on His throne in "Person", we constantly vex His "spirit". We repeatedly go against His "Will" as though it means nothing.

56. That is why much judgment came against Israel and the world today, the vexing or grieving GOD's "spirit".

57. **(Genesis 6:6)** "And it repented the LORD that he had made man on the earth, and it grieved him at His heart".

58. When we grieve or vex GOD's *"spirit"* we hurt His heart. We literally break His heart. GOD's heart was broken when Adam sinned. Adam made his will more important than GOD's "Will". Adam and Eve used their minds, will and emotions over GOD's.

59. Every time we pick our will over the will of the Father, we break His heart. We grieve him, we vex him. We say loud to GOD "that our will is more important than His".

60. **(1 Thessalonians 4:8)** "He therefore that despiseth, despiseth not man, but GOD, who hath also given unto us His Holy Spirit"

61. The Word *"despiseth"* means to *"dishonor"*. Whenever we go against the "Will" of GOD, whenever we use our minds over the mind of GOD, we "dishonor" him. We "dishonor" Him with sin. Sin is the ***end*** result of choosing our understanding over the understanding of GOD.

62. **(Genesis 7:1)** "And the LORD said unto Noah, come thou and all thy house into the ark; for thee have I seen righteous before me in this generation".

63. Noah functioned with the “*spirit*” of GOD, not going by his own will, but by the “spirit” of GOD. Therefore, he remained righteous, rejecting his own will and the will of Satan.

The Person, The Spirit
Questionnaire

1. We have the __________________________ because it is through the "spirit" of GOD that we developed our will, and our ability to think.

2. Understand, Adam received his ability to have His __________________ from the "spirit" of GOD.

3. Why did GOD have to give everyone a will and/or mind?

4. Explain the three things that left man, when he sinned?

5. What does the word "vexed" and "despised" mean?

Lesson 7
The Person, The Spirit

1. Now, let us talk about the *"Person"* of the Holy Spirit and the *"spirit"* of the Holy Spirit.

2. **(John 15:26)** "When the Advocate comes, whom I will send to you from the Father—the Spirit of truth who goes out from the Father—he will testify about me".

3. The Holy Spirit is a *"Person"* who is /was with the Father. His position in heaven was to always be with the Father. He came to earth once he was sent.

4. The Holy Spirit is a *"Person",* not an *"it"* or thing. The *"spirit"* of the Holy Spirit is the Holy Spirit. The "Person" of the Holy Spirit is the Holy Ghost.

5. In the scriptures, often the words Holy Spirit and Holy Ghost are interchanged. You must also know who they are referring to according to the scripture. As you study and understand the "Person" versus the "spirit", it will become clearer to you.

6. The *"spirit"* of the Holy Spirit gives us their living ability. It is the very personality of GOD. That is why he is the ***"fruit"*** of the Spirit. He is what brings life back to men. The Holy Spirit is what gives men the ability to walk and to live a holy and righteous life. He is what gives man the ability to understand and receive truth. Again, he is the personality of GOD.

7. **(Acts 1:8)** "But ye shall receive power, after that the Holy Ghost is come upon you: and ye shall be witnesses unto me both in Jerusalem, and in all Judaea, and in Samaria, and unto the uttermost part of the earth".

8. The *"Person"* (the Holy Ghost) is what empowers man. Jesus made it noticeably clear that the "Person" (the Holy Ghost), would come to bring power.

9. He would enable man to work on a whole different level. The *"Person"* (the Holy Ghost) would make man a *"witness"*. The word "witness" means evident.

10. **(Matthew 3:11)** "I indeed baptize you with water unto repentance, but He who is coming after me is mightier than I, whose sandals I am not worthy to carry. He will baptize you with the Holy Spirit and fire.'"

11. If you notice in the scripture, John said *"the Holy Spirit and fire."* He declared, the *"Spirit"* (which is the Holy Spirit), and fire, which is the "Person" (the Holy Ghost), is power.

12. Again, the Holy Spirit always gives you your living power. The Holy Ghost gives you your working power. That is why it is called "fire".

13. **(John 16:7)** "Nevertheless I tell you the truth; It is expedient for you that I go away: for if I go not away, the Comforter will not come unto you; but if I depart, I will send him unto you."

14. The word "*Comforter*" means **intercessor, consoler, and advocate. The Holy Spirit and Holy Ghost became on earth what Jesus is to us, in heaven. There must always be a divine connection.**

15. **(Acts 2:4)** "And they were all filled with the *Holy Ghost*, and began to speak with other tongues, as the *Spirit* gave them utterance".

16. You will see in scripture the **"Person"** of the Holy Spirit and the *"spirit"* of the Holy Spirit, came the earth at the same time. GOD knew we would need living power and working power.

17. You now see, it is noticeably clear how they work together and how they enhance one another.

18. **(John 14:26)** "But the Advocate, the Holy Spirit, whom the Father will send in my name, will teach you all things and will remind you of everything I have said to you."

19. The Holy Spirit will teach us all things. We do not have to be ignorant (unlearned) concerning anything in the kingdom of GOD because of the Holy Spirit. He even teaches us how to handle the Holy Ghost, the power source.

20. The *"Person"* of the Holy Ghost is what empowers us. The Holy Spirit is what teaches us. The Holy Ghost empowers us to do everything. The Holy Spirit teaches us the "*spirit* "of excellence.

The Person, The Spirit
Questionnaire

1. The Holy Spirit is a person he is not a ______________ or _________________.

2. What is the difference between the Holy Spirit and the Holy Ghost?

3. What is "fire"?

4. The person of the Holy Ghost is what _______________________ man. The Holy Spirit is what _________________________ man.

5. The Holy Spirit is the ___________________of GOD.

Lesson 8
Jesus the Will of GOD

1. Jesus, (*the "Will" of the Father*) no longer being present in man's life is how man became a product of the world, Satan's system.

2. Because we do not have the "*Will*" of GOD in us anymore, (which is Jesus), we have the will of Satan in us, (our own will). Now we are subject to do anything, because we do not have the "Will" of the Father in us anymore, once Adam and Eve sinned.

3. When we talk about the world, this is what the world is. The word "world" is the will of Satan. It is not per- say a place, it is a will. It is the Kingdom of Satan.

4. Everyone is born into the will of Satan and the will of Satan is in them. It will show up even in a little baby. When babies become frustrated, or do not want their bottle anymore, they will bend backward or even throw the bottle.

5. Another example would be putting paper on a table and telling a two-year-old not to touch it. More often than not, the child will go there and touch it anyway. You must slap its little hand, why? That child already has a will of rebellion in them that came straight from Satan.

6. No parent would teach a child to be rebellious or stubborn. But the child already knows how to do this. The knowledge of transgression and iniquity (which is a will of Satan), is already in the child.

7. **(2 Corinthians 4:4)** "In whom the **GOD of this world** hath blinded the minds of them which believed not, lest the light of the glorious gospel of Christ, who is the image of GOD, should shine unto them".

8. *"The god of this world"* means that Satan's will rule this world. He decides what goes on. As long as a person is in the world, in the system of Satan, they are being ruled by his will.

9. Why do you want to drink? Have you ever thought about why you want to drink? Why do you want to curse? Why do you want to do certain things? You know they are wrong, but why would you want to do them?

10. Why do you want to smoke? Think about it for a moment. Think about why you would want to do something that you know is not necessarily good for you. Man has a desire for it because Satan is the will of this world.

11. Jesus is not in us until we get saved. Until then, we have Satan's will in us. Even though we know it might not be good for us, we still have a desire for it because of the will of Satan in us.

12. The *"god of this world"* means Satan's will. Because of the fall of man, Satan's desires rule now. That is why Paul said, "when I would do good, evil is always present".

13. As holy as Paul was supposed to be, he was saying "because the will of Satan is always somewhere around me, it makes me do things I should not. I struggle daily with my choices.

14. **(John 8:44)** "Ye are of your father the devil, and the lust of your father ye will do. He was a murderer from the beginning, and abode not in the truth, because there is no truth in him. When he speaketh a lie, he speaketh of his own: for he is a liar, and the father of it".

15. **"Ye are of your father the devil, and the lust of your father ye will do".** When we are not saved, our will is being controlled by the will of our father, which is the devil. He is everyone's spiritual father before we get saved. That is why Jesus said, "Your father".

16. *"Lust"* means we desired unclean stuff. Even after you are saved, if you do not get delivered, you will not surrender your will in that area. Your will, will still be controlled by Satan.

17. That is why many will say, *" I am saved, I know I am saved, I know I'm trying to do this thing right. But why is it that I keep still slipping up"*? Do not forget that man is still dominated in certain areas by Satan's will, even after salvation. He can still control you even though you are saved.

18. While you were in the world, Satan filled you up with his will; lust, lying, crazy desires, tattoo, earring wrapped around your head. You have all these crazy desires, because these are all wills of Satan, he has put in you. You still want to drink a little. You still want a beer or a shot every now and then.

19. Now you are saved. GOD rescued you out of the system of Satan. Guess what Satan's has done to your life, while you were in the world? He has put all these desires in you. Even though Jesus is in your life, until you recognize they are there, there will still be struggles. You are going to have to get rid of these desires daily.

20. Until you get rid of them, you will still want to do stuff you did in the world. Satan's desires are still in you, even though you have the "Will" of GOD in you.

21. Though you are saved, you can still have the desire to smoke. The will of Satan still resides in you. That desire is rooted in you. Even though the "Will" of the Father is in you, your will is still struggling in you. You can get saved, but you will fornicate. You still will lie. You still will to drink. This is not picking on anyone. You must understand, your will still *"will to"*. You are going to try and have your way. Your will is still powerful, though the *"Will"* of the Father is living inside of you.

22. Until you are delivered out of the wills of Satan, until you are delivered out of your own personal will, you are still going to will these other things. Jesus is perfect. Jesus is in you, which is the perfect "Will" of the Father. But the inward battle is there all the time, willing *"To Will"*.

Jesus the Will of GOD
Questionnaire

1. What does "world" mean?

2. Everyone one is born with what, concerning Satan?

3. What does it mean to be controlled by the "Will" of your father"?

4. Why does man have crazy desires?

5. What does the word "lust" mean?

Lesson 9
GOD With Us

1. **(Matt. 1:23)** "Behold, a virgin shall be with child, and shall bring forth a son, and they shall call His name Emmanuel, which being interpreted is, **GOD with us".**

2. What does *"GOD with us"* mean? What, was He saying when he said, *"Jesus was going to be born"?* When He said, *"GOD with us"* He was saying, "The *"Will"* of the Father will be with you or back with you".

3. Please keep that in mind. Just saying He is Emmanuel, or that He is the Son of GOD, we know all of that. But if you do not know what He really means in your life, then you are just simply saying He is the "Son of GOD", or that "He is Emmanuel". Beyond that, you must "know" who he really is.

4. It is time to learn who the Son really is, understand who He is, because of the Father. We often say, "I know Jesus the Christ, and I know the Son". But if we really knew who Jesus is, we would have total victory.

5. You know that He is the Savior, but you have got to know who he is as Savior. You think because you do not fornicate and lie any more, you do not commit adultery or do not steal any more, that makes you spiritual.

6. He is way beyond that. The average person does not do any of that; yet they do not have him. Because man lost the *"Will"* of GOD, the Will of the Father had to be born; born back into the world.

7. Before Adam and Eve sinned, when Adam was created, the Father simply placed the Son inside Adam and Eve; thus connecting them to the Son. He connected them to His perfect *"Will"*. After they sinned, GOD's *"Will"* left, which was the Son.

8. Thereafter, everything on the earth had to be born. Jesus then came back into this world as the legal *"Will"* of the Father. He could not just be

9. He could not just be here on earth anymore. The legal way to enter the earthly realm is to be born into this world. That is why he said, *"Behold, a virgin shall be with child".* GOD's *"Will"* is pure and perfect. It could not be contaminated by man's will. So, Mary had to be a virgin.

10. Not only that, but the Father had to be literally the perfect Will of GOD. GOD had to be the father because He is the Will. He placed His perfect *"Will"* in Mary, which was His Son, who is the perfect "Will" of the Father.

11. Therefore, when a mother gets pregnant, guess whose blood type the baby will have, the father. The mother's blood cannot cross over into the baby. The father is the one who must determine the blood type. GOD perfectly design that system, so that Mary's blood in no way could contaminate Jesus.

12. Mary was a virgin, but the father was the Father of the *"Will".* When Jesus was born, he was born as the perfect "Will" of the Father, so Mary's blood could not contaminate him.

13. All of us have an earthly, natural father, whose blood has already contaminated us. The babies born will automatically be contaminated with a worldly will. Their desires will already be tainted when they enter natural life.

14. Our father's blood was contaminated. Our father's desires were contaminated. That is why we have contaminated desires, even though some have been raised in church.

15. We grow up in church and still end up departing. We go out there and do foolish things because of contaminated blood. Cain rose and kill his brother because he was born with contaminated blood.

16. Even though we had what may look like good desires, though some desires did not seem wrong, they were wrong. When desires do not line up with the *"Will"* of the Father, they are wrong.

17. When we talk about the world concerning GOD, always understand when the scripture says, "GOD so loved the world" He was talking about the people in the world.

18. When we talk about the world concerning Satan, it is talking about a *"system"* or his will. Its talking about Satan's will.

19. **(John 3:16)** "For GOD so loved the world, that He gave His only begotten Son, that whosoever believeth in Him should not perish, but have everlasting life".

20. What is that saying? "GOD so loved the people in Satan's system". When we were under Satan's will, GOD gave His Will to rescue everyone back from the will of Satan.

21. Once a person becomes saved, the *"Will"* of GOD will began to push the will of Satan out, if you will allow it to.

22. There are three wills, the will of Satan, the will of man, and the "Will" of GOD. You determine which one will control your will, either Satan or GOD. As you allow the will of GOD to dominate, soon or the later, your will and the will of Satan will completely disappear.

GOD With Us
Questionnaire

1. What does "GOD with us" mean?

2. The mother's blood cannot ____________________ into the baby.

3. The Father is the one who has to determine _______________.

4. What does "GOD so love the world" mean?

5. Why was Mary a virgin?

Lesson 10
The Will to Believe

1. **(John 3:16)** "For GOD so loved the world, that He gave His only begotten Son, that whosoever **believeth in Him".**

2. When the Father is telling us to believe in His Son, what is He telling us who to believe in? "He is telling us to believe in His *"Will"*.

3. The word *"believe"* means to accept and agree with. So, when you say, *"I believe in Jesus"* you are saying, "I accept and agree with the perfect "Will" of the Father".

4. This is how Jesus starts to rescue us from out of the world, and the will of Satan. When someone says, *"I believe in Jesus",* they are saying, "Father I believe in your perfect "Will".

5. When we start understanding the Son, we begin to make the Father proud. We do not make the Father proud by just being saved. When we do not understand the Son, which is GOD's *"Will",* we are wasting the work GOD put into, sending His *"Will"*.

6. **(Romans 10:9)** "That if thou shalt confess with thy mouth the Lord Jesus, and shalt believe in thine heart that GOD hath raised him from the dead, thou shalt be saved".

7. When you confess Jesus, you are confessing the *"Will"* of the Father. When you believe in your heart, you are saying, "I accept and agree that GOD raised His "Will" to live again.

8. Please understand this. It was more than just Jesus getting up out of a physical grave. It was the fullness of the *"Will"* living again.

9. The minute that Adam sinned, Jesus left, and the Will of the Father died on earth. The Father's "Will" died on earth in Genesis because of Adam and Eve.

10. Now the *"Will"* of the Father has been resurrected again. The Father's *"Will"* had to be resurrected. Understand, Jesus is that resurrected "Will" of the Father.

11. When Jesus went into the grave and into hell, he took the keys from Satan. He took the power of *"Will"* again.

12. What were the keys? Jesus took the right for man to freely have the *"Will"* of GOD back in his life. That is why when the Father raised Jesus from the grave, it was the power of the *"Will"*. Why is that significant? It is significant because the Father did not just raise a man from the grave, He raised his own *"Will"* from the grave.

13. He awakened the fullness of His *"Will"* back to life for man. So, now we have the right to the fullness of the *"Will"* of GOD in us, which is Jesus. He did not just resurrect a man; He resurrected His own Will.

14. When His Will got up, man now have a right to be healed, a right to be delivered, and a right to be set free. That is what His *"Will"* declares.

15. When you start understanding, accepting, and agreeing; then you will recognize, you do not have to work for your blessing. You already have the *"Will"* for your blessing.

16. **(Philippians 3:10) "That I may know Him**, and **the power of His resurrection**, and the fellowship of His sufferings, being made conformable unto His death.

17. Why did Paul want to know Jesus? He wanted to know the *"Will"* of the Father, and the power of the resurrection.

18. What was the power of His resurrection? It was to know the *"Will"* and the Power, of the Fullness of GOD's Will.

19. Paul understood, it was not just a man that got up out of the grave. Paul said, "if I can get to know the *"Will"* and the Power of the *"Will"*, no devil in hell can bring me down.

The Will to Believe
Questionnaire

1. What does "believe" mean?

2. When you start really understanding the Son, that is when you going to make ______________________________.

3. What were the "keys"?

4. Why did Paul want to know Jesus?

5. What is the "power of his resurrection"?

Theology of the Trinity
Assignments

(All homework, practical, and scripture information, must be on a separate sheet of paper. If it is written on this paper, there is a 50% deduction from your grade automatically.) Homework, practical, and Bible study observation must be a paragraph long or more).

Homework

Explain two incidents where the will of GOD had truly left the Old Testament Saul

Practical

Give an example where you can recognize when the Will of GOD has left an individual.

100 Word Essay

Please try and type all essays if possible. If you cannot type your essay, please make sure your teacher is aware of it. Your essay and Bible study lessons must be turned in with all of your homework. Your essay must be 100 words. Please be aware that your homework and essays count 20%each of your total of grade.

Please write a 100-word essay on how Satan is the GOD of this world. Please use scripture.

Name ___________________________

Site ____________________________

Instructor _______________________

Date ___________________________

The Theology of the Trinity
Test

(Each Question is Worth 10 Points)

1. Why is the "Word" capitalized in John 1:1?

2. What is the difference between "made" and "create"?

3. How did Adam know what to name the animals?

4. Why did GOD ask Adam "Where are you"?

5. How is when the Father has no connection with us?

6. What does it mean for man to become a god?

7. Why did Jesus have to go and prepare a place for man?

8. Explain the difference between the person of GOD vs the spirit of GOD.

9. Explain the difference between the person of Jesus vs the spirit of Jesus.

10. Explain the difference the between the Holy Spirit and the Holy Ghost

THE THEOLOGY OF PRAYER

Safe Haven Interdenominational Bible College and Training Institute
PO Box 457
Zebulon, NC

THE THEOLOGY OF PRAYER
TABLE OF CONTENTS

Lesson One
Mysteries of the Church

1.**(Ephesians 6:18-19)** “Praying always with all prayer and supplication in the Spirit, and watching thereunto with all perseverance and supplication for all saints; [19] And for me, that utterance may be given unto me, that I may open my mouth boldly, to MAKE KNOWN THE MYSTERY OF THE GOSPEL”

2.GOD is ready to reveal the mysteries to the church, to the true body of Christ. Mysteries will not come by how much word you know. (Ephesians 6:18-19) Mysteries are revealed by how much prayer you do. Mysteries are sacred or heavenly secrets, reserved just for the body of Christ. To know and understand, in right timing and due season.

3.**(Ephesians 6:18-19)** “And for me, that utterance may be given unto me, that I may open my mouth boldly”.

4.Utterance is a declaration of understanding. GOD wants to bring the church into true understanding of his voice, but it will ONLY be done through prayer. Prayer will cause our spirits to become truly available to the voice of the Holy Spirit.

5.The devil does not want the body of Christ to pray, because it positions us to hear GOD, and to hear His voice clearly. If, we really know how to pray. That is why learning to pray correctly, is so important in the kingdom of GOD.

6.The last day anointing will be prayer. The greatest gift in the last days will not be the apostle, prophet, pastor, teacher, or evangelist; it will be the power of intercession. Those that will allow themselves to be commissioned to pray.

7.**(Luke 2:36-40)** “And there was one Anna, a prophetess, the daughter of Phanuel, of the tribe of Aser: she was of a great age and had lived with a husband seven years from her virginity;[37] And she was a widow of about fourscore and four years, which departed not from the temple, but served GOD with fastings and prayers night and day”.

8.One of the greatest intercessors in the Bible other than Jesus, was the prophetess Anna. She never left the temple. She lived in fasting and prayer. Her life was centered around hearing the voice of GOD. She interceded so must that she knew who the Messiah was, when he was brought to the temple.

9.In the last days, GOD will raise back up the spirit of Anna, in the church. It is through the spirit of Anna, that the true church will recognize the true Messiah from the antichrist spirit. The Anna anointing will sense the very coming of Jesus Christ for His bride.

10. The Anna spirit will come from selfless people. People who will make their lives about prayer; and not about themselves. This last day anointing will be people who will be sold out to become watchman, and a voice for the kingdom of GOD.

11. The Anna spirit will reveal the mysteries of GOD, because of prayer. The Anna spirit will uncover things need for the local house of GOD, and specific individuals. The Anna spirit will uncover things for leadership. Because of her prayer life, she will often make leadership aware of the wheat and tare.

12. The Anna anointing will help leadership come into true understanding of the last days and hours, because of the power of intercession. She will help reveal time and season, for the true body of Christ. Because of the power of intercession, her revelation will be that of the deepest level of the prophetic.

13. Intercessors are people who recognize they "NEED GOD". They understand they are not to move without God, without answers from God. They do not move on their own terms; they move strictly by the voice of the heavenly Father, through and by the Holy Spirit.

14. Their need for God comes directly out of the power of prayer. They surrender to prayer. They need prayer like they need food. It is a necessity to them. Their life and time schedules are centered around prayer, because of their need for GOD.

15. Intercessors get answers from GOD. They MUST have answers from GOD. They create a direct line of communication to GOD. Intercessors are people who will pray because they truly understand the exchange program. Therefore, intercessors:
    a. *Communicate with GOD.*
    b. *Let GOD communicate with them.*

16. Intercessors do not go into prayer with a one-track mind. They understand intercession is a two-way conversation. They must communicate with GOD, but they must allow GOD to communicate back TO them. Because intercessors understand, they are looking for heaven to respond by word, deed, or change.
17. Before Adam and Eve sinned, there was no such thing as prayer. There was no need for prayer. Because GOD walked in the cool of the day with Adam and talked directly to him.

18.Once sin came, Satan became the prince of this world. Prayer became the restored communication TO GOD. We are now ruled by prayer. Even though we have the Holy Spirit that speaks to us, our communication to the Father must be through prayer. We must talk to him and allow him to talk back to us.

19.However, all prayer must be done through and by the name of JESUS. Because of the broken relationship of Adam and Eve, there had to be restored communication. And it had to come through and by Jesus Christ. Because of sin, we do not have direct access to the Father, even with prayer, unless we go through and by the name of Jesus.

20.There are three major things you will come into understanding with prayer, as well as learning the types of prayer:

a. Legality –the right to have.
b. Anointing –the power to have.
c. Favor –the supernatural influence too have.

21.The word "*legal*" means the right by law. Because of the blood of Jesus, by law; We have a right to access heaven. But, because of the many things that we do in life, it can also make us "illegal" in our prayers. Things that can make us "illegal" are things like unforgiveness, bitter roots, and sin. We will learn about those, as we go forth.

22.Satan knows when we are *"illegal"* in the kingdom and GOD. Therefore, he can use that to stop our prayers. He can use our *"illegal"* status, to block our answers.

23.The "anointing" means our power through and by prayer. There is an "anointing" that can come to our lives, simply because of fasting and prayer. Many things have not happened, because we have not empowered ourselves through prayer. We often working out of flesh; not power.

24.Then there is favor. Favor comes through prayer. Favor is supernatural influence, through the power of prayer. If the people of GOD would pray, there would be influence. There would be a supernatural influence over the enemy.

The Theology of Prayer
Questionnaire

1. Explain “legality”.

2. Explain the “anointing”.

3. Explain “favor”.

4. Explain recognizing the “need for GOD”.

5. Explain the “Anna spirit”.

The Theology of Prayer
Assignments

Practical

Explain what it means to go into prayer with a *"one track mind"*.

Lesson Two
The Kingdoms of Heaven

(Matthew 11:12) "And from the days of John the Baptist until now, the Kingdom of Heaven suffereth violence, and the violent take it by force".

1. The heavens have three levels, the three levels of heaven are:
    a. Heaven 1 -Atmosphere.
    b. Heaven 2- Satan's kingdom.
    c. Heaven 3- GOD's throne.
2. The first heaven is the atmosphere. It is the stars and moon. It is an area where GOD and Satan control. GOD controls the stars and moon. However, Satan uses the atmosphere as his working ground. It is where familiar spirits operate.
3. When people deal with the stars, zodiac signs, and things like that, it is operated out of the first heaven; and controlled by Satan. When people go to palm readers and witch doctors, these are people using the power of the first heaven. They use familiar spirits to deal in a person's personal life.
4. The second heaven is where Satan's personal kingdom is set up. Satan still desires to be as close to GOD as possible; because he knows who GOD is. Satan was kicked out of the third heaven.
5. The second heaven is yet where wicked angels and Satan gather. Because he wants His kingdom as close to the kingdom of GOD as possible. It is also where he is set up, to block prayer access to the third heaven.
6. The third heaven is where GOD has His throne and kingdom set up. It is now where Jesus set on the right hand of the Father. And where the born-again believer is taken after death. It is the place of true perfection. It is the place where all desire to go one day. It is where prayers are answered from.
7. Satan's ultimate goal for setting up His kingdom in the second heaven was to still have access to the third heaven, again. Also, it was to block man's access to heaven again, through prayer.
8. Satan knew that man could not physically come into heaven at that time, but it was His prayers that would access heaven. It was His communication. It is man's true way of communicating with the Father. And Satan's desire is to block that communication.

9. **(Matthew 11:12)** "And from the days of John the Baptist until now, the Kingdom of Heaven suffereth violence, and the violent take it by force".

10. There are three major words you must understand in this scripture above:

    a. Violence –war.
    b. Violent- warrior.
    c. Force – exercising our spiritual abilities against the enemy.

11. When it declares that, the kingdom of heaven *"suffereth violence"*. The word *"violence"* means war. There is war going on in the second heaven. That war is Satan and his wicked angels, fighting against the prayers of the saints.

12. When a child of GOD prays, the devil does not want those prayer to get to GOD. Most of all, he does not want the answer to get back to mankind. His desire is to block constant communication to the Father.

13. Satan knows because of the fall of man, GOD does not come anymore and walk and talk with man, like he did with Adam before sin. So therefore, man must release his request, straight to the throne of GOD. And Satan is waiting constantly on the defense, to stop it.

14. **(Daniel 10:12-13)** "Then said he unto me, Fear not, Daniel: for from the first day that thou didst set thine heart to understand, and to chasten thyself before thy GOD, thy words were heard, and I am come for thy words.[13] But the prince of the kingdom of Persia withstood me one and twenty days: but, lo, Michael, one of the chief princes, came to help me; and I remained there with the kings of Persia".

15. This is what happened to Daniel's prayer. He prayed his prayer, and it got through to the Father the very first day. But Satan set out to block the answer. Therefore, the angel Michael had to come and war for the answer to pass through the second heaven, to Daniel.

16. Satan's goal is that you never get the answers to your prayers. One way or another, he desires to block our answers. Because he knows, if he can block your answers long enough, you will either stop praying or totally give up on the situation.

17. That is the war that is constantly going on in the heavens. There are certain angels that are always at war with Satan in the second heaven, on behalf of a righteous prayer. Satan's goal is to stop a righteous prayer. Because a righteous prayer gets results.

18. The *"violent"* are the intercessors. It means warrior. Because it is the person that will not stop praying, until the answer comes. Daniel did not stop praying for 21 days, until his answer came. The intercessor cannot get tired of praying.

19. The intercessor must remain in war, until the answer breaks through the heavenlies. Many people pray one time and when they do not see the answer, they want or need; they give us. You must have a warrior spirit when it comes to prayer. You must know what is going on in the heavenlies, therefore, you must not give up.

20. **(Matthew 5:4)** "Blessed are they that mourn: for they shall be comforted".

21. The mourner is an intercessor. It is one that cries out in warfare prayer for themselves or someone else, until the breakthrough answer comes. They refuse to give up hearing from GOD. They pray until peace comes. That is what the word "comforted" means.

22. **"By force"** means we must exercise our spiritual power and authority in the spiritual world, by prayer. We do not fight or even attempt to deal with the spiritual world with our natural abilities or our minds. Because Satan is a supernatural being with power beyond our GREATEST imagination. But *"by force"* means we pray with our right of spiritual authority, until he must release. We pray with our *"legal"* right to have.

23. You see when we continue to pray, we give angels the supernatural beings; that work on our behalf, the continuous power to work. Our continuous praying gives the angels their power in the heavenly realm, for the earthly realm. Had Daniel stopped praying, it would have appeared that Daniel gave up. Therefore, the angelic host warring power would have been weakened, by his lack of prayer.

24. We cannot physically work in the supernatural realm. It must be done through and by angelic host or the Holy Spirit. So many people end up losing their minds because they attempt to deal with the supernatural world, with their little finite mind or mental abilities. Your natural nor mental abilities have no power in the supernatural world. It is the spirit through and by the Holy Spirit. *(Not by power or by might, but by my Spirit, "say the Lord")*

25. When someone plays with a Ouija board, that is an individual trying to deal in the supernatural world, using their natural mind. That is a dangerous place to be. There have been people who literally lost their mind, because doing this. Again, your

natural mind cannot handle the supernatural world. That is why when you pray, the angelic host intervenes on your behalf.

The Kingdoms of Heaven
Questionnaire

1. Explain what goes on in the first heaven.

2. Explain what goes on in the second heaven.

3. What does the word violence mean?

4. What does the word violent mean?

5. What does the word force mean?

The Kingdom of Heaven
Assignments

Practical

Explain how Satan block Daniel's prayers.

Essay

Write a 350-word essay on how you would pray for a situation with someone that is sick, and then how you would pray for someone who is demon possessed. Please use full examples and scriptures. Detail your examples out. Make sure to explain in detail the difference between bind and loose.

Lesson Three
(Binding and Loosing)

1. **(Matthews 16:19)** "And I will give unto thee the keys of the kingdom of heaven: and whatsoever thou shalt bind on earth shall be bound in heaven: and whatsoever thou shalt loose on earth shall be loosed in heaven".

2. *Keys mean legal rights to access.* Prayer is one of the first keys that give us the legal right to enter into the heavenly realm to totally access GOD.

3. Prayer takes you into the decision-making process of the kingdom into the destiny of the kingdom, GOD has given man those keys because of the blood, death, and resurrection of Jesus Christ.

4. When man is binding and loosing, in the heavenly realm, he is operating in the decision-making process of the kingdom of GOD for the earthly realm. That is why GOD put the keys back in our hands through and by the power, blood, and name of JESUS.

5. We must understand the word *"keys"* Jesus gave us more than one key to the kingdom of GOD. Therefore, we must know the key and how to use the keys. The keys that Jesus gave us was:

a. Prayer
b. The name of Jesus
c. The blood of Jesus

6. You must understand all keys represent authority. If we do not know how to use our authority which are our keys, we will remain bound and defeated in our own house. Think about when a person has a key it means freedom of access. But if they do not use that key or know how to use the key, they will remain shut out of everything that should belong to them.

7. You must recognize what he gave us keys to. He gave us keys to the kingdom of heaven. Because when Adam and Eve sinned, they lost all keys. They lost the alignment for heaven and earth. Before Adam sinned, whatever was going on in heaven it was aligned with earth.

8. To align man, back up he must have open access back to heaven. But this is why Satan set up his kingdom in the second heaven so that he could stop the alignment. Earth belongs to man, therefore for the alignment to happen man must do it. GOD gave him what he needed to do it. He gave him the keys he needed.

9. Now what is *binding and loosing*? There are two forms of binding and losing. We will discuss both of them. When it comes to natural things, you use binding and losing in one way. When it comes to Satan and his demonic force you use it in another way.

10. The word *"bind"* when it comes to natural things means to make a legal agreement with and the word "lose" means to divorce. When you bind, it means you make a contract. If we use the words properly then we want to make a contract with what we want and divorce what we do not want.

11. For example, if I want my healing then I must make a contract with healing and I must divorce sickness. Many times, people do the opposite. Sometimes making a contract with the sickness and divorcing the healing.

12. In this scripture Jesus said *"What" not "Who".* Therefore, Jesus is not talking a person, He is talking about things or substance. Jesus declared, *"whatsoever you make a legal contract with on earth, there will be a legal contract made heaven".* Whatsoever you divorce on earth it will be divorce in heaven".

13. If we make a legal contract with healing, then there will be a legal contract made in heaven. If we divorce sickness in earth, it will be divorced in heaven. If we make a legal contract with prosperity on earth, there will be a legal contract made in heaven. If we divorce poverty on earth, then poverty will be divorced in heaven.

14. Now you must understand in the third heaven there is no sickness or poverty but in the second heaven there is. Because that is where Satan's kingdom is set up. That is where he holds up blessings. So, once we on earth, make legal contract on earth then the Father through the name of Jesus make new contracts in the third heaven. Changing and breaking all contracts in the second heaven.

15. Because of sin, Satan made negative contracts over all of our lives. That is why certain things are happening to us and in the earth. Every nature of sin gives Satan rights to make legal contracts of destruction. But through the power of prayer through declaration, we can make new contracts by true binding agreement. But we must know how to use that key.

16. That is why many times we are asking GOD to do certain things in prayer and GOD is saying *"I can't because I gave you the key"*. He cannot make the kingdom contract until you make the earthly contract. Heaven is always awaiting again to align itself back up with earth. But the wait is on us.

17. Again, please understand the clarity of these two words "binding and loosing". When it comes to natural things not people. Whatever you want to keep or want to attach to you, you must blind it to you. You must make a spiritual legal contract with it. What every you do not want, you "loose it. To *"loose"* something means you divorce it.

18. When you divorce something, you are breaking a legal contract that has been made. You are breaking complete covenant with something. That thing or person has no more legal rights to you. Once you divorce sickness and poverty then they have no more legal right to your life.

19. **(Matthew 12:29)** "Or else how can one enter into a strong man's house, and spoil his goods, except he first binds the strong man? and then he will spoil his house.

20. **(Mark 3:27)** "No man can enter into a strong man's house, and spoil his goods, except he will first bind the strong man; and then he will spoil his house.

21. **(Luke 4:34-35)** "Saying, Let us alone; what have we to do with thee, thou Jesus of Nazareth? art thou come to destroy us? I know thee who thou art; the Holy One of GOD.[35] And Jesus rebuked him, saying, Hold thy peace, and come out of him. And when the devil had thrown him in the midst, he came out of him, and hurt him not".

22. When it comes to dealing with the strong man or Satan you must use the word in the opposite way. When it comes to dealing the enemy, the word *"bind"* means to take the authority of.

23. Whenever you are going to defeat the enemy, you must understand he is the strong man. And you must take his authority. You lock down his authority. If a person is possessed by a spirit you blind up the spirit. You take his authority from over that person. You cannot get to that person until you take the power from the strong man.

24. If you are going to free someone from prison you must first bind up the guards so that you can loose the prisoner to their freedom. The person that is guarding the door is the strongman. The person inside of the prison is the one that needs to be loosed.

25. For Jesus to free this young man of the demon he had to blind up the strong man. He told him to *"Hold thy peace"* he took the demonic force of authority. And then He demanded that he come out of him. Once the demon came out, victory was loose upon this young man's life. Therefore, he was free to go and live his life in fullness.

26. Whenever you are dealing with a strong man in any area to stop his work, you must bind him. You must take his authority, if his authority is not taken then he will continue to rule. Then you must loose victory. When you lose victory, you are giving them the freedom to go on and live the life that was intended before the strong man took over.

Questionnaire

1. What does the word "keys" mean?

2. Explain binding for things?

3. Explain binding when it comes the Satan.

4. Explain loosing when it comes to things?

5. Explain loosing when it comes to Satan.

Lesson Four
Kingdom Atmosphere

1. **(Job 1:7)** "And the Lord said unto Satan, Whence comest thou? Then Satan answered the Lord, and said, from going to and fro in the earth, and from walking up and down in it".

2. **(1 Peter 5:8)** "Be sober, be vigilant; because your adversary the devil, as a roaring lion, walketh about, seeking whom he may devour":

3. **(James 5:16)** "Confess your faults one to another, and pray one for another, that ye may be healed. The effectual fervent prayer of a righteous man availeth much".

4. The word legal means one who has the right to have by spoken or written standards or laws. Satan knows the legal spiritual system very well. Again, the word legal means permitted by law/rights.

5. Because covenants and promises were put in place by GOD, because *they are established by GOD*, it gives GOD legal rights to do certain things. But it also gives Satan legal rights to do certain things, especially when covenants or promises are disobeyed or broken by man.

6. A covenant is a spiritual or natural agreement by sign, such as blood or as simply as a handshake. A promise is spoken words used for agreement, through trust and honesty.

7. The kingdom of heaven is set up like a legal system. Therefore, GOD must operate in the earthly realm legally because heaven and earth yet operate in a form of alignment. That is why covenants and promises were made.

8. GOD blesses you through His legal rights. God curses through His legal rights. God also know that Satan know this when it comes to the children of God. That is why he is always roaming about the earth and especially when it comes to the children of God, looking for something he can legally use against us.

9. One of the key places that Satan works in the legal realm concerning a believer, is prayer. Because he is always looking for that legal thing, he can use to stop the answers to our prayers.

10. When the scripture above declares "*the prayer of a righteous man*", it is talking about one the is in legal standards and standing with GOD. If a person is out legal standing with GOD, then their prayers mean nothing. They have no legal right for the answers from GOD. Because they are not righteous.

11. Many times, we will ask people to prayer for us not knowing if they are in legal standing with GOD. Do they even have a legal right to enter the heavenly realm? Do they have a legal right to get answers from heaven? You are only righteous if you are legal with GOD. Your life mut be pure and holy, which places you in right standing, which is legal standing.

12. That is why the scripture James 5:16 declares *"Confess your faults one to another"*. You must not even attempt to start the prayer until you are legal. The atmosphere of your very surroundings must be right for your prayers to be heard and answered.

13. **(Mark 11:25)** "And when ye stand praying, forgive, if ye have ought against any: that your Father also which is in heaven may forgive you your trespasses".

14. There are many things that can make us illegal on the earth which make us illegal in the heaven realm. Again, many prayers are hindered because we are operating in a spiritual illegal place. Heaven and earth must align legally for there to be effectual and fervent prayers. If not, one is just using up air or being loud for their own personal sake.

15. Again, intercessors are warriors that is why it is call a *"fervent"* prayer. The word "fervent" literally means with fire. When a true intercessor prays it has supernatural fire, that disintegrate the forces of the devils. Satan must let go. Satan will recognize he has no more legal right to be there.

16. The word *"availeth"* again means our prayers forces things to happen no matter what. Intercessors prayers will overtake if the person is righteous. The word *"avail"* means much work. When a person is legal in the kingdom of GOD their prayer will do much work. It can change a situation, family, town, city, and state. But the prayer must be legal. The prayer becomes legal because of righteousness.

17. **(John 10:10):** The thief cometh not, but for to steal, and to kill, and to destroy"

18. One of the main ways that Satan can steal, kill, and destroy, is through prayer. He knows that many times we are illegal in the kingdom of GOD therefore we miss getting what belongs to us. Through our illegality he can steal our healing, deliverance, and blessings right out from under our nose, and we will not even know it.

19. **(2 Samuel 21)** "Then there was a famine in the days of David three years, year after year; and David enquired of the Lord. And the Lord answered, it is for Saul, and for his bloody house, because he slew the Gibeonites".

20. Saul broke a covenant that Joshua had made with Gibeonites 70 years before then. David did not do anything, yet the land was under famine. He could not get his prayers answers because he was illegal in heaven, because of a broken vow of Saul.

21. There are many things that can make you illegal in heaven, especially broken vows. Broken bows are broken promises or broken sworn commitments. These are things that will block answers, Satan knows that.

22. There are people who have broken financial, marriage, and other vows. These same people have not repented for these broken vows therefore, causing their prayers to be hindered. They are illegal in the kingdom of GOD. Therefore, their prayers are continuously hindered. And many times, they do not know why. Satan can come before GOD accusing that person of their illegal status and again because the kingdom of heaven is a legal realm, it must be handled legally.

23. When a person desire to get out of jail, the prosecutor will bring up as much illegal and legal stuff against that person to block their parole or total freedom. By the time, the prosecutor is finish sometimes that person cannot get out.

24. Satan is a prosecutor in the presence of God. He has worked extremely hard to gather information on each individual again, especially a child of God. He has his stuff together all the time. He never goes to God unprepared. If your defense is not in place which is, forgiveness, repentance, deliverance, and conversion, you very well can remain in bondage.

Kingdom Atmosphere
Questionnaire

1. Explain the "prayers of the righteous".

2. Explain how GOD blesses and curses through legal rights.

3. Explain covenants and promises.

4. Explain the word availeth.

5. Explain how Satan steal, kill, and destroy, through prayer.

Please do an observation, interpretation, and word study on this scripture:

Scripture
(1 Peter 5:8) "Be sober, be vigilant; because your adversary the devil, as a roaring lion, walketh about, seeking whom he may devour":

Word study

a. Vigilant
b. Adversary

Lesson Five
Kingdom Atmosphere (Continued)

25. There are seven major covenants:
    - **a.** The covenant of creation.
    - **b.** The covenant of Noah.
    - **c.** The covenant of Abraham.
    - **d.** The covenant with Israel.
    - **e.** The covenant of David.
    - **f.** The covenant of Jesus (New Covenant).
    - **g.** Man spoken or willed covenant.

26. When covenants are not in order with people, they cause prayers not to be heard or answered. Many people have not done anything wrong, yet Satan can tempt you, limit you, afflict you, and hinder you, by the iniquity of the blood and man/willed covenants or broken covenants that have not been repented for or corrected. Now Satan is controlling your prayer life.

27. There are such things as willed covenant such as:
    - a. Wrong covenants.
    - b. Broken covenants.

28. These are man willed covenants. These are covenant agreements that you make on your own in words and then you refuse to fulfill them. Such as a person saying" Lord if you get me out of this situation, I will come to church every Sunday". Yet after you get out of the situation you never come to church. That is a broken will covenant now Satan can use that against you until you repent.

29. Wrong covenants are when you make exchange deals out of flesh. This is actually witchcraft. For example, if a man tells a woman, he will marry her if she will sleep with him. This is a sexual covenant that can be passed down through generations.

30. Broken covenants and wrong covenants bring curses or hold up blessings. Ancestors/family/relationships, this is where many in the church are operating now.

31. There has been a lot of unanswered prayer because Satan had a legal right to hold up answers because of broken covenants. The enemy has been denying answers because of this.

32. In 2 Samuel 21 year after year; and David enquired of the Lord. Why is there so much famine? David kept asking GOD the same question not realizing what Saul had done.

33. Some of you have been saying "*Why Lord*"? For many of us we are not realizing there is a broken covenant somewhere that was never repented for. Again, because broken covenants make you illegal in the kingdom of GOD.

34. You must inquire of the Lord concerning covenant and make sure there are no wrong or broken covenants. If so, then correct them immediately. This spirit can pass from bloodline to bloodline, affection generation to generation. There is too much at state. It is not worth the continuous loss. It is not worth years of unanswered prayer.

35. When you are in legal standard, in covenant that is when you can pray the prayer of obedience. What is the prayer of obedience? It is when you pray a prayer based on the fact that you have done what GOD asked of you.

36. It is a prayer based on righteousness and being in the Perfect Will of GOD. A life which has been conditioned by the Word of GOD.

37. **(2 King 20:1-3)** "In those days was Hezekiah sick unto death. And the prophet Isaiah the son of Amoz came to him, and said unto him, Thus saith the Lord, Set thine house in order; for thou shalt die, and not live. Then he turned his face to the wall, and prayed unto the Lord, saying, I beseech thee, O Lord, remember now how I have walked before thee in truth and with a perfect heart, and have done that which is good in thy sight. And Hezekiah wept sore."

38. When Hezekiah prayed, he prayed on obedience. He prayed legally and in covenant. When Hezekiah got sick and he turned his face to the wall, his request was on the fact that he had done what GOD asked him.

39. Hezekiah said, "Lord I have walk before thee in truth, I have done that which is good." Hezekiah was saying, "I am expecting you to respond based on what I have done right."

40. Hezekiah did not even ask for his healing. He just told GOD of his obedience. He knew that GOD responded to those who followed His commandments.

41. **(Malachi 3:10-12)** "Bring ye all the tithes into the storehouse, that there may be meat in mine house, and prove me now herewith, saith the Lord of hosts, if I will not open you the windows of heaven, and pour you out a blessing, that there shall not be room enough to receive it. And I will rebuke the devourer for your sakes, and he shall not destroy the fruits of your ground; neither shall your vine cast her fruit before the time in the field, saith the Lord of hosts. And all nations shall call you blessed: for ye shall be a delightsome land, saith the Lord of hosts."

42. There are times when we can have certain needs in our lives and if we know we have followed His commandments, then your request is through obedience, not a request of need.

43. For example, when you know that you have been faithful in your tithes and offering and you have met your vows and seeds, then your prayer for a financial blessing would be about your obedience and not your need.

44. When you pray the prayer of obedience, you are only asking GOD to honor His Word. He said He would honor His Word before He honored His Name.

45. GOD's loves to honor His Word. Honoring His Word is honoring His Name.

Kingdom Atmosphere
Questionnaire

1. Explain a wrong covenant.

2. Explain a broken covenant.

3. Explain the prayer of obedience.

4. Explain being legal in covenant.

5. Explain Hezekiah's prayer.

Homework

Write out how you would pray a prayer of obedience concerning a situation in your life,

Lesson Six

Curse of the Law

1. **(Galatians 3:13)** “Christ hath redeemed us from the curse of the law, being made a curse for us: for it is written, Cursed is everyone that hangeth on a tree”.

2. You must understand Jesus redeemed us from the curse of the law. The law was in place because people could not access heaven anymore because of the fall of man. People had so much natural and spiritual disorder in their lives.

3. Once the veil was ripped, it gave man access back to the Father that we might receive back legally everything the devil had stolen, or the devil had legally put in place through Adam’s fall.

4. Please recognize because of the fall of Adam, Satan had a right to put certain things in place on earth legally because of him being in charge. It also gave him the right to set up his heavenly kingdom blocking man’s access to heaven. It was not just the un-ripped veil. This is why there is battle in prayer.

5. Because of that, being redeemed just from the curse of law is not enough, if so, we would not need deliverance. We must pull down strongholds; we must destroy generational curses through the anointing of GOD, because of Satan’s spiritual kingdom. We must come back into legal ramification through prayer for total victory.

6. **(2 Samuel 21:3)** “Wherefore David said unto the Gibeonites, ‘What shall I do for you? And wherewith shall I make the atonement, that ye may bless the inheritance of the Lord’”?

7. Once David understood what happened, he made the atonement. There had to be a spiritual deliverance. He knew what to do to get back in legal standing. JESUS is our blood atonement. But we make our atonement by repentance, obedience, and deliverance.

8. Because of the blood of Jesus, we do not have to go and kill a lamb or bull, but we must get ourselves back in legal standard by doing certain things to please the Father. We must understand our part of atonement for our legal sake.

9. The first type of prayer that makes us legal in the kingdom of GOD is *"the prayer of confession."* The word *"confession"* in the Greek means acknowledge. I acknowledge Jesus as Savoir and Lord. He must be known in my life as Savior and Lord.

10. Satan knows when a sinner attempts to come to GOD and he has not confessed Jesus as Lord, he has no legal right unless he is coming to confess Jesus.

11. When you confess Jesus, you position yourself to come legally before the Father. Because the Father does not see you, He sees His Son and the blood of His Son which covers all of our sins. When the Father look upon us to hear our prayers because of confession he can receive them through and by His Son.

12. When you confess, you acknowledge:

a. Sin.
b. Helplessness.
c. Your lack of ability to do it on your own.
d. You are seeking for GOD's grace and mercy.

13. **(Psalms 51:3-4)** "For I acknowledge my transgressions: and my sin is ever before me. Against thee, thee only, have I sinned, and done this evil in thy sight: that thou question be justified when thou speakest, and be clear when thou judgest." David did the prayer of confession. He acknowledged his sins and transgressions before the Lord.

14. **(Psalms 51:1-2)** "Have mercy upon me, O GOD, according to thy lovingkindness: according unto the multitude of thy tender mercies blot out my transgressions. Wash me thoroughly from mine iniquity and cleanse me from my sin."

15. David requested the Lord to wash him and cleanse him. David also needed mercy from the Lord. He needed GOD to give him time for change. David needed GOD to understand his shortcomings.

16. We must pray the prayer of confession daily. We must ask GOD to forgive us of all our sins. First, we must acknowledge our shortcomings and sins. It is the prayer of confession that help keep us in right standing with the kingdom system.

17. When we confess, we are praying for mercy and time for GOD to understand our shortcomings.

18. **(Romans 10:9)** "That if thou shalt confess with thy mouth the Lord Jesus, and shalt believe in thine heart that GOD hath raised him from the dead, thou shalt be saved."

19. "*The Prayer of Salvation*" is the prayer of confession. When we acknowledge Jesus Christ as Savior, we are doing the prayer of confession. We are legally placing ourselves in the kingdom of GOD, for him to receive us.

20. **(Luke 18:13)** "And the publican, standing afar off, would not lift up so much as his eyes unto heaven, but smote upon his breast, saying, GOD be merciful to me a sinner."

21. In the New Testament, the publican carried out the prayer of confession. When he asked forgiveness of his sin, he asked GOD to have mercy on him for being a sinner.

22. **(Luke 15:20-21)** "And he arose and came to his father. But when he was yet a great way off, his father saw him, and had compassion, and ran, and fell on his neck, and kissed him. [21] And the son said unto him, Father, I have sinned against heaven, and in thy sight, and am no more worthy to be called thy son."

23. One of the greatest stories of the prayer of confession is the lost son. The lost son made a prayer of confession to his father. The prodigal son acknowledged his sin and requested mercy for his shortcomings.

24. The prayer of confession is needed in the church for every:

    a. New convert
    b. Backslider
    c. Believer

25. Because we of the prayer of confession, it shows us our deliverance from the curse of law. Our confession through and by the blood of Jesus now free us from this law. The curse of the law can no longer control our personal life nor our prayer life.

Curse of the Law
Questionnaire

1. Explain why the law was in place.

2. What does the word confess mean?

3. Explain why David needed mercy from the Lord.

4. What are we legally doing through the prayer of salvation?

5. When you pray the prayer of confession, what are positioning yourself to do concerning the Father?

Practical

Explain a situation where you would need to pray a prayer of mercy.

Lesson Seven
Main types of Prayer-
Positioning Prayer

1. Again, there are four types of prayer that bring victory. These prayers position us to get our legal rights back, and get back in legal position:
   a. Positioning prayer-repentance and forgiveness.
   b. Worship prayer- sacrifice, praise, and thanksgiving.
   c. Weeping Prayer-request.
   d. Warfare Prayer-defense and demand.

2. The first prayer that we will talk about is the positioning prayer. It is the positioning prayer that places us in right standing with GOD. It positions us so that GOD can answer prayer and Satan working power concerning that area of my life, become limited.

3. **(2 Samuel 21:3)** "Wherefore David said unto the Gibeonites, what shall I do for you? And wherewith shall I make the atonement, that ye may bless the inheritance of the Lord"?

4. Once David understood what happened, and he made the necessary spiritual corrections, GOD delivered the land and blessing began to flow. Once the people became legal again in the heavenly realm the prayer was answered, and the famine ended.

5. You must examine and see are prayers being held up because of things that are illegal in the heavenly realm. Are there things from my past that the enemy is still using against me and or my family because you out of position?

6. **(Matthew 6:12)** "And forgive us our sins, as we have forgiven those who sin against us". Now we will deal with" The Prayer of Forgiveness." The word "forgiveness" in the Hebrew means "to be pardoned." In the Greek, the word "forgiveness" means "to be given freedom or given back freedom."

7. Understand that "the prayer of confession" and *"the prayer of forgiveness"* are not the same. *Confession means to acknowledge. It means to actually put the sin or the situation in the air. Forgiveness is when you actually get freedom. It is when true liberty comes.* With forgiveness, true freedom comes.

8. In the teaching of the Lord's Prayer, Jesus taught His disciples how to pray for forgiveness. He knew that they had to stay in a place of forgiveness. The "prayer of forgiveness" opens up access for every other prayer. Many people need forgiveness from GOD before they can go on to anything else.

9. There are 4 types of forgiveness:
    1. Forgiveness from GOD.
    2. Forgiveness from others.
    3. You are forgiving others.
    4. Forgiving yourself.

10. **(Luke 6:27-28)** "But I say unto you which hear, love your enemies, do good to them which hate you, [28] bless them that curse you, and pray for them which despitefully use you."

11. In your prayers, you must pray for forgiveness for others. Others could have done things due to the lack of knowledge or the fact that they are just your enemy. Also, your prayers of forgiveness for others will help them get in a legal place in their prayer life. It can also bring conviction.

12. **(Acts 7:59-60)** "And they stoned Stephen, calling upon GOD, and saying, Lord Jesus, receive my spirit.[60] And he kneeled down, and cried with a loud voice, Lord, lay not this sin to their charge. And when he had said this, he fell asleep".

13. **(Luke 23:34)** "Then said Jesus, Father, forgive them; for they know not what they do. And they parted His raiment and cast lots".

14. Stephen and Jesus prayed the prayer of forgiveness for others. Because they did not know really what they were doing. They did not know that they had place themselves in a very illegal position with GOD. And they had made themselves very available to Satan.

15. It is through the power of the request for forgiveness from Jesus and Stephen, that it repositioned them back with GOD for forgiveness and divine protection. Again, going back to marriage, that is why a husband, wife, mother, and father, should ask forgiveness for their spouse and their children. Because sometimes that person or child has done something knowingly or unknowingly. And with your request of forgiveness for them it place them back in the ark of safely. Also, through your request, it places them back in a legal place.

16. **(I Peter 3:7)** "Likewise, ye husbands, dwell with them according to knowledge, giving honour unto the wife, as unto the weaker vessel, and as being heirs together of the grace of life; that your prayers be not hindered."

17. It is very important for husbands and wives to stay in a prayer of forgiveness because if there is not true forgiveness, it will hinder the rest of their prayers. Many husbands and wives are illegal in the kingdom of GOD because of their unforgiveness for one another. They walk around for weeks in a home not speaking to one another making then illegal and most of all the whole family. Sometimes parents have not forgiven children and children have not forgiven parents, therefore, there is a lack of restoration.

18. Many pastors come into the pulpit and attempt to preach to a congregation with unforgiveness in their heart towards their wives. They even lay hands on individuals at the altar. Not realizing that their prayers are illegal in the kingdom of GOD. It was simply a warm touch from a contaminated illegal hand. That touch or hand mean nothing to GOD until it become legal.

19. You cannot bootleg GOD you must be legal in the kingdom. Bootlegging was an illegal liquid. People made it at home without getting the Federal Government to approve it. Because it was made illegal and not properly tested many people died from it.

20. There are many pastors and different types of leaders bootlegging. Therefore, they are killing people right there in the congregation preaching illegally, prophesying illegally, and praying illegally. Your natural legal ministerial license does not make

you spiritually legal. You may be legal in man's eyes, but it means nothing if you are not legal in GOD's sight.

21. Forgiveness should be your opening to prayer because you do not want anything in the way of your prayer. Forgiveness clears the air way for everything that needs to be said in the kingdom of GOD.

22. Many times, as people of GOD, we lose our connection with GOD because of the lack of forgiveness. We break the bond with our Savior because of sin. Therefore, we must reconnect through forgiveness. We must become legal again.

23. Many people lack the ability to hear from GOD because they first need to pray *"The Prayer of Forgiveness"*. When there is lack of forgiveness, it will block answers and it can block the anointing. Remember the anointing will not flow in an illegal place. The anointing is holy and righteous.

24. We can affect the anointing on our lives because of the lack of forgiveness. The anointing is your keeper and your power source. However, the anointing is very sensitive. It will not function in an unclean vessel. It will not function in an illegal place.

25. We have such a *"division spirit"* in the church because there is a lack of forgiveness. The church does not flow properly in the anointing because of the lack of forgiveness. In many local churches because the spirit of unforgiveness is so strong in that ministry, the entire ministry is illegal in the presence of GOD.

26. The leader himself must recognize when there is much tension in the house because of the spirit of unforgiveness. He must deal with it quickly to get the ministry back in legal status. If not, then the church will spiritually be operating in a spiritual illegal status possibly inviting the Ichabod spirit. The Ichabod spirit is when the glory of GOD is gone, the anointing is gone. Man is operating in flesh only. We must pray the prayer of forgiveness so that we can create an atmosphere for the anointing.

27. **(2 Chronicles 7:14)** "If my people, which are called by my name, shall humble themselves, and pray, and seek my face, and turn from their wicked ways; then will I hear from heaven, and will forgive their sin, and will heal their land".

28. When GOD told Israel to humble themselves and turn, he was telling them to repent. Because of sins, evilness, and wickedness. Israel had become illegal in the kingdom of GOD. Therefore, they had lost access to the Father's protection. Israel was always finding themselves in an illegal place with GOD. Just like they are today.

29. Again, positioning prayer is one of the first ways that you are made legal in the kingdom of GOD. Positioning prayer speaks for itself. It places you in legal access in the kingdom of GOD for the Father to hear you.

Main types of Prayer-
Positioning Prayer

Questionnaire

1. What does the positioning prayer do for us?

2. Explain the difference between the confession prayer and the prayer of forgiveness.

3. How did Jesus and Stephen prayer of forgiveness help the people?

4. Explain the division spirit.

5. Explain “bootlegging”.

<u>Homework</u>

Write a detail break down of the four types of forgiveness and use scripture to back up each one.

Lesson Eight
Main Types of Prayer-
Worshiping Prayer

1. **(Matthew 21:13)** "And He *said to them, "It is written, 'My house shall be called a house of prayer".

2. It is called the house of prayer because prayer builds an altar for GOD. *"Altar"* means a place of sacrifice. The house of GOD is a place of sacrifice.

3. **(II Corinthians 4:4)** "In whom the *god of this world"*. GOD must be invited in by the children of GOD through prayer, into this world because Satan is the prince of this world.

4. GOD can only enter this earthly realm if there is an altar built for HIM. Because HE is not the GOD of this world, the system of the earth, Satan is.

5. Even though GOD's house is called a house of prayer, GOD's house can be just a building if it is not truly established as a house of prayer with the true altar of sacrifice.

6. There are three major things that build an altar of sacrifice:
   1. Prayer
   2. Giving
   3. Praise and Worship

7. There are three types of prayer that build an altar:
   1. The prayer of sacrifice
   2. The prayer of praise
   3. The prayer of thanksgiving

8. We must learn to build an altar for GOD through our prayer, so that he can come and consume the sacrifice. GOD wants to do so much for the body of Christ, but he is simply waiting on the altar to be built.

9. **(Genesis 12:7)** "And the LORD appeared unto Abram, and said, Unto thy seed will I give this land: and there builded he an altar unto the LORD, who appeared unto him".

10. **(Genesis 13:18)** "Then Abram removed his tent, and came and dwelt in the plain of Mamre, which is in Hebron, and built there an altar unto the LORD".

11. Abraham built an altar of sacrifice of prayer where GOD could come and consume the sacrifice. Every time people come together and make time for true prayer, it is the beginning of building an altar of sacrifice.

12. GOD is always looking for an altar where His presence can come. Most churches do not build him an altar therefore His presence will never come. It is on the true altar of sacrifice where you call on the name of Lord.

13. **(Genesis 12:8)** "And he removed from thence unto a mountain on the east of Bethel, and pitched his tent, having Bethel on the west, and Hai on the east: and there he builded an altar unto the LORD, and called upon the name of the LORD".

14. **(Romans 12:1)** "I beseech you therefore, brethren, by the mercies of GOD, that ye present your bodies a living sacrifice, holy, acceptable unto GOD, which is your reasonable service.

15. You see we do not bring lambs and goats to the altar; we bring ourselves. We become the sacrifice on the altar for GOD to come and consume. We are the living sacrifice. We are the laid-out sacrifice on the altar, not an animal.

16. When you come to build the altar of sacrifice, this is called the prayer of worship. Because as you build the altar of sacrifice you have already completed the positioning prayer. That is why the scripture say, *"holy and acceptable"*. The word *"acceptable"* means GOD agrees with the sacrifice.

17. Many prayers are not received because they are trying to build an altar or worship prayer, without first going through the positioning praying prayer. Again, this is what causes our prayers to be illegal in the kingdom GOD. Causing us to have an illegal altar before GOD.

18. **(2 Chronicles 29:10-13)** "Then David praised the Lord in the presence of the whole assembly: O Lord, the GOD of our ancestor Israel, may you be praised forever and ever! Yours, O Lord, is the greatness, the power, the glory, the victory, and the majesty. Everything in the heavens and on earth is yours, O Lord, and this is your kingdom. We adore you as the one who is over all things. Wealth and honor come from you alone, for you rule over everything. Power and might are in your hand, and at your discretion people are made great and given strength. "O our GOD, we thank you and praise your glorious name!"

19. The *"The Prayer of Praise."* Is part of building the altar of GOD. The word "praise" in the Greek means *"to invoke or invite."* The *"Prayer of Praise"* is a prayer of *"acknowledging GOD for who He Is and what He Has done."*

20. The prayer of praise invokes and invites GOD to come. Because the prayer of praise is always presenting a form of sacrifice. Because anytime you acknowledge who he is and what he has done, it creates an altar for him to come.

Main Types of Prayer-
Worshiping Prayer
Questionnaire

1. What is an altar?

2. Explain Satan being the god of this world.

3. Explain the living sacrifice.

4. Explain the prayer of worship.

5. Explain the prayer of praise.

Lesson Nine
Main Types of Prayer-Worshiping Prayer
(Continued)

21. GOD will never share the altar of sacrifice with man or any other gods. That is why when the prophet was dealing with the people who worship the idol god Baal, he said "you build an altar for him and I will build an altar for the almighty GOD".

22. David said, *"I will bless the Lord at all times for His praises shall continually be in my mouth"*. David was saying *"I will empower the Lord to come at all times." Because* the word *"bless"* means to empower. David declared *"His sacrifice will always be in my mouth"*. David always had an altar for the Lord to come to through and by His praise.

23. David prayed *"The Prayer of Praise"* for who GOD was to him. He adored GOD for being the GOD of Israel. GOD would always respond to David because his altar always consists of His praise.

23. **(Luke 1:46-47)** "Mary responded, Oh, how my soul praises the Lord. How my spirit rejoices in GOD my Savior!"

24. Mary presented the prayer of praise. She adored the Lord for who he was. She adored the Lord for all that he had done.

25. **(Matthew 6:9)** "After this manner therefore pray ye: Our Father which art in heaven, Hallowed be thy name." When Jesus taught the disciples the Lord's Prayer, part of the prayer was a "Prayer of Praise."

26. When JESUS said, *"Hallowed be Thy Name,"* the word "*hallow*" means "praise thy name, exalt His name, or make His name holy." When we pray that state There are three major things that build an altar of sacrifice:
    1. Prayer
    2. Giving
    3. Praise and Worship

27. There are three types of prayer that build an altar:

1. The prayer of sacrifice
2. The prayer of praise
3. The prayer of thanksgiving

28. We are saying His Name is great and that we highly exalt His Name. We recognize His Name as Holy above everything else. Therefore, through and by the Lord's prayer, when we understand it, we build an altar of sacrifice.

29. **(Exodus 15:1-3)** "Then sang Moses and the children of Israel this song unto the Lord, and spake, saying, I will sing unto the Lord, for he hath triumphed gloriously: the horse and his rider hath he thrown into the sea. The Lord is my strength and song, and he has become my salvation: he is my GOD, and I will prepare him an habitation; my father's GOD, and I will exalt him. The Lord is a man of war: The Lord is His name."

30. Moses prayed *"the Prayer of Praise"*. Moses was so excited about GOD. Moses brought forth the prayer of praise because of the power of GOD, the Lord was a GOD of war, and the Lord is His Name.

31. Moses knew the Lord was his strength. The only way you can pray "the Prayer of Praise" is you must know who He is. *"The Prayer of Praise"* can be prayed by those who truly know His Power and His Works.

32. **(Philippians 4:6)** "Be careful for nothing; but in everything by prayer and supplication with thanksgiving let your requests be made known unto GOD".

33. Now we will deal with "*The Prayer of Thanksgiving.*" The word "thanks" or "thanksgiving" means "gratitude." It means to be grateful. The Worship prayer is when we are grateful for His goodness. The prayer of thanksgiving truly establishes the altar of GOD.

34. Now there are two types of *"Prayer of Thanksgiving." There is the prayer of thanksgiving "for what he has done based on what you can see" and "there is the prayer of thanksgiving for what he has done based on what you can't see".*

35. **(Luke 2:38)** "And she coming in that instant gave thanks likewise unto the Lord, and spake of him to all them that looked for redemption in Jerusalem."

36. "*The Prayer of Thanksgiving*" is for what he has done based on what you can see. It deals with facts like: He woke you up this morning. Again, you are dealing with he revelation of just how good GOD is. You express it to him in the prayer of worship.

37. This prayer is a prayer that everyone can pray because He had done something for everyone based on what they can see. Even though the sinners may not believe in GOD at this time as their savior, they can still thank GOD.

38. The true prayer of gratitude states to GOD that, "I am grateful for what you have taken time to do for me, and that you took the time to bless my life no matter what."

39. **(John 11:41-42)** "Then they took away the stone from the place where the dead was laid. And Jesus lifted up His eyes, and said, Father, I thank thee that thou hast heard me. And I knew that thou hearest me always: but because of the people which stand by I said it, that they may believe that thou hast sent me."

40. Jesus prayed the worship prayer first a prayer of gratitude before His Father before he even asks for the life of Lazarus. This is the prayer of thanksgiving based on what you cannot see. Jesus did not see the miracle happen, yet he thanked Him for what He was going to do.

41. This prayer of thanksgiving is based on faith because you thank Him based on the fact that you know He is GOING to do it. You are thanking Him based what you see in the Spirit, not the natural.

42. The worship prayer, the prayer of praise, and thanksgiving operates according to faith. Because you are also operating in the finish work of Jesus Christ. Because he really is not going to do anything. It is already done. All we are waiting for is the manifestation from the spiritual or supernatural world to the natural world.

43. When you know GOD has heard your prayer by faith, you must thank Him. When you thank GOD like that, you are thanking Him for a finished work. You are thanking Him for something completed in the Spirit. When a person can pray this prayer of thanksgiving, thanking Him for what you cannot see represents trust.

44. You are saying to GOD, "I truly trust you. I believe in you and your work." Also, when The Prayer of Thanksgiving is prayed, you are saying to GOD, "I agree

with you. I agree with the way you are doing things; I agree with what you have to do."

45. Going back to faith, you can thank GOD for the plan that He has for your life. You may not understand the plan, but you can release the prayer of thanksgiving for the plan.

Main Types of Prayer-
Worshiping Prayer
Questionnaire

1. Explain "hallow be thy name".

2. Explain Mary's prayer of praise.

3. What is the only way you can pray the prayer of praise?

4. Explain the prayer of thanksgiving.

5. Explain Jesus's prayer before the resurrection of Lazarus.

Lesson Ten
The Weeping Prayers

1. A weeping prayer is one of:
a. Request
b. Petition
c. Intercession

2. *"Request Prayer"* is when one desires answers from GOD for himself or other. To do "request prayer" correctly, one must know the word correctly.

3. **(I John 5:14)** "This is the confidence we have in approaching GOD: that if we ask anything according to HIS will, HE hears us."

4. If we do "*Request Prayer*" wrong, we can bring on a permissive will, verses a perfect will:
A. "Permissive Will" is allowed will.
B. "Perfect will" is planned will.

5. Many people do request prayer according to a permissive will. This will cause people to not get answers at all or just get wrong allowed answers. The key word is ALLOWED. GOD never planned it for your life nor wanted it for your life. But if you continue to request out of a permissive will, he will just let it happen. However, it will cost you in the long run.

6. Because of what Abraham stood for, when Sarah asked him to sleep with her handmaid, she released a permissive will request. Our desires cannot override the perfect will of GOD. That is why you must check your desires closely when asking for something from the kingdom of GOD. Also, we read books or look at the television. That is where we get our desires from not from the almighty GOD.

7. Many people do not get their healing because they are asking according to a permissive will. This is why it is so important to seek GOD for direction to get the right answers.

8. Request prayers takes you into the decision-making process of the kingdom IN TO THE DESTINY OF THE KINGDOM.

9. Request Prayer is:
   A. My legal request.
   B. My persons request.
   C. My mercy requests.
   D. Personal request.

10. **(Philippians 4:6)** "Be careful for nothing; but in everything by prayer and supplication with thanksgiving let your requests be made known unto GOD".

11. Do not move too quickly with request prayer until you know the legality of your petition. That is what supplication is, it is a true interview. Making sure that your request is legal according to the word of GOD. And also, with your personal request it is also align in His perfect will. Many personal requests can come out of your emotions not His will.

12. Request Prayer is:
    a. My mercy requests:
    b. I need compassion because of error.
    c. I need compassion because of time.

13. A mercy request is the fact that someone has just messed up and now I truly need GOD to intervene because of my mess.

14. When I need compassion because of error it literally means that someone has to suffer on my behalf because of a mess that was made. This happens often with David. Sometimes members of David's army had to die because of compassion, because of error.

15. Compassion of time is simply you need someone to suffer because of the missed timing of GOD. Someone will suffer on your behalf because of being off in time.

16. **(Psalm 27:7)** "Hear me, O Lord, when I cry out. Have mercy on me and answer me".

17. **(Romans 8:29-30)** For whom he did foreknow, he also did predestinate to be conformed to the image of His Son, that he might be the firstborn among many

brethren. [30] Moreover whom he did predestinate, them he also called: and whom he called, them he also justified: and whom he justified, them he also glorified.

18. Prayer will show you if you are in the proper timetable of GOD. Your petition becomes legal according to your calling, purpose, and destiny. If you ask out timing of GOD, it can so easily place you in the permissive will of GOD. Answered prayers coincide with your calling purpose and destiny. GOD is a GOD of alignment. Therefore, your answers must have alignment.
19. GOD knows when you need to move or have a mate. Because of the destiny on your life. He knows when you need to be released. Because it has to align with your end results. You cannot get there too early or too late.

20. Moses had a legal right to go to GOD according to Israel's purpose and destiny. This is why it is important for you to pray correctly concerning yourself and your children.

The Weeping Prayers
Questionnaire

1. Explain what will happen if we do request prayer wrong.

2. Explain how Sarah released a request prayer wrong.

3. How do you make sure your request is legal?

4. Explain how your prayer will show you the timetable of GOD.

5. Explain needing compassion because of an error.

Homework

Give an example of praying in proper timetable concerning your purpose and destiny.

Lesson Eleven
The Prayer of Petition

21. The next prayer that we will deal with is *"The Prayer of Petition."* The word "*petition*" in the Hebrew means to request or to seek. The word *"petition"* in the Greek means "to require or obligation." The request prayer and petition prayer at times overlap with each other. However, petition goes deeper because it places a greater demand.

22. **(Daniel 6:12)** "Then they came near, and spake before the king concerning the king's decree; Hast thou not signed a decree, that every man that shall ask a petition of any GOD or man within thirty days, save of thee, O king, shall be cast into the den of lions? The king answered and said, the thing is true, according to the law of the Medes and Persians, which altereth not."

23. When Daniel prayed, he petitioned GOD. Three times a day, Daniel requested an answer from GOD. We have a right to put our request out before GOD. We have a right to seek GOD while He may be found.

24. **(1 Samuel 1:17)** "Then Eli answered and said, go in peace: and the GOD of Israel grant thee thy petition that thou hast asked of him."

25. When Hannah wanted a child, she put out a specific petition before the Lord. The Lord granted the specific petition that Hannah put before Him.

26. The Lord wants us to petition Him because we are His children. He desires to meet our needs and desires.

27. We must petition GOD according to His Word. We must petition GOD according to His Will. Many attempts to petition GOD are based on personal desires, but it will not work.

28.**(1 John 5:14)** "And this is the confidence that we have in him, that, if we ask anything according to His Will, he heareth us." When we petition according to His Will, he hears us. He is always waiting to hear us according to His will.

29.The word *"petition"* also means *"to obligate when we petition according to His Will."* He is obligated to do so. GOD wants to be obligated to His people by His Word and His Will.

30.You cannot obligate GOD to just anything. You cannot hold him accountable to just anything. It has to be according to His Will. When Moses petition for the lives of Israel he had a right to obligate GOD because it was the will of GOD.

31.**(John 5:30)** "I can of mine own self do nothing: as I hear, I judge and my judgment is just; because I seek not mine own will, but the will of the Father which hath sent me."

32.One of the main things you should do in a petition prayer is *"to seek or petition to know His Will."* JESUS always sought out what the Father's Will was for His life. We must do the very same thing. I must have a desire to know His Will.

33.**(Act 17:27)** "That they should seek the Lord, if haply they might feel after him, and find him, though he be not far from every one of us."

34.You may have to continue to petition until you have peace. Do not stop until you know that G od has heard you or that there is something different GOD wants to do.

35.When David's child was sick, he did not stop seeking GOD until they told him the child was dead. Many just quit, but we must not quit on GOD. We must not be afraid to search Him out until the end.

36.**(Isaiah 55:6)** "Seek ye the Lord while he may be found, call ye upon him while he is near." *One of the greatest times to seek or petition GOD is in an anointed service.*

37. When the anointing is highly present, that is when He is so available or easily found. This is a great time to petition GOD or touch and agree with someone. That is why He said, *"Petition while I am available."*

38. We must not be afraid to petition GOD on demand. There may be times when you are praying for someone, and a general prayer will not work. It will be at that time that you must petition for a certain word on a certain way of praying.

39. This could be a life of death situation. You may be in a personal situation, and you must petition GOD for a quick answer or a "*right now*" answer before you make a certain decision.

40. The petition prayer is used everywhere and by everybody. But again, if you are going to petition GOD, study His Word so that your petitions are in His Will.

The Prayer of Petition
Questionnaire

1. What does the word petition mean?

2. How must we petition GOD?

3. How can we obligate GOD?

4. Explain how you cannot just obligate GOD to just anything?

5. What does it mean to petition on demand?

Homework

Explain Moses obligating GOD and use scripture.

Lesson Twelve
The Prayer of Intercession

41. Now we will talk about *"The Prayer of Intercession."* The prayer of intercession is making a request on someone else's behalf. Another name for intercession is "*standing in the gap."*

42. The church needs more intercessors, but the church as a whole is so selfish. People are so focused on their own problems and needs.

43. **(John 17:9)** "I pray for them: I pray not for the world, but for them which thou hast given me; for they are thine." One of the most powerful intercessors was and is Jesus Christ Himself. When he was here on earth, he was always standing in the gap for those that GOD gave him.

44. As a pastor or a leader, you should be an intercessor for the people that GOD has entrusted into your hands. However, this does not take the place of them having their own prayer life.

45. Also, parents are intercessors. They should stand in the gap for their children. We have such a lost generation because parents have dropped the ball.

46. They stopped praying and standing in the gap for their children. We have a whole generation of people who got more caught up in their lives, their careers, and material gain.

47. **(Luke 23:24)** "And Pilate gave sentence that it should be as they required." Intercession can be used to stop destruction on ignorance. These men were casting lots to divide Jesus' garments. They were totally ignorant as to who they were dealing with.

48. Because of Jesus' compassion and love, he stood in the gap and asked GOD "to forgive them." They did not realize the Son of GOD could have destroyed them right then.

49. There are many who come up against the Power of GOD. They come against the true men and women of GOD. It is only by the power of grace and/or the spirit of intercession that they do not drop dead.

50. The Bible states *"Touch not my anointed one."* Many take this very lightly. If you do not like a leader or agree, *"Just leave them alone."*

51. Do not bring accusation against them. *"Let GOD do the judging."* Even as wicked as Saul had become, David knew not to come up against Saul.

52. David knew that Saul had lost his anointing, but he still had his position. There are many who have lost their anointing, but they still have their position.

53. Therefore, you must respect the title and position. For example, there may be a father in a house, and he may a drug addict. He may not appear to be doing his husband nor his fatherly duties, but as long as he is in the house, you must respect him.

54. **(Act 7:57-60)** "And they stoned Stephen, calling upon GOD, and saying, Lord Jesus, receive my spirit. And he kneeled down, and cried with a loud voice, Lord, lay not this sin to their charge. And when he had said this, he fell asleep."

55. Stephen stood in the gap for the people who stoned him to death. He realized how ignorant they were. Stephen asked GOD to not lay the sin to their charge.

56. **(Exodus 32:11)** "And Moses besought the Lord his God, and said, Lord, why doth thy wrath waxes hot against Thy people, which Thou hast brought forth out of the land of Egypt with great power, and with a mighty hand?"

57. Moses stood in the gap for Israel because of their disobedience. Because of the wickedness of their heart, GOD was getting ready to destroy the whole nation of people. Moses stopped him by being an intercessor.

58. GOD could wipe out a whole family, community, city, or town, but GOD chooses an intercessor to stand in the gap.

59. Intercession blocks the hand of the enemy, or it delays the timing of God. When God decided to destroyed Sodom and Gomorrah, He did.

60. Abraham's intercession delayed timing until Lot and his family could get out. *Again, intercession can delay timing for many people.* Because of their disobedience and rebellious spirit, they should have been dead.

The Prayer of Intercession
Questionnaire

1. Explain how a pastor should be an intercessor.

2. Explain how a parent should be an intercessor.

3. Explain how intercession can stop destruction on ignorance.

4. Explain respecting title or position.

5. How did Moses stand in the gap for Israel?

Lesson Thirteen
Defending Prayer

1. *"Defending prayer"* is a prayer of blocking the:
   a. Enemies' destruction.
   b. Judgment of GOD.

2. **(Ezekiel 22:30)** "I looked for someone among them who would build up the wall and stand before ME in the gap on behalf of the land so I would not have to destroy it, but I found no one."

3. Defending prayers are the kinds of prayer that most of the older saints prayed all of the time. They prayed prayers that would stop destruction from coming on their children. Many old mothers defended the family from the power of the enemy.

4. Many people would be dead today if they had not had a praying grandmother, mother, or father. When people were living unsaved lives, the enemy had great plans to kill them. But there was someone holding back the destruction of the enemy, giving them time for salvation.

5. Again, these are the kinds of prayer that:
   a. Parents should pray for their children.
   b. Pastors should pray for the congregation.

6. **(Esther 4:15-17)** "Then Esther bade them return Mordecai this answer, [16] Go, gather together all the Jews that are present in Shushan, and fast ye for me, and neither eat nor drink three days, night or day: I also and my maidens will fast likewise; and so will I go in unto the king, which is not according to the law: and if I perish, I perish. [17] So Mordecai went his way and did according to all that Esther had commanded him".

7. Haman representing the enemy set out to destroy the people. Esther had to stand in the gap to stop the destruction of the enemy through and by the king. Esther prayed the defending prayer. Esther went on a fast and through prayer even receive a defending answer for GOD's people.

8. Mordecai recognized the plan of the enemy, therefore making Esther aware of his plan. They call together fasting and praying to block the enemy. Mordecai recognized the need for defending prayer.

9. **(Esther 7:9-10)** "And Harbonah, one of the chamberlains, said before the king, behold also, the gallows fifty cubits high, which Haman had made for Mordecai, who spoken good for the king, standeth in the house of Haman. Then the king said, Hang him thereon. [10] So they hanged Haman on the gallows that he had prepared for Mordecai. Then was the king's wrath pacified".

10. As individuals, especially pastors, we must recognize when the enemy has put together plans to bring down the body of Christ or just individuals in the church.

11. Even pastors must recognize when spiritual hits have been put out on their individual ministry. One must go into defensive or defending prayer. You do not attempt to fight the battle through your own strength, you fight it in prayer.

12. Defending prayers will:

    a. Block the enemy.
    b. Delay the enemy.
    c. Stop the enemy.
    d. Overcome the enemy.

13. Defending prayers are also there to block the judgment of GOD. There are many things that GOD would have done and can do now if someone does not block His judgment.

14. Anything that Satan finds in your blood he has a legal right to bring a legal lawsuit against you in heaven. Against you and your bloodline, which is a form of legal judgement.

15. Many saints are dealing with spiritual lawsuits. Satan is using things against us still in the heavenly realms. Until the lawsuits are thrown out, you will be defeated. There are certain things that must be overturned by prayer only. YOU overturn these lawsuits against you as a believer by understanding the legal operation of prayer.

16. **(Genesis 18:21-23)** "I will go down now and see whether they have done altogether according to the cry of it, which is come unto me; and if not, I will know. [22] And the men

turned their faces from thence and went toward Sodom: but Abraham stood yet before the LORD. [23] And Abraham drew near, and said, wilt thou also destroy the righteous with the wicked?

17. GOD declares that he was going to destroy the entire city of Sodom and everything and everyone that was in it. However, Abraham's family was there, which was Lot. Because of the prayers of Abraham, he held back judgment until Lot had a chance to get out.

18. There can be places, families, and even individuals that GOD will judge; however, because of the prayers of saints we can delay judgment.

19. Moses delayed judgment on Israel. Because GOD had planned immediate destruction until Moses spoke up for the people.

20. **(Hebrews 10:31)"** It is a fearful thing to fall into the hands of the living GOD".

21. When men make GOD angry, it can open the door for personal or corporate judgment. If it were not for the prayers of the righteous many cities, families, and individuals would be doomed. Thank GOD for defending prayers. Thank GOD for those who were operating in defending prayers.

Defending Prayer
Questionnaire

1. Who often prayed defending prayers?

2. Explain the four things that defending prayers will do concerning the enemy.

3. Explain spiritual lawsuits.

4. Explain delaying judgment.

5. What can happen when men make GOD answer?

Practical

Explain how judgment was delayed concerning Lot and his family and use the scripture.

Lesson Fourteen-
The Defense of the Word

1. We must require all illegal words be removed out of the heavenly kingdom. Illegal words are used constantly against the children of GOD in the kingdom GOD by Satan.

2. Illegal words are words spoken contrary to the word of GOD, negative, or defensive to the kingdom system of God. They are words spoken totally against the power and the plan of faith.

3. **(Daniel 7:10)** " A stream of fire issued forth and flowed *from His presence* ; [a] thousands *upon* thousands served him and ten thousand *upon* ten thousand stood before him. The judge sat, and *the* books were opened".

4. Heaven is an open court system. Many people have spoken things against themselves and now Satan is using those words in the open heaven court.

5. Many people open their mouths and speak words against their children, their mates, and other given situations. In the midst of those words, Satan will hold up blessings and answers to prayers because of those negative words. Words defend you, curse you, or bless you. That is why your words are so important.

6. **(Psalm 19:14)** "Let the words of my mouth, and the meditation of my heart, be acceptable in thy sight, O LORD, my strength, and my redeemer".

7. The word acceptable means agreeable. David checked his words. He wanted his words to be approved by almighty GOD. When our words are agreeable with GOD there is nothing the enemy can do to stop the flow of return from GOD.

8. Many Christians do not check their words before they come out of their mouths. Because words are legal contracts, made in heaven for the good or the bad. That is why when the police pick you up for a crime, he will make a very clear statement, *"You have a right to remain silent. Anything you say can and will be used against you in the court of law".*

9. But because Satan knows the written word, he knows what the Father will and will not accept. Satan at one time was in the very presence of the Father; that is how he knows how to use our word against us.

10. **(Mark 11:22-23)** "And Jesus answering saith unto them, Have faith in GOD. [23] For verily I say unto you, That whosoever shall say unto this mountain, Be thou removed, and be thou cast into the sea; and shall not doubt in his heart but shall believe that those things which he saith shall come to pass; he shall have whatsoever he saith.

11. Because of words there are spiritual mountains built against many Christians. They must repent or speak against those mountains before their blessings can come forth. That is why you can be praying for hours, and nothing will happen because of the illegal words you have already put in place.

12. **(Proverbs 18:21)** Death and life are in the power of the tongue: and they that love it shall eat the fruit thereof.

13. Many people have spoken death with their tongue. Therefore, Satan will use the words of death against each man in prayer in the heavenly realm. You must cancel death to get to life.

14. **(Isaiah 54:17)** "No weapon that is formed against thee shall prosper; and every tongue that shall rise against thee in judgment thou shalt condemn".

15. Weapons are instruments that are chosen by the devil to destroy:
    a. Every tongue—words.
    b. Judgment -sentence.
    c. Condemn-punish.

16. **(Revelation 12:10)** "And I heard a loud voice saying in heaven, Now is come salvation, and strength, and the kingdom of our GOD, and the power of His Christ: for the accuser of our brethren is cast down, which accused them before our GOD day and night".

17.. Satan will bring legal accusations to stop our victory.

18. **(Zechariah 3:1-3)** "And he shewed me Joshua the high priest standing before the angel of the Lord, and Satan standing at his right hand to resist him. [2] And the Lord said unto Satan, The Lord rebuke thee, O Satan; even the Lord that hath chosen Jerusalem rebuke thee: is not this a brand plucked out of the fire? [3] Now Joshua was clothed with filthy garments and stood before the angel.

19. Satan brought open accusation against Joshua in the heavenly realm because Joshua's dirty clothing represented the sin and filth of Israel. But because of the power of GOD, he brought open rebuke on the devil.

20. This is the same way Satan can do us. The only thing that we have truly covering us as believers, is the blood of JESUS Christ.

The Defense of the Word
Questionnaire

1. What are illegal words?

2. Explain how words can defend you.

3. What does the word "acceptable" means?

4. Explain Satan's legal accusation concerning words?

5. Explain weapon.

Homework

How would you know that illegal words have been spoken over someone's life?

Lesson Fifteen
Warfare Prayer

1. Warfare Payer is:
    a. Deliverance
    b. Altar deliverance
    c. Demand deliverance
    d. Spiritual Demand

2. Warfare is demanding legal freedom because I have a right to my legal freedom. Many people do not understand that they have a right to freedom because it was legally promised to them through and by the blood of Jesus Christ.

3. "*Warfare prayer*" is when we untangle what belongs to us. Because it is held up by the enemy. It is when one puts a demand on heaven. There is very little warfare prayer going on in this generation because they do understand the spiritual fight.

4. **(Daniel 10:13)** "But the prince of the Persian kingdom resisted me twenty-one days. Then Michael, one of the chief princes, came to help me, because I was detained there with the king of Persia".

5. Warfare Prayer is where you find out:
    1. Legal words.
    2. Illegal words.
    3. Prophetic words.

6. You must go into the spiritual world and find out what types of legal things according to the word can be used for your victory. You also must find out what words have been used to cause you to be illegal into the kingdom of GOD that Satan is using against you. Therefore, holding up your prayers or the answers to your prayers.

7. That is why prophetic words can be a blessing or a curse when it comes to prayer. Because if someone prophecy over your life dangerous words, Satan can use those words against you in the prayer. Because one must remember life and death is I the power of the tongue.

8. Warfare is used to bring one out from under attack. Many people are being attacked by the devil constantly. But they have no one to war on their behalf or they do not know how to war themselves.

9. We wonder why so many children are under attack. Why so turmoil is in the government system because there are no true warriors in the kingdom of GOD. Our prayers today are passive not aggressive. There is no real boldness on prayer.

10. When people come to the altar, we must know how to war for them to get their true deliverance. Because people are not trained in warfare prayer, people come and go back the same way. Because we do not know how to deal with a real enemy.

11. We pray a general prayer and send them back to their seats because we do not know how to deal with a real enemy. He knows when the pastor does not know how to confront or legally deal with him.

12. I must know how to demand and spiritually demand. Jesus did not pacify the enemy. He told him what to do and where to go. He put a legal demand on the devil, and he had to respond.

13. Because we do not understand warfare prayer, we just pamper the devil. We do not really deal with the devil. We do not understand what is really going on in the spiritual realm, we are often operating in the natural.

14. There are nine areas of warfare:
    1. Messenger from Satan (when he constantly bothers you).
    2. Strongholds.
    3. Imaginations.
    4. High things.
    5. Thoughts.
    6. Principalities.
    7. Powers.
    8. Rulers of darkness of this world.
    9. Spiritual wickedness in high places.

15. In deliverance ministry these are dealt with greatly because in deliverance ministry is where you must understand warfare prayer. If not, you will not accomplish true deliverance.

16. Warfare prayer is to take legal right from Satan such things as:
    1. Sickness
    2. Attacks
    3. Premature death
    4. Destructions
    5. Bloodline
    6. Cross contamination.

17. Warfare prayer will make you have true encounters with GOD and Satan. Jacob wrestles with an angel all night. It was a form of warfare prayer with God. He was not warring against the devil he was warring with his belief and faith. He was warring with assurance in God.

18. **(Romans 8:26-27)** "Likewise the Spirit also helpeth our infirmities: for we know not what we should pray for as we ought: but the Spirit itself maketh intercession for us with groanings which cannot be uttered. [27] And he that searcheth the hearts knoweth what is the mind of the Spirit, because he maketh intercession for the saints according to the will of God."

19. Praying in the Spirit is a form of warfare prayer. Praying in the Spirit is praying in your prayer language or in tongues. When you pray in the Spirit you are supernaturally putting a demand on heaven directly through the Holy Spirit. Because you are praying in tongue it is not about your understanding, it is simply about your obedience.

20. There are two types of praying in tongues:
    1. Praying in an unknown tongue.
    2. Praying in other tongues.

21. Praying in an unknown tongue is the language of the Holy Spirit. When we do not know what we should pray for we can allow the Spirit of GOD to pray through us. He knows exactly what to pray for. When you are praying in the Holy Spirit the Holy Spirit is confronting the devil head on.

22. The scriptures states that the "*Holy Spirit helpeth our infirmities.*" This means that we have a fleshy weakness when it actually comes to praying. In a lot of situations,

we do not know exactly what the needs of a specific individual or situation may be. We are weak when it comes to the spiritual realm because we are flesh.

23. The Holy Spirit will pray the perfect prayer. The perfect prayer is the will of GOD. The Holy Spirit knows exactly what the will of the Father is, and He will pray the will of the Father through us.

24. There are times you may wake up at night and have an urge to pray for someone, but you do not know exactly what to pray. It is at that time that the Holy Spirit will step in.

25. The Holy Spirit is constantly standing in the gap for the saints and making intercession on our behalf. The saints are always in need in ways that we do not even know. Therefore, the Holy Spirit is always standing in the gap.

26. The Holy Spirit is always keeping the saints out of danger or protecting them in danger by the spirit of intercession through the Spirit.

27. Many times, people do not develop their prayer language because they do not really understand the true significance of their language. They think it was only a sign of them receiving the Holy Spirit.

28. Praying in your prayer language is so much greater than that. You should spend as much time in your prayer language as possible because your ultimate goal should be to pray the perfect will of GOD.

29. Also, when you are praying in the Spirit, you are always waring against Satan in the supernatural world. And he hates that. Because he hates it when the Holy Spirit takes over. That means he has to encounter the fulness of the power of the Father.

Warfare Prayer
Questionnaire

1. What does warfare prayer demand?

2. What will warfare prayer make you have?

3. Warfare prayer is used to bring people out from under what?

4. Explain warfare prayer concerning praying in the Spirit.

5. What is pampering the devil?

Lesson Sixteen
Preventive and Corrective Prayer

1. There are four types (Timed) prayer:
    1. Preventive prayer
    2. Corrective prayer
    3. Sanctification prayer
    4. Benediction prayer

2. These are called "*Timed Prayer*" because one has a certain amount of time to do prayer. Prayer must be done at a certain time to be effective. For example, as you study benediction prayer, you cannot pray a benediction prayer two days later after the service. It will not be effective. It must be prayed at the right time.

3. Preventive prayer is when you pray prayers that will stop certain things from happening ahead of time. If the church, fathers, and mothers would spend more time in prayer for their families, there would be a lot of things that could be prevented.

4. Mothers should start praying for their children in their wombs. They could prevent things before the child is even born. They could prevent generational curses and bitter roots right there in their womb.

5. But because people lack spending true time in prayer, the enemy is allowed to invade our territories therefore we spend more time on corrective prayer versus preventive prayer.

6. Corrective prayer when one must pray after the fact. This when things have already gotten out of hand and now one has to try and fix the problem by prayer. Sometimes it may take years because things may have gotten so deep in the situation.

7. When major things happen in the world, then all of a sudden everyone wants to call a great prayer session. Those things should have been called before the situation happened, not after. This is what you call corrective prayer.

8. Israel spent so much time in corrective prayer. They would always call on GOD after the fact. Israel would get in trouble with their enemies and then call on GOD in corrective prayer.

9. Often when situations happen in a home with the marriage, or with the children, then people want to call a onetime fast and prayer attempting to move GOD in corrective work. But as it was said prayer should have been done in a preventive manner vs a corrective manner.

10. Often in many situations it is too late. Because by the time you start to pray the enemy has already set up camp. And many times, roots have taken their place in the family. Now as you start doing corrective prayer, you must be willing to set back and wait the course out.

11. Corrective prayer is costly just like corrective work is costly. Anytime someone has to fix another man's mess they are usually going to charge you much more.

12. In corrective prayer, you will have to deny your flesh. Accept the consequences for a period of time. While corrective prayer is going on, remember Satan has set up camp therefore, he will not just give up place that easily.

13. As see the results of change happen, then you must continue the corrective and start the preventive prayer. The preventive prayer is declaring that we will never go down this road again,

14. For example, if someone end up on drugs because of a generational curse. Then as you are praying the corrective prayer, you must start the preventive prayer, that they never go down that road again. Because in the preventive prayer you are closing all old doors.

15. This is also where the sanctification prayer starts. In the sanctification prayer, you are asking GOD to set you that person totally apart from everything. You are asking GOD to bring divine cleansing and separation.

16. **(John 15:15-17)** "I pray not that thou shouldest take them out of the world, but that thou shouldest keep them from the evil.[16] They are not of the world, even as I am not of the world.[17] Sanctify them through thy truth: thy word is truth.

17. When Jesus was preparing to leave His disciples, he prayed the preventive prayer and the prayer of sanctification. He wanted them to be sanctified from the world. Through the prayer of sanctification, he knew they would remain separated from the things of the world even though they had to be in the world.

18. Through the prayer of sanctification, it would prevent them from being contaminated with things that they did never need to be involved in ever again. Jesus knew through Satan he would attempt to draw them back in somehow. But it could be prevented.

19. The prayer of sanctification can also be prayed with sicknesses, deliverance, or as a total preventive prayer. When a person has an illness going on in their lives such as cancer one can prayer for GOD to sanctify their bodies. Separate their bodies from that cancer.

20. Now you can pray the prayer of sanctification with every disease. But it will not work, if it is a type of illness that you must do a certain thing to bring under control such as diabetes and high blood pressure. Once you do your part sanctification will begin.

21. The last "*timed*" prayer is "*the Prayer of Benediction*." The word "*benediction*" actually means "*the end*" or a prayer of conclusion.

22. Many times, when people are leaving the church, they pray a prayer of benediction because people are getting ready to separate. The "Prayer of Benediction" is used to release each person to go their own separate way.

23. **(Jude 1:24)** "Now unto him that is able to keep you from falling, and to present you faultless before the presence of His glory with exceeding joy, Lives."

24. **(Jude 1:24 NIV)** "Now all glory to GOD, who is able to keep you from falling away and will bring you with great joy into His glorious presence without a single fault."

25. We pray "*the Prayer of Benediction*" because as we are released from each other, we desire that GOD keep us from falling. The word falling or falling away in the Greek mean I will not forsake GOD or things of the kingdom.

26. The desire is that we come back together again in the same place or another occasion showing where the enemy has not had opportunity to rob us of anything.

27. At any time when the people of GOD can come back together and present the success of GOD then we immediately defeat the enemy. We show that we can stand, GOD can keep us, and that we give no place to devil.

28. **(Genesis 31:49)** "And Mizpah; for he said, The Lord watch between me and thee, when we are absent one from another." Many people use this scripture as a prayer of benediction. But this scripture is not a positive prayer for benediction.

29. Jacob and Laban did not trust one another. Therefore, when they separated, they wanted the Lord to watch over them as they were apart. They wanted the Lord to watch between them at all times.

30. When we pray this pray as a benediction we are really saying to the congregation "I do not trust you and therefore I want the Lord to watch between us."

31.. We are saying to someone, you might steal from me. You might try and hurt me, so therefore I want the Lord to keep His Eyes on you.

32. Again, this prayer would be a prayer that you pray because you do not have confidence in the individual you work with or live with.

33. It would be a prayer that you would pray if you were in an area and you did not trust the area. Therefore, it would be a prayer of benediction to protect you and your possessions.

34.. Also, the "Prayer of Benediction" is a prayer of favor. It is a time to pray great favor on you and anyone else that you are getting ready to leave.

35. You should desire to pronounce great blessing on anyone that you can. It is a time to pronounce favor on your family, your children, and yourself.

36. **(Genesis 27:28-29)** "Therefore GOD give thee of the dew of heaven, and the fatness of the earth, and plenty of corn and wine: [29] let people serve thee, and nations bow down to thee: be lord over thy brethren and let thy mother's sons bow down to thee: cursed be everyone that curseth thee and blessed be he that blesseth thee."

37. Isaac prayed a Pray of Benediction on Jacob. Isaac pronounced great favor on Jacob. It was a prayer of conclusion. It could not be taken back and that is why Esau was so angry. This is a prayer that you should always be prayed because it cannot be taken back.

38. We must get back to true intercession. We must get back to where we are bombarding heaven with prayer. We must get back to preventive prayer versus corrective prayer.

Preventive and Corrective Prayer
Questionnaire

1. What is preventive prayer?

2. What is corrective prayer?

3. What is sanctification prayer?

4. What is a prayer of benediction?

5. Explain “Timed Prayer”.

Homework

Give an example of a preventive prayer.

Name ______________________

Site ________________________

Instructor ___________________

Date _______________________

Preventive and Corrective Prayer
Test
(Each Question is Worth 10 Points)

1. Explain legality.

2. Explain the three heavens.

3. Explain binding and loosing when it comes to things.

4. What does the word "*confess*" mean?

5. What is an altar?

6. How can we obligate GOD?

7. Explain delaying judgment.

8. What does the word "*acceptable*" mean?

9. What is pampering the devil?

10. What is preventive and corrective prayer?

THE PACKAGE OF SUFFERING

Safe Haven Interdenominational Bible College and Training Institute

PO Box 457

Zebulon, NC 27597

The Package of Suffering
Table of Contents

Lesson One
What is Suffering?

1. What is suffering?
   A. Pressure on the flesh
   B. Pain to the flesh

2. All will suffer one way or another. Whether:
   1. (**Matthew 25:45**) As a sinner in Hell eternally.
   2. (**John 15:20**) As a Christian because you belong to GOD.

3. (**Luke 16:19-25**) You must understand that a Christian's suffering is always on a time schedule. It may not end here on earth, but it will end in Heaven. There is no suffering in Heaven. There are some Christians who may suffer on earth because they are suffering for the kingdom of GOD. But a sinner will suffer for ever in hell if they do not come out of sin.

4. Suffering is a part of the Christian walk, and we must accept that. But we have a GOD who know how to get us through it. Sometimes preacher do not like to talk about suffering to their congregation, but you must. People must be made aware of the entire package of Christianity. This is why people get mad at the church because sometimes minsters teach salvation one-sided.

5. Often pastors teach the blessing plan of GOD but not the suffering side. If you do that, then people will not be ready for the struggles ahead. No, often in the old days people thought the more you suffer, the more holy you were. That is not so. But suffering must be included in the whole process of salvation. This will prepare people for entire package of salvation.

6. There are the three P 's you must understand when it comes to suffering:
   1. Praise
   2. Prayer
   3. Prophecy

7. You can't praise your way out of suffering, you can't pray your way out of suffering, and no one can prophecy you out of suffering. However, you can praise your way through suffering, you can pray your way through suffering, and someone can prophecy you through suffering.

8. You should praise to keep yourself encouraged through suffering. You should pray to keep open communication through suffering. It is a wonderful thing when people are giving you encouraging words or directions through your suffering.

9. This is why it is so important for you to understand these three words in the correct ways. Because there have been people who thought the more I shout or praise GOD the suffering was just going to go away. And when it did not, they became angry and shut down their praise.

10. There are also people who pray in desperation thinking that it will also stop suffering. But some things you must go through. Prayer will not always totally stop suffering. Again, you must continue to pray for answers and direction during suffering.

11. There are people who will run down prophets trying to get words during their suffering. Hoping that someone will give them a word to excuse the suffering. Many people have even gotten false prophecies during the time of suffering. Because Satan knows your desperation, so he will give you what you want to hear not necessarily the truth about your situation. Again, no one can prophesy you out suffering.

12. The first type of suffering we will talk about is **"SUFFERING FOR OUR SINS".**

13. We must know exactly what sin is. Sin is:
    1. Breaking the laws of GOD.
    2. Doing wrong according to the laws of GOD.
    3. Breaking the Ten Commandments.

14. As you learned earlier, there are general sins and personal sins. General sins are wrong for everyone, such as killing and stealing. But personal sins relate directly to you. When it is something, GOD has told you to do or not to do. when you refuse to follow through on either. you will suffer for your sin.

15. GOD is not fair, he is just. This means:
    a. He punishes us for our wrongdoing.
    b. He punishes us according to our heart, not our sin or wrongdoing.

16. If we were under the law, we would be punished because of our sin and according to our sin. But because we are under grace, it is according to our heart. Also,

grace gives us time to make corrections even though we may receive punishments. And mercy measures the punishment.

17. When JESUS died on the cross, he died for our sins for the purpose of reconnecting us to the Father and allowing us to receive forgiveness by confession and belief. We don't need to sacrifice an animal any more for the forgiveness of sin. However, His death does not excuse us from being dealt with for our sins.

18. Even though we get saved, it does not excuse us from paying for our sins. If you sow the seed, you must reap the harvest. There are people who get upset in the church because sometimes people think they can get saved to avoid certain punishments.

19. Once salvation comes and forgiveness is in place, you can go to Heaven. However, while on earth and there is still breath in your body, there are consequences to sin. There are some things you pay for no matter what. There are things you must face. There is no way around it.

20. For example, if a young lady gets pregnant out of wedlock and then she come to church and get saved, the baby will not just disappear. She will still have to deal with having the baby. She will still have to deal with being a single parent.

21. There are times when people have been selling drugs in the world and they get caught. They will attempt to come to church, and get saved or so called saved, to avoid jail time. This will not be. Sometimes GOD will give mercy, but you did the crime, and you must do the time.

22. Again, when you sow seeds, you will reap those harvest. The idea is never to sow those same seeds again. However, many of the seeds you sowed in the world are already in the ground. Therefore, you must deal with the harvest. The seed won't just go away just because you got saved.

23. The idea is to start pulling up and cursing as many bad seeds as possible. Then start putting down as many good seeds as possible.

24. **(Colossians 3:25)** This scripture declares that ***"He that does wrong shall receive for the wrong he has done, for GOD has no respect of person".***

    1. We will suffer because of our wrong.
    2. We will be dealt with because of our wrong.

3. It doesn't matter who or what you are.

25. **(Matthew 9:1-2)** In this particular story, this man was very sick with palsy because of sin. That is why when Jesus went to heal him, He said "Thy sin be forgiven thee." He made that statement because sin was the reason behind the sickness.

26. There are those who are suffering because of sin. When you sin in your unsaved life or saved life, you may suffer in your physical body, finances, relationship, or other areas because of sin.

27. You may get by, but you do not get away. Pay day is always coming. You must be dealt with because of sin. That is why GOD is always trying to get us out of sin as soon as possible. Satan wants to keep us in sin as long as possible, because knows the consequences of sin.

28. **(II Samuel 12:14)** "Howbeit, because by this deed thou hast given great occasion to the enemies of the LORD to blaspheme, the child also that is born unto thee shall surely die".

29. David's child died because of him committing adultery with Bathsheba. The child died because of sin. David and Bathsheba had to pay for the consequences of their sins. GOD told David the child was going to die.

30. **(John 5:14)** In this scripture, JESUS healed another man due to sin. When JESUS met this man later, He told him "Do not go and sin again or it will get worse the second time."

31. We must make people aware that when they go back and repeat sin, they may suffer two times worse the second time around.

32. Many times, when people come into the church and get saved, they tend to think that they can get away with sin. They assume the church is a hiding place from sin. GOD deals with sin no matter what side of the fence you are on. They tend to think they can repeat sin, but even as Christian it will get worse the second time around.

33. **(Genesis 4:9-13)** There is such a thing as the curse of sin. The curse of sin is when there are long term effects from sin. Cain had the curse of sin on him because he killed his brother.

34. There are people right now who have the curse of sin such as:
    1. Life in prison.
    2. Death row.
    3. Long term guilt.
    4. A baby suffering from a drug addict parent.
    5. A sickness from substance abuse.
    6. Female problems from multiple sexual partners.

35. **(I Peter 4:15)** "But let none of you suffer as a murderer, or as a thief, or as an evildoer, or as a busybody in other men's matters".

36. Once someone is born again, one should never have to suffer for sin again. As a child of GOD, you should not be practicing a lifestyle of sin anymore.

37. You may have to suffer in the beginning of your spiritual walk for a sin that you committed in the world, but once that is over, you should not have to suffer in that area ever again.

38. It is sad when saints are suffering for repeated sins. We are known as repeat offenders. It literally makes Jesus's suffering in vain. We literally put Jesus back on the cross again.

39. If you are suffering for a sin, there are seven major things you must do:
    1. Repent (turn away from).
    2. Ask for forgiveness (be released from).
    3. Denounce the sin (to recognize as wrong and be convicted of, to feel sorrow for).
    4. Be delivered (getting it internally out of you).
    5. Renounce the sin (abandon or resign from).
    6. Do the time (Go through the suffering).
    7. Declare your freedom (declare it over).

40. It is important not to hide the truth concerning this type of suffering so that people will take it seriously concerning their salvation. Also, so that people will be aware of the consequences to sin.

41. Pastors must make their congregation aware of the consequences of sin. We must stop pacifying the truth. We will be held responsible for lives when we don't make them aware of the punishment for sin. Whether it is earthly punishment or eternal damnation in Hell, there will be punishment.

What is Suffering?

Questionnaire

1. What is suffering?

2. Explain praise concerning suffering.

3. Explain GOD not being fair but just.

4. Explain suffering for sin.

5. Explain what can happen if you repeat sin.

Lesson Two
Suffering Due to Flesh

1. **(John 1:13)** The second type of suffering we will discuss is *"SUFFERING DUE TO FLESH"*. Suffering due to flesh is called his permissive will. There are two types of suffering due to flesh and that is "
   a. Will of man-own human desires
   b. Will of the flesh-carnality (immaturity or ignorance)

2. The permissive will is GOD's allowed will. It is not what GOD wants for us but because it is what we want so badly, therefore, it is what will be allowed. GOD will simply let it happen even though he does not want it to.

3. The permissive will can be with a:
   a. Person
   b. Place
   c. Things
   d. Timing

4. For example, He will let you marry that person even though He knows it is wrong, He will let you move to that place even though you should not, He will let you have that car even though He knows it is going to break down, and He will let you have that job even though He knows that you are not mature enough to handle it. It is totally wrong timing.

5. The key to fleshly suffering or the permissive will is:
   a. Unnecessary hardships.
   b. Unnecessary struggles.
   c. Unnecessary troubles.

6. The word is "*UNNECESSARY*" when you are in the permissive or fleshy will, you will go through unnecessary things. Things that you just should not have to go through, face, or deal with. You should never want unnecessary hardship. They bring on so much unnecessary pain and hard work.

7. **(Proverb 10:22)** This scripture declares that "*The blessing of the Lord adds no sorrow*". The word sorrow in the Hebrew means unnecessary trouble. In anything in our lives there are going to be challenges but if you are in the will of GOD, they will not be unnecessary.

8. The word "*blessing*" in that scripture means wisdom. When you are in the perfect will of GOD, he will give you wisdom, the way to carry out each plan in your life. Therefore, it will not add any unnecessary struggles. Unnecessary struggles come because when you are out of will, you are having to use your mind or your own plans to make things work. GOD's plans does not work on our wisdom, they work on GOD's wisdom.

9. Such as GOD telling you to buy a certain car that is within your price range, but you go and buy a very expensive car that you can't afford. Now you are having "*UNNECESSARY*" hardship making the payment. Now you must come up with your own plan, which unusually will only complicate your life even more.

10. **(I Corinthian 3:1-13)** Many people are in the permissive will because they are carnal. The word carnal means ignorant, immature, childlike, or spoiled.

11. There are many people who get into trouble because they are unlearned and inexperienced in many areas of life and ministry. They are simply too immature for what they want to do at that time.

12. Moses was carnal and he brought on unnecessary hardship when he killed the Egyptian. He knew he was different and there was something different about his life, but he was yet immature. We can know we have a calling or a gift but we can still be too immature to walk in it at that time of our lives.

13. GOD had to quickly get him out of Egypt before he could have caused the whole nation of Israel to be out of the will of GOD. That is why GOD will at times shut things down in our lives, block certain things from happen because of our immaturity. It is not that GOD does not want us to have it or that GOD does not want to bless us. But he will not give you something to destroy you.

14. That is like when parents give 16 years kids very expensive fast running cars. You must recognize those children cannot handle that kind of power at their age. There was a young man in Virginia, his father gave him a 5.0 mustang. He and five other boys were out one night riding around. He decided to test the speed of his car. He hit a tree running 120 miles per hour. Killed all five of them. His father kept saying "*what happened*"?

15. Paul was declaring to the people that he could not trust them with certain information because they were carnal, they were immature. He knew because of their immaturity they would use the information in error.

16. **(I Timothy 3:6)** The Bible tells us not to ever put a novice in position. A novice is one that is immature, inexperienced, or unlearned. Because of their immaturity they can easily be lifted up in pride, making decisions according to flesh not the spirit, causing themselves and many others to end up in a permissive will.

17. There are many young leaders in the permissive will of GOD bringing on unnecessary struggles to themselves, their families, and even their churches.

18. Carnality is a dangerous thing in the Kingdom of GOD it has destroyed so many people. That is why when Joseph had a dream concerning his ministry; GOD had to separate him quickly because he was unlearned. He could so easily have gotten himself and his brother in the permissive wills of GOD, causing unnecessary suffering.

19. Satan knows when you are immature and unlearned therefore using it against you, especially when you are anxious and impatient. He has set many Christians up based on their immaturity. That is why it is important to be accountable to someone, so that your level of immaturity can always be put in check.

20. Wisdom is the key to staying out of the permissive will when it comes to carnality. You must be willing to sit, hear, learn, and wait. If not, you will end up in unnecessary hardship.

21. Many young people end up like this because they think they know more than their parents, therefore ending up in the permissive will. They get in wrong relationships, financial problems, and many other things because they are unlearned and immature.

22. This is also what happens in the church because many young leaders think titles mean maturity. A title is only a name or a position, it has nothing to do with your level of maturity. Many times, a pastor will start a church they assume this make them mature. Just because a group of people will follow you does not make you mature.

23. Knowledge without maturity will just make you foolish. Increase without maturity will just bring destruction. There was a great musical artist who was talking about his life. He was telling someone how he went through 30 million dollars in one year because of being immature and foolish.

24. Carnality will cause one to get connected to wrong people, places, things, and do things out of timing. That is how people really got caught up in wrong places and relationships. Even when it comes to ministry the devil will hook you up with all the wrong things and people if you are immature.

25. Weakness is not necessarily carnality. There are many people with a weakness, but they are mature enough to handle it. However, it is a very dangerous thing to have a weakness and be carnal. That will be a time that Satan will truly use it against you, because of your ignorance and immaturity.

Suffering Due to Flesh
Questionnaire

1. What is suffering for the flesh?

2. Explain the permissive will.

3. Explain the word of carnality.

4. What is the key to staying out of the permissive will?

5. Explain being foolish.

Lesson Three
Suffering Through Afflictions

1. **(Psalms 34:19)** The third suffering of a believer, SUFFERING THROUGH AFFLICTIONS. Afflictions are pressures on the flesh:
    a. Allowed by GOD.
    b. Carried out by Satan.

2. Allowed by GOD means that GOD takes the hedges down so that the enemy can get to a believer in a certain area. He actually allows the devil to attack you. Not because of what you have done wrong but actually because of what you have done right.

3. Afflictions are pressures on your:
    a. Finances
    b. Marriage
    c. Health
    d. Children
    e. Many other things

4. **(Job 1: 1)** "There was a man in the land of Uz, whose name was Job; and that man was perfect and upright, and one that feared GOD, and eschewed evil".

5. Afflictions only come on righteous people not the ungodly or sinners, because afflictions are based strictly on righteousness. Job was noted to be perfect and upright that is why he was allowed to be afflicted.

6. **(Psalms 34:19)** The Bible declares that "Many are the afflictions of the righteous". Job had pressures or afflictions on every area of his life. Job had to face every affliction, he:
    a. Lost his children.
    b. Lost his homes.
    c. Lost his finances.
    d. Lost all his property.
    e. Lost his health.
    f. Lost his wife.

7. Every believer will have many afflictions in their lifetime. Afflictions will attack every area of your life one way or another, at one time or another. As a righteous person there is no way around afflictions.

8. Afflictions come on a believer or a righteous person to:
   a. To prove their trust in GOD.
   b. To show that they will not deny GOD.

9. That is what happen to Job, he had to prove his trust and in GOD and he had to show he would not deny GOD. That is why Satan used his wife to see if she could get Job to deny the heavenly Father. Even Job's friend tried to put Job in a distrusting place and a place of denial.

10. Satan is always trying to prove that a believer or a righteous person only serves GOD because he continues to bless them. Job proved that he trusted GOD and that He would not deny him. Even in the process of complaining, Job never denied him.

11. **(Job 1:8)** "And the LORD said unto Satan, Hast thou considered my servant Job, that there is none like him in the earth, a perfect and an upright man, one that feareth GOD, and escheweth evil"?

12. Afflictions again must be approved by GOD. Satan must get permission from GOD before he can bring an affliction on any RIGHTEOUS man. When it comes to afflictions. Satan can not just attack a Christian. He must be allowed to get to that individual. Because when a believer is in the will of GOD, he is divinely protected.

13. GOD knows every righteous man; therefore, your afflictions are only allowed based on:
   a. Commitment
   b. Faith

14. **(Job 1:12)** "And the LORD said unto Satan, Behold, all that he hath is in thy power; only upon himself put not forth thine hand. So Satan went forth from the presence of the LORD".

15. GOD will not allow an affliction that would cause you to fall away from the Kingdom of GOD or that is bigger than your faith. That is why afflictions are measured by GOD. Afflictions show you where you are, and they show the devil where you really are. GOD already know your level of faith and commitment.

16. Afflictions are subject to the grace of GOD, which is GOD's timing. GOD knows exactly how long to allow Satan to afflict someone. The timing is based on GOD not us as individuals.

17. Israel was afflicted by Pharaoh and Egypt. The affliction was allowed for 400 years. After 400 years GOD released Israel from the pressure of the affliction.

18. Every righteous man will have afflictions, but just remember that the timing is on GOD and he knows exactly when to get you out. It may feel like it is going to kill you. But again, GOD has it timed out not Satan. Satan is just allowed to implement it.

19. It will never be longer than:
    a. What you need.
    b. What you can bare or handle.

20. **(2 Timothy 2:3)** "Thou therefore **endure** hardness, as a good soldier of Jesus Christ.

21. All one has to do in an affliction is <u>ENDURE</u>. The word *"endure"* in the Greek means to *"Hold up against"*. It means to maintain under pressure.

22. One will maintain and endure mainly by knowing that GOD is in charge. and he knows exactly what someone can handle and how long one will need to suffer.

23. **(Psalms 34:19)** In afflictions, it is GOD's responsibility to get you out. The scripture declares that "The Lord will deliver them all". Again, you will not have any affliction that you have to get yourself out of. The exit plan is GOD's responsibility.

24. When praying for afflictions the only thing that one really will need to pray for is an individual's mind. Satan's ultimate goal is to take one's mind by applying so much pressure on the flesh during a given situation. Therefore, causing the person to snap under pressure.

25. Satan can't take anyone's life in an affliction. However, he can attempt to apply so much pressure that the person may consider giving up, because they do not understand what is really going on.

26. Job talked constantly about death during his time of afflictions because he did not understand what was going on.

27. You must allow GOD to give you a discerning spirit, therefore being able to recognize an affliction versus something else. This will allow you to minister to the person in the right way.

28. To be able to bring proper reassurance to someone concerning righteousness and their exit plan brings much value to that person. It is a great thing to allow a person to know that GOD really is going to get them out and also that they did not do anything wrong.

29. During afflictions, many people will feel as though they have sinned or may be accused of sin by others, causing the person to feel very despondent. You must reassure them of their righteousness during their afflictions.

Suffering Through Afflictions
Questionnaire

1. Explain suffering through afflictions.

2. Explain the areas that afflictions will attack a person.

3. Why do afflictions come on a righteous person?

4. Explains afflictions being subject to the grace of GOD.

5. What does one need to pray for during afflictions?

Lesson Four
Suffering in Burdens

1. The second pressure on a believer is a burden. A burden is a weight on the spirit or the flesh that one is expected to carry out.

2. Burdens are brought on by:
    a. *GOD*
    b. By oneself
    c. Others

3. **(Matthew 11:30)** The weight of GOD 's burden is measured according to what one can carry. GOD will never give you a burden above that which you can carry. The weight is measured by GOD not you.

4. GOD declares that *"His burden is light"*. GOD's burden means service. GOD's burden is a requirement in an area where you are to serve him and or a situation.

5. For example, when we work in a certain area of ministry, GOD places that thing on us as a burden, which is a service. We have the burden of evangelism, pastoring, and teaching.

6. When GOD states "*That His burden is light*" the word light means balanced. GOD's burdens are always well balanced. He will not place anything on you that will throw you off balance or cause disorder in your life.

7. When people are carrying out a leadership position in their life, such as pastoring and it becomes overwhelming or starts to cause everything to be off balance, then it is not GOD's burden anymore.

8. Many times, we add to things in our lives and make them our burdens not GOD's, causing conflicts and struggles. Sometimes the weight becomes so heavy that you cannot bear it anymore.

9. GOD releases His burdens according to where you are:
    a. In your availability.
    b. Your faith.
    c. Your gifting.
    d. Your anointing.

10. GOD never releases His burden beyond where you are. That is what it means when it states, "He will not put more on you than you can bear".

11. If at any time you have a burden on you that you feel as though it is too much, then it is your choice to ask GOD to remove the burden or even give the burden up.

12. **(Galatian 6:5)** Every man is to bear his own burden. Each person we have an individual burden that he is to carry. He is to prove his own work. If our personal burdens are too hard. then we have taken on something that is not required of us.

13. We live in a society that we have taken on unnecessary burdens. We attempt to compete, live up to man's standard and not GOD's. We are weighted down daily with overwhelming struggles.

14. **(Psalm 55:22)** When a personal burden becomes overwhelming then it is your job to cast that burden on the Lord. The word cast means to throw quickly. But if I do not get rid of it quickly it will eventually destroy you.

15. For example, it is a person's burden to work and take care of themselves in every way, financially, physically, and spiritually. However, if I lose my job or an illness comes upon that I can do nothing about them, I am to cast it on the Lord quickly.

16. However, I can't cast something on Him that is not His responsibility. Such as I have the money to pay a bill and I go out and use it on something else that is not GOD's care.

17. It is each person's responsibility to monitor their burden and do not take on more than what is required on them. This is happening so much in the church, again people are taking on unnecessary burdens.

18. When it comes to taking on the burdens of others. There are required burdens of others and no requirements. Required burdens of others are things such as raising your children dealing with your mate (In sickness and in health).

19. If you are a pastor, you have a required burden to meet the basic needs of the people, such as feeding the Word of the truth, and meeting the needs of the people based on what the church can handle.

20. Many times, we take on the burden of others that is not a requirement. Many times, parents get burned out taking grown children's burdens. Parents are taking on responsibilities that are no longer theirs becoming a heavy burden.

21. Pastors take on burdens of the church that do not belong to them. They attempt to bear the burdens of people who just do not want to live right or change.

22. They take on the financial burden concerning the church. We are required to be a financial blessing to the church, but GOD never will lay it in your lap as a burden.

23. Many people are just worn out because of taking on the burden of others that are not requirements. If someone is sick you can't wear that sickness for them.

Suffering in Burdens
Questionnaire

1. What is a burden?

2. Explain "His burden is light".

3. Explain how GOD releases his burdens.

4. What does it mean when our personal burdens are too heavy?

5. Explain required and nonrequired burden of others,

Lesson Five
Suffering with a Yoke

1. **(Matthew 11:29-30)** "Take my yoke upon you and learn of me; for I am meek and lowly in heart: and ye shall find rest unto your souls. For my yoke is easy, and my burden is light".

2. A yoke is:
   a. A requirement.
   b. An obligation from GOD.

3. For you to be victorious in GOD, you must learn and meet His requirements. However, GOD will never give you requirements or obligations that you can't meet.

4. Man will ask for unnecessary requirements. That is why so many people are frustrated in the church, because man has attempted to put more biblical requests on them.

5. A yoke is:
   a. A requirement.
   b. An obligation from GOD.

6. You become educated by the Word and as you practice it you become disciplined.

7. As you meet the requirement to be disciplined, it will be "*Easy*". The word "*easy*" means manageable.

8. The yoke or the requirements of GOD are always manageable. He will not give you something that will cause your life to be out of hand or out of order.

9. GOD does not put requirements on man that overwhelm them. If you are overwhelmed by a requirement of GOD, then it is usually not of GOD, or you just refuse to obey, or you have put yourself in a position where you can't obey.

10. With the yoke of GOD, you find rest in Him. The word "*rest*" in the Greek mean belief or to believe. When you take on the yoke of GOD, it will bring belief in Him; therefore, bringing the peace of GOD.

11. God does not force His yoke on anyone you must take it. To *"take it"* you must receive it by choice. You must choose to learn to be disciplined by the principles of GOD.

12. GOD's yoke is external. It is placed upon you. It can be removed at any time. It is there to truly bring spiritual order.

13. **(Isaiah 10:27)** "And it shall come to pass in that day, that his burden shall be taken away from off thy shoulder, and his yoke from off thy neck and the yoke shall be destroyed because of the anointing".

14. The second type of yoke is a yoke of:
    a. Internal bondage.
    b. Internal strongholds.

15. This type of yoke is self – inflicted. It has nothing to do with GOD, but all to do with man and Satan.

16. These types of yokes come from:
    a. Habits.
    b. Generational curses.
    c. Biter roots.
    d. Contact with demonic sources.

17. These types of yokes must be dealt with quickly or they can be very destructive to one's personal and spiritual life.

18. These yokes are destroyed by the anointing, which is the power of GOD. The word "destroy" means taken totally away from or put in a position that it can no longer be repaired.

19. These yokes are not light or easy; therefore, they must be dealt with as quickly as possible or they will get worse as time goes on.

20. Pastors must attempt to deal with the negative yokes as soon as possible so that the person can quickly take on the yoke of JESUS Christ.

21. The negative yokes in a person's life can hinder a person from taking on the yoke of Christ. The negative yokes are strongholds.

22. The yoke of JESUS is so important because it brings you into alignment with the word, power, and positions of JESUS Christ.

Suffering with a Yoke
Questionnaire

1. What is a "yoke"?

2. Why are so many people frustrated in the church?

3. What does the word "rest" mean?

4. What does it mean that GOD's yoke is external?

5. Explain a self-inflicted yoke.

Essay
Write a 350-word essay on the four types of self-inflicted yokes.

Lesson Six
Suffering of a Care

1. **(1 Peter 5:7)** "Casting all your care upon him; for he careth for you". Now we will talk about the word "*care*". The word "*care*" in the Greek actually means your obligation.

2. The word "*care*" does not have an "s" on it, because as a Christian you only have one "care" and that is your life. If "care" had an "s" on it, then you would or could individualize things in your life.

3. You could pick and choose what you want to give to GOD and what you want to keep for yourself. For example, if you wanted GOD to work on your finances, then you would give them to him. But if you did not want GOD to work on your marriage, then you would keep that for yourself.

4. Many people suffer from their "*care*" or life itself, because they will not turn their life over to GOD.

5. **(Luke 12:22-26)** "And he said unto His disciples, Therefore I say unto you, take no thought for your life, what ye shall eat; neither for the body, what ye shall put on. [23] The life is more than meat, and the body is more than raiment.[24] Consider the ravens: for they neither sow nor reap; which neither have storehouse nor barn; and GOD feedeth them: how much more are ye better than the fowls? [25] And which of you with taking thought can add to his stature one cubit? [26] If ye then be not able to do that thing which is least, why take ye thought for the rest"?

6. We are to take no thought for our lives. We are not to figure out how we are going to survive. It is our job to obey GOD and allow GOD to figure out everything else.

7. When you see people always worried about their day-to-day survival, it is because they are carrying their care, which is their life. They are suffering unnecessarily.

8. The word "*cast*" means to throw off or throw onto immediately. You are not to play with your care because it will attach itself to you and turn into a worry.

9. “*He careth for you*” you must understand GOD is obligated to your needs. He is obligated to supply your needs.

10. The disciples did not have to figure out how to take care of themselves. They did not have to figure out where to eat, drink, or live. All they had to do was do what GOD wanted them to do.

11. **(Psalms 23:1)** “The Lord is my shepherd I shall not want”. The word “*want*” in the Hebrew means “no need of”. David understood that he would not have a need that GOD would not fulfill.

12. GOD knows what each individual need and the timing in which they need it. Therefore, all you have to do is allow GOD to supply the right thing at the right time.

13. When the people of GOD understand the Lord really is their shepherd and it is His job to take care of every need. Then as a believer, they will not worry.

14. The reason why people do not cast their “*care*” on GOD is because they do not trust GOD. They do not believe he really will take care of them. So, they keep their lives to themselves, therefore, living in distress and frustration.

15. They would rather trust their own ability or intellect, instead of relying on the one who has all of the true insight to every situation in the life of a believer.

16. Most pastors are stressed out for their personal lives and ministry because they will not cast their care on GOD, signifying their lack of trust in GOD.

17. They spend more time providing for themselves instead of allowing GOD to provide for them. Therefore, their concentration is more natural than spiritual.

18. Therefore, it is very difficult for them to teach people something that they themselves are not doing. From headship throughout the congregation is a spirit of distress.

19. As a pastor, it is not about fleecing the people. It is about trusting GOD for your every need.

20. Once the people can see the pastor's true trust in GOD, then they can develop the same trust.

Suffering of a Care
Questionnaire

1. Why is it that the word "care" does not have a "s" on it?

2. What does it mean to "take no thought for your life"?

3. What will happen if you do not throw your "care" off immediately?

4. Why is it that people will not "cast their care"?

5. Explain why pastor are stress out concerning "their care".

Lesson Seven
Suffering for Your Faith

1. **(James 1:2-3)** "My brethren, count it all joy when ye fall into divers temptations; 3
knowing this, that the trying of your faith worketh patience".

2. The next area, in which a believer will suffer in or because of, is their "*faith*". "The trying of your faith" means that you will take a test for the level of faith that you have developed.

3. For example, how does one know that they have learned a certain thing without taking a test? How will you know that you have truly developed faith if you do not take a test.?

4. For each thing that you learn, believe, and begin to practice is a type of faith. How do you know that you really learn that or believe that?

5. You know that, by the test you take in your life in a certain area that causes you to apply that certain information.

6. Another example would be, you learn the Word concerning healing, but how do you know you know that you really learned it or believe that without a test?

7. How often have we thought children were prepared to leave school, and then a test is given to discover, they do not know what you thought.

8. The test on your faith is measured according to your faith. Your test will never be bigger than the measure of your faith.

9. GOD will never allow the devil to put more on you than your faith can stand. That would be like the teacher in school giving someone a second-grade test, when she has only taught first grade work.

10. GOD measures your test according to where your faith is. He is a Just GOD.

11. The timing on your test will also be measured based on the endurance of your faith. Your test will never outlast your faith.

12. You must understand this; GOD will never set you up to fail. If He did, then His dying would have been in vain.

13. **(Isaiah 54:17)** "No weapon that is formed against thee shall prosper; and every tongue that shall rise against thee in judgment thou shalt condemn. This is the heritage of the servants of the Lord, and their righteousness is of me, saith the Lord".

14. When you understand the trying of faith, then you will understand how no weapon formed against a believer can prosper. Because GOD allows weapons to form according to the size of your faith.

15. The word "*weapon*" means an offense or a tool of defeat. Satan will form a tool of defeat against a believer, but it can't be bigger than one's faith.

16. That is why that weapon can be formed but it can't overcome you. As a believer you must come out on top.

17. The tools of defeat that Satan formed against Job were very strong, but they were not bigger than Job's faith. Job complained but his faith remained.

18. GOD let Satan know what he could and could not do according to the faith of Job.

19. We are the same way. GOD will make it very clear to Satan what he can and can't do to us as individual saints, according to our faith.

20. Again, the test on your faith is measured according to your faith not your flesh. The test is not on you or your flesh, it is on your faith.

Suffering for Your Faith
Questionnaire

1. Explain the "trying of your faith".

2. How is the test of your faith measured?

3. GOD will never allow the devil to do what?

4. The timing of your test will be measured based on?

5. Why is it that a weapon cannot prosper?

Lesson Eight
Suffering for a Weight

1. **(Hebrew 12:1)** " [1] Wherefore seeing we also are compassed about with so great a cloud of witnesses, let us lay aside every weight, and the sin which doth so easily beset us, and let us run with patience the race that is set before us".

2. The next suffering of a believer is a *"weight"*. A *"weight"* in the Greek means a distraction or hindrance.

3. Many believers are suffering because of distractions in their lives. They are distracted by sin, family problems, children's issues and many others.

4. We are to lay aside weights. The phrase "*lay aside*" means to put away or forsake. There are a lot of things we forsake if we are going to be victorious in the kingdom of GOD.

5. For GOD to use Abraham, he had to get Abraham to forsake his family for a season. Even though we don't want to believe it, but there are things that we love that can be a weight or distraction.

6. The phrase *"beset us"* means there are things that literally take our focus off of the things that we should be focusing on.

7. When Nehemiah was working on the wall, the young men came to beset or distract him. They came to take his focus off of what he was doing to please GOD.

8. However, Nehemiah easily laid the weight aside. He did not lose his focus, because he knew he was doing a good work.

9. When you carry a weight or a distraction, you are carrying unnecessary suffering.

10. The word "*run*" in the Greek means to have course. We have a path or a course we must stay on. And if we allow weights to be a part of our course, it will cause us to either get off balance, or be slowed down.

11. When Abraham left his kindred, he carried a weight with him, a distraction, which was Lot. Lot slowed him down.

12. There came a time when tension came up between him and Lot's livelihood, separation had to come.

13. As a pastor or leader, you must be careful when you are carrying unnecessary weights or distractions. You must stay on course.

14. **(Act 6:1-4)** "And in those days, when the number of the disciples was multiplied, there arose a murmuring of the Grecians against the Hebrews, because their widows were neglected in the daily ministration. [2] Then the twelve called the multitude of the disciples unto them, and said, it is not reason that we should leave the word of GOD, and serve tables. [3] Wherefore, brethren, look ye out among you seven men of honest report, full of the Holy Ghost and wisdom, whom we may appoint over this business. [4] But we will give ourselves continually to prayer and to the ministry of the word".

15. Peter understood his position in the kingdom of GOD. He could not allow himself to get distracted by the everyday business of the church. It would have become a weight to him.

16. Peter found the brethren that were to carry the day-to-day concerns of the operation of the church.

17. Many pastors take on things that should not be their concern, causing them to be under a weight, therefore being distracted from the spiritual wellbeing of the church.

18. Distractions can easily creep in. You must pay close attention to when you find yourself overwhelmed by weights.

19. Weights will bring on a bad attitude. We are to run with patience. The word "*patience*" in the Greek means attitude. When you are carrying weights, you eventually become angry and stressed out.

20. That is why it is so important to lay them aside before your attitude become negative concerning your situation, others, and especially ministry.

Suffering for a Weight
Questionnaire

1. What is a weight?

2. What does it mean to lay aside?

3. Explain “beset us”.

4. Explain how a weight can bring on s bad attitude.

5. Explain what Peter did concerning his weight and distraction.

Lesson Nine
Suffering for Infirmities

1. **(Galatians 4:13)** "Ye know how through infirmity of the flesh I preached the gospel unto you at the first".

2. The word "infirmity" in Greek means sickness or disability. Many of us will suffer because of sicknesses or disability. Paul had an infirmity in the flesh. No one really knows exactly what it was.

3. **(2 Corinthians 12:7-10)** "7 And lest I should be exalted above measure through the abundance of the revelations, there was given to me a thorn in the flesh, the messenger of Satan to buffet me, lest I should be exalted above measure. [8] For this thing I besought the Lord thrice, that it might depart from me. [9] And he said unto me, my grace is sufficient for thee: for my strength is made perfect in weakness. Most gladly therefore will I rather glory in my infirmities, that the power of Christ may rest upon me. [10 Therefore] I take pleasure in infirmities, in reproaches, in necessities, in persecutions, in distresses for Christ's sake: for when I am weak, then am I strong".

4. Paul's infirmity was there to keep him humble. GOD knew it was very possible was Paul's head to become swollen because of the revelation he had received.

5. Infirmities are in our lives for different purposes. They bring:
   a. Humility
   b. Forgiveness
   c. Deliverance
   d. Exposure
   e. Evidence of the power of GOD.
   f. Glory to GOD.

6. An infirmity comes from Satan, but it is regulated by GOD. It is there to worry you. It is there to get on your very last nerve.

7. You can seek the Lord concerning an infirmity, but GOD knows the timing in which you need to be in that situation.

8. GOD's grace is sufficient concerning an infirmity. Again, that means that GOD's timing is just right. His timing is measured for the given situation.

9. Everyone will be used out of their infirmity. It is out of your infirmity that GOD is made strong in your life. It is out of that weakness that GOD can truly manifest himself.

10. It is out of your infirmity that GOD will get all the glory, not you. That is why Paul declared "*When I am weak is when I am strong*".

11. Your infirmities are not for your sake yet for Christ sake. He will never put us in a position where we could dare touch His Glory or be glorified.

12. It is through that weakness that the power of GOD has the ability to rest upon you. That is why Paul said, *"I rather glory in my infirmities that the power of GOD rests upon him"*.

13. The flesh itself is an infirmity because it is a weakness. It is always subject to weakness. However, if it is kept under subjection to the Holy Spirit, it can be controlled.

14. Your weakness or infirmity does not dominate when you allow GOD to be in control. Yes, at times they can be painful and uncomfortable. But GOD's grace is sufficient.

15. It is in your infirmity that you really rely on GOD not yourself. All of us will have some type of infirmity. It is for GOD's Glory.

16. As a pastor recognize your infirmity and glory in it. GOD has allowed it to be to keep you humble.

17. Also realize that GOD will always surround you with people who have the ability to strengthen you.

18. This is not a one man show. Our abilities are there to enhance one another.

19. Your handicap will be someone else's strength. Rely on it.

Suffering for Infirmities
Questionnaire

1. What is an infirmity?

2. Why was Paul's infirmity in his life?

3. What does it mean for an infirmity to come from Satan but be regulated by GOD?

4. Explain how God's grace is sufficient concerning an infirmity.

5. How will God get the glory out of an infirmity?

Lesson Ten
Suffering for Righteousness

1. **(1 Peter 4:12-16)** "Beloved, think it not strange concerning the fiery trial which is to try you, as though some strange thing happened unto you: [13] but rejoice, inasmuch as ye are partakers of Christ's sufferings; that, when His glory shall be revealed, ye may be glad also with exceeding joy. [14] If ye be reproached for the name of Christ, happy are ye; for the spirit of glory and of GOD resteth upon you: on their part he is evil spoken of, but on your part, he is glorified. [15] But let none of you suffer as a murderer, or as a thief, or as an evildoer, or as a busybody in other men's matters. [16] Yet if any man suffers as a Christian, let him not be ashamed; but let him glorify GOD on this behalf".

2. The last type of suffering for a believer is *"righteousness."* When you suffer for righteousness sake, you are then considered part of Christ suffering.

3. When you are suffering for Christ sake or righteousness sake, don't be surprised when things just come out of nowhere to attack you.

4. When you are dishonored or abused for Christ sake then GOD said, *"Be happy"*. That word "happy" means to be satisfied, that is it is for the right reason.

5. We should never have a bad name because of sin or unrighteousness. We are never to suffer for the wrong reason.

6. You do not have to be a shame for suffering for the gospel or for the kingdom of GOD. We are to exalt GOD for doing the right thing.

7. Adam and Eve had to be a shame; they had to feel condemnation or guilt because of their wrongdoing.

8. **(Roman 8:1)** "There is therefore now no condemnation to them which are in Christ Jesus, who walk not after the flesh, but after the Spirit".

9. You do not have to feel guilty when you have done the right thing.

10. **(1 Peter 4:19)** "Wherefore let them that suffer according to the will of GOD commit the keeping of their souls to him in well doing, as unto a faithful Creator".

11. When you are suffering for righteousness, you are suffering according to the Will of GOD. That is why Jesus had to suffer in the Garden, because he had to suffer according to the will of His Father.

12. All of the disciples had to suffer for righteousness sake. They ended up in jail, beaten, even killed. We must recognize that as a child of GOD every now and then we are going to suffer for the sake of the kingdom.

13. When you are suffering for righteousness, sake the devil will try to run you crazy. He will truly mess with your mind. He will torment you in your mind.

14. You must commit your mind to the Holy Spirit. You must commit it to well doing. *"Well doing"* in the Greek means virtue, it means purity.

15. When you are suffering, all kinds of thoughts are going to come to your mind, even impure thoughts. Therefore, you must protect your mind.

16. **(Philippians 4:8)** "Finally, brethren, whatsoever things are true, whatsoever things are honest, whatsoever things are just, whatsoever things are pure, whatsoever things are lovely, whatsoever things are of good report; if there be any virtue, and if there be any praise, think on these things".

17. You must know what to think when you going through. You must think the right things at all times. You must think truth, lovely, and pure.

18. GOD will keep you in the midst of suffering for His sake.

Suffering for Righteousness Questionnaire

1. What is suffering for righteousness sake?

2. What are you considered when you suffer for righteousness sake?

3. What does it mean to not be a shame?

4. When you suffer for righteousness sake, what are you suffering according to?

5. What will the devil try and do when you are suffering for righteousness sake?

Works Cited

6. Rapids, M. (2002). *Holy Bible: King James Version.* Grand Rapids, Mich.: Zondervan.

7. Dockery, D. S. (1998). *Holman concise Bible commentary: simple, straightforward commentary on every book of the Bible.* Nashville, Tenn.: Broadman & Holman Publishers.

8. Strong, J., Kohlenberger, J. R., & Swanson, J. A. (2001). *The strongest Strong's exhaustive concordance of the Bible* (Larger print Ed.). Grand Rapids, Mich.: Zondervan.

9. *Life application Bible: New Revised Standard Version.* (1990). Iowa Falls, Iowa: World Bible Publishers.

THE PACKAGE OF SUFFERING

Safe Haven Interdenominational Bible College and Training Institute

PO Box 457

Zebulon, NC 27597

The Package of Suffering
Table of Contents

Lesson 1
Wilderness *Experiences*

1. **(Matthew 4:1-10)** The process of discipleship is for all believers to master or overcome the wilderness experience. Jesus overcame the wilderness experience.

2. The wilderness experience is when one must overcome:
    a. The world or sin.
    b. The flesh or personal sins.
    c. The devil.

3. Jesus went into the wilderness for forty days and forty nights to be tempted of the d evil.

4. **(Hebrew 4:15)** "But with all points tempted like as we are, yet without sin". He was tempted of every possible sin and yet he never failed. He proved in the flesh that man could overcome sin, sins, and the devil.

5. Discipleship is being disciplined, orderly, or balanced, in one's life. It is having spiritual control or again spiritual, mental, emotional, and physical order.

6. **(James 4:7)** Discipleship prepares you to resist the devil. You have a responsibility to overcome the devil in every area of your life. The word "resist" in the Greek means to withstand or oppose.

7. You must be able to oppose or withstand the devil in your day-to-day walk, or you will not be able to overcome him in your ministry. You must be able to resist him concerning finances, family, job, and all daily encounters.

8. **(Matthew 6:13)** "And lead us not into temptation but deliver us from evil: For thine is the kingdom, and the power, and the glory, forever. Amen".

9. When JESUS set His disciples down to pray, he taught them in the Lord's Prayer to say, "Lead us not into temptation". This meant, help us to stay away from anything that would cause us to fall into the hands of Satan.

10. **(Matthew 26:41)** "Watch and pray, that ye enter not into temptation: the spirit indeed is willing, but the flesh is weak".

11. We are to watch as well as to pray, because at any time we can encounter temptation, which is something that is trying to cause us to fall into sin.

12. JESUS was always aware when the enemy was trying to set him up to fall, and that is what he was trying to teach the disciples. Judas failed the wilderness test because he fell right into the hands of temptation.

13. JESUS kept the disciples very close to him. He wanted them to see if they drew close to GOD, they could resist temptation. JESUS always stayed very close to His father.

14. You must build up your resistance by staying in the word and practicing the word. You also must have a life of fasting and prayer to resist Satan.

15. **(Galatians)** Paul spent years in the presence of the Lord being disciple, building up a resistance against the devil.

16. **(Luke 8:13)** "They on the rock are they, which, when they hear, receive the word with joy; and these have no root, which for a while believe, and in time of temptation fall away".

17. When you are being discipled you are developing a root. Without being disciplined you will have no true root in the Word. Therefore, when temptation comes, you will fall away.

18. You must develop a root or right foundation to stand against the enemy. He knows when our foundation is not right. Therefore, Satan will use that against us.

19. Every great man or woman in the Bible that GOD used was first properly disciple, given a proper foundation, so that they could resist temptation.

20. **(1 Corinthian 10:13)** "There hath no temptation taken you but such as is common to man: but GOD is faithful, who will not suffer you to be tempted above that ye are able; but will with the temptation also make a way to escape, that ye may be able to bear it".

21. When you have been properly discipled, you learn to escape temptation properly. You learn to get out properly and in a timely manner. GOD knows

exactly how much temptation you can handle. Therefore, He will always give you a way out.

22. (James 1:12) "Blessed is the man that endureth temptation: for when he is tried, he shall receive the crown of life, which the Lord hath promised to them that love him".

23. When you are discipled, you are instructed how to endure temptation. The word ``*endure*" in the Greek means to come through in a proper manner. To come through in the proper manner means with the right attitude, with character and integrity.

24. Discipleship brings balance and order, again it makes you effective in everything that you do. Therefore, you will come through temptation with discipline, balance, and order if you have been properly discipled. Lesson 2

Wilderness Experiences
Questionnaire

1. What is the wilderness experience?

2. Why did Jesus go into the wilderness?

3. Explain “lead us not into temptation”.

4. What was Jesus always aware of?

5. What is that you must build up to overcome temptation?

Lesson 2
The Garden Experience

1. **(Matthew 26:39)** "He went on a little farther and bowed with His face to the ground, praying, "My Father! If it is possible, let this cup of suffering be taken away from me. Yet I want your will to be done, not mine."

2. To properly be discipled one must go through the garden experience. The garden experience is when one must deny or die to their will, and embrace the will of GOD.

3. Most people will get stuck in the garden. Over 90% of the body of Christ is their right now, because they can't give up their will. It very hard to get pass:
   a. Me
   b. Myself
   c. I

4. JESUS was completely human and he was completely GOD. His battle was between His human side and the deity side of him. There was a tug of war between flesh and spirit.

5. The battle of every Christian is what GOD wants for you versus what you want for self.

6.**(John 4:34)** "Jesus saith unto them, My meat is to do the will of him that sent me, and to finish His work"

7.The word *"meat"* in the Greek means true fulfillment. It means survival also to satisfy the father.

8.GOD is looking for a people whose true survival is first satisfying the Father. GOD had a heart to satisfy His father.

9.**(Matthew 26:44)** " And he left them, and went away again, and prayed the third time, saying the same words."

10.You can't pray away the will of the Father. JESUS went back and forth three times, but nothing changed.

11.You can't pray away the will of GOD because it is designed to:

a. Fulfill purpose.
b. A purpose in an individual life.

12.You may not like where you live, go to church, work, go to school, or even who you are married to, but it is not about you, it is about the will of GOD.

13.Jesus had to go to the cross to fulfill a purpose of salvation. So many people will miss purpose for their lives by trying to get out of the will of GOD.

14.To walk away from will is to walk away from purpose. GOD's approval is on His will.

15.GOD will two things concerning His will, He will:

a. Delay it for a time period to give man response time
b. Give the will to someone else.

16.**(Hebrew 10:9)** "Then said he, Lo, I come to do thy will, O GOD. He taketh away the first, that he may establish the second."

17. **(Matthew 28:20)** "Teaching them to observe all things whatsoever I have commanded you: and, lo, I am with you always, even unto the end of the world. Amen."

18.The command in the Greek means will. They were to teach all new disciples to follow GOD's will completely.

19. Two types of commands:

a. Written commands-will (His written word).
b. Personal commands-will (Specific instructions for a certain individual).

20.Before GOD could use Abraham, he had to be disciplined concerning the will of GOD:

a. Leave your country

b. Leave your kindred
c. Leave your father's house
d. Go to a strange land

21. Favor is on the will of GOD. He told Abraham:
1. I will make thee a great nation
2. I will bless thee
3. I will make thou name great
4. Thou shall be a blessing
5. I will bless them that bless thee
6. I will curse them that curse thee
7. In thee shall all the family of the earth be blessed

22.**(Matthew 6:33)** "But seek ye first the kingdom of GOD, and His righteousness; and all these things shall be added unto you."

23.The garden is where one must seek the will of GOD first. To seek the will of GOD means to seek what matters to GOD first. It is to seek the mind of GOD.

24.When you are subject to the will of GOD it is then recognize that you are available to GOD.

25.JESUS had three years to find people who would be totally available to the will of GOD. GOD has no respect of person; He will use whoever is available.

26.**(Psalms 91:1)** "He that dwelleth in the secret place of the Most High shall abide under the shadow of the Almighty."

27.The secret place of the Lord is the:
a. Fear of GOD.
b. Will of GOD.

Questionnaire

1. What is the garden experience?

2. Explain why most people get stuck in the garden.

3. What is the battle of every Christian?

4. Explain the word "meat".

5. Why is it that you can not pray away the will of GOD?

The Cross Experience

1. **(Matthew 16:24)** "Then said Jesus unto His disciples, if any man will come after me, let him deny himself, and take up his cross, and follow me. Now we will talk about the cross experience concerning discipleship".

2. Discipleship is about learning to suffer, not only to suffer but how to suffer correctly. Even in your suffering it must be pleasing to GOD.

3. To suffer means to bear weight or have pain against the flesh. If you are going to walk this Christian walk there is going to be some suffering.

4. The cross suffering is due to choosing to go against the world and the enemy, therefore, following the plans of GOD.

5. Do not get suffering or the cross experience and consequences mixed up. The consequences are due to sin and disobedience. The cross experience is due to self-denial for righteousness sake.

6. The cross experience is the willingness to suffer to become:

   a. Obedient to the word.
   b. Like Christ.
   c. Pleasing to the Father.

7. Everyone will have their own cross. No two will have the same cross experience.

8. There are three types of cross, the first one is suffering for oneself such as:

   a. Exposure
   b. Humility
   c. Correction
   d. Direction

e. Change

9. **(Hebrews 11:25)** "Choosing rather to suffer affliction with the people of GOD, than to enjoy the pleasures of sin for a season".

10. Then there is suffering for other such as:

a. Salvation.
b. Meeting needs.
c. Manifestation of spiritual requirements in the Kingdom of GOD.

11. **(Mark 8:34)** "And when he had called the people unto him with his disciples also, he said unto them, whosoever will come after me, let him deny himself, and take up his cross, and follow *"Me"*.

12. Last there is suffering for the kingdom sake such as:

a. Manifesting the works of the Kingdom.
b. To bring glory to the Father.

13. It is in the cross experience that you truly learn to deny yourself:

a. Putting what matters to GOD first.
b. Establishing Kingdom order.

14. (Luke 14:27) "And whosoever doth not bear his cross, and come after me, cannot be my disciple".

15. To bear the cross means to:

a. Carry—support the weight
b. Endure—go through
c. Overcome it—victory out of

16. **(Matthew 10:38)** "And he that taketh not his cross, and followeth after me, is not worthy of me".

17. The word *"worthy"* means suitable or usable. You will never be suitable to be u sed in the kingdom of GOD without the cross experience. You must be willing to suffer.

18.**(Philippians 1:29**) "For unto you it is given in the behalf of the messiah, not only to believe on him, but also to suffer for his sake".

19.Many will be saved but they will not be workable material without true discipleship, which includes the cross experience.

20. **(2Timothy 2:12)** "If we suffer, we shall also reign with him".

21.To reign with Christ means to have authority, the right to His power.

The Cross Experience
Questionnaire

1. The cross experience is willing to suffer to become?

2. What is suffering for oneself?

3. What is suffering for others?

4. What is suffering for the kingdom sake?

5. What do you truly learn in the cross experience?

Lesson 4
Death Experience

1. **(John 19:30)** "When Jesus therefore had received the vinegar, he said, It is finished: and he bowed His head, and gave up the ghost".

2. To walk in discipleship everyone must have a death experience. The death experience for discipleship is to render up emotions.

3. In the soul area man is made up of three parts the mind, will and emotions.

4. Man is controlled by many emotions. Another name for emotions is flesh. Satan uses the five senses which are the main attachment to our emotions, which causes us to fall and disobey.

5. When you go through the death experience you are no longer controlled by feeling, you truly began to operate on and in faith.

6. When Lazarus became sick and Mary and Martha wanted Jesus to come, he was not moved by emotions. He was only moved by the will of His father.

7. **(Roman 8:1)** "There is therefore now no condemnation to them which are in Christ Jesus, who walk not after the flesh, but after the Spirit".

8. Another name for condemnation is guilt. Guilt is an emotion of the flesh that will hold an individual to their pass.

9. **(Roman 8:6)** "For to be carnally minded is death; but to be spiritually minded is life and peace".

10. A carnal minded person is an immature or emotionally minded person. You must die to the emotional of the mind if you are going to be controlled by the Spirit.

11. The mind will play tricks on you if you are being controlled by the emotional part of the mind. That is why you have so many Christians yet losing their minds.

12. **(Roman 8:8)** "So then they that are in the flesh cannot please GOD".

13.Your emotions will cause you not to satisfy or please GOD. Because of emotions, one will base their decisions on how they feel, not the word or the voice of G OD.

14.Emotions must truly go through a death experience for you to be used by GOD. It is not that you don't love or feel pain, but the emotions can't be the determining factor for the work of the kingdom.

15.You do not owe your emotions anything.

Questionnaire

1. What is the death experience?

2. What is condemnation?

3. What is a carnal minded person?

4. What will your emotions cause you to do?

5. When you go through the death experience you are no longer controlled by?

Lesson 5

Resurrection Experience

1. **(John 20:9)** "For as yet they knew not the scripture, that he must rise again from the dead".

2. To be discipled all must go through the resurrection experience. The resurrection experience is your ability to recover or come back. You can't stay down forever.

3. Your victory is determined in your recovery or your resurrection experience.

4. As a disciple. you learn to rise up and out of any given situation.

5. **(Mark 16:18)** "They shall take up serpents; and if they drink any deadly thing, it shall not hurt them; they shall lay hands on the sick, and they shall recover".

6. There are two types of resurrection or recovery power, the ability to bring:
    a. Recovery to yourself
    b. Recovery to someone else

7. **(Luke 22:32)** "But I have prayed for thee, that thy faith fail not: and when thou art converted, strengthen thy brethren".

8. Jesus told Peter *"when thou has come out of your shortcoming, your downward spiral, then recovery and restore your brethren"*.

9. It is part of our job to help others resurrect, however we must be able to resurrect yourself. It is sad to see so many people who are supposed to be Christian who have no *"come back power"*.

10. They constantly lay and wallow in their graves of situations. You must know how to rise again.

11. Peter was able to repent, cry out, receive deliverance, and recover again. That was part of His disciple training from being with JESUS for three long years.

12. Judas represented failure in discipleship because he could not resurrect again. He hung himself dying in his own bed of iniquity.

13. If we have not been properly discipled in our spiritual walk, we very well can end up in the same predicament. Not able to recover from the attacks of the enemy.

14. **(2Timothy 2:26)** "And that they may recover themselves out of the snare of the devil, who are taken captive by him at his will".

15. You must be able to come back after the attacks or the snares of the devil. The word snare in the Greek means:

a. Traps
b. Displeasures
c. Stumbling block

16. There are going to be many traps, displeasures, and stumbling blocks in a believer's life but you must be able to resurrect, or you will be defeated just like Judas.

Resurrection Experience

Questionnaire

1. What is the resurrection experience?

2. What are the two types of resurrections? Explain each.

3. Explain why Judas represent failure.

4. What is you victory determined by?

5. How did Peter resurrect?

Glorified Experience

1. **(John 20:22)** "And when he had said this, he breathed on them, and saith unto them, Receive ye the Holy Ghost: 23 whosesoever sins ye remit, they are remitted unto them; and whosesoever sins ye retain, they are retained".

2. Now we will deal with the last experience of discipleship, and that is the glorified or the approval experience. The glorified or the approval experience is when GOD has approved your ability to work.

3. Jesus spent three years making the disciples so that they would be ready to truly pick up the mantle and move forward with the work of the kingdom.

4. There are three forms of receiving the Holy Ghost:
   a. Holy Ghost with you-your ability to be kept.
   b. Holy Ghost in you-your ability to live right (Fruit of the Spirit).
   c. Holy Ghost upon you-your ability to effectively work.

5. In the scripture above JESUS breathes on them keeping power. Then he told them to go to the upper room and wait. It was in the upper room, that they would receive the power to live and the true power to work.

6. **(Acts 1:8)** "But ye shall receive power, after that the Holy Ghost is come upon you: and ye shall be witnesses unto me both in Jerusalem, and in all Judaea, and in Samaria, and unto the uttermost part of the earth".

7. Once you have GOD's approval then you have working power. We must understand, Jesus walked around for thirty years and he did no real work until the Holy Ghost came upon him.

8. Part of discipleship for those twelve men, was about proving they could handle the power of GOD. Judas proved he could not handle GOD's power.

9.Just because you have been called into ministry, does not qualify you for the power of GOD. You must go through the qualifying process to be glorified.

10.**(Romans 8:30)** "Moreover whom he did predestinate, them he also called: and whom he called, them he also justified: and whom he justified, them he also glorified".

11.To be glorified means GOD renders His approval on you. Many are working in the ministry and GOD has not rendered His approval on them. They very well are working on man's approval but not GODs.

12.You must truly go through the process of discipleship to truly handle the work of the kingdom. There are many who are Christians but not yet disciples. Even the disciples were first Christians.

13.Many Christians followed JESUS but they never became disciples, because they could not be discipled or disciplined. That is why Jesus only ended up with eleven before His death.

14.Discipleship is about truly preparing your life, your overall being for His mighty work. Many can handle the life of the kingdom but that does mean you can handle the work.

15.Before really wanting the true work of the kingdom of GOD, truly ask yourself, have I really been properly disciple? Don't be afraid to ask GOD, do I really have your approval? GOD have I been glorified by you?

Glorified Experience Questionnaire

1. What is the glorified experience?

2. What do you have once you have GOD's approval?

3. If you do not have GOD's approval, what are you working on?

4. What is discipleship really about?

5. What questions must you truly ask yourself?

Works Cited

1. The Strong's Exhaustive Concordance of the Bible

2. The Holy Bible King James Version

3. Holman Concise Bible Commentary

The Three Attacks of Suffering

Safe Haven Interdenominational Bible College and Training Institute

PO Box 457

Zebulon, NC 27597

The Three Attacks of Suffering
Table of Contents

Lesson 1
Temptations

1.**(Matthew 26:41)** "Watch and pray, that ye enter not into temptation: the spirit indeed is willing, but the flesh is weak".

2.**(I Corinthians 10:13)** "There hath no temptation taken you but such as is common to man: but GOD is faithful, WHO will not suffer you to be tempted above that ye are able; but will with the temptation also make a way to escape, that ye may be able to bear it."

3.Attacks come to block and stop your double blessings. His desire is to stop everything that GOD is attempting to get to us.

4.Satan's goal is to con you out of your victory. *"Attack"* means to invade to overcome.

5.When it comes to attacks, there are three things you must do with prayer:

1. You pray the prayer of prevention.
2. The Lord's Prayer.
3. You must pray your way through the attack.

6.Satan tempts your flesh. His ultimate goal is to make you fall into sin. The word *"tempt"* means to prove your ability to stand and or resist sin or shortcomings.

7.A *"temptation"* is something "SET UP BY THE DEVIL" to cause you falter or completely fall.

8.It's set up for spiritual and natural destruction. Temptations come straight from the devil.

9.Temptations tempt your:

a. *Flesh/desires and needs*
b. *Emotions/feelings*
c. *c. Overall your weaknesses*

10.Temptations will expose your fleshly weakness, or your spiritual strength.

11.When Joseph had to encounter Potiphar's wife, it exposed Joseph's strength. However, when David encountered Beersheba, it exposed his weakness.

12.**(Matthew 4:1)** "Then was Jesus led up of the Spirit into the wilderness to be tempted of the devil"

13.**(Mark 1:13)** "And He was there in the wilderness forty days, tempted of Satan".

14.**(James 1:13)** "Let no man say when he is tempted, I am tempted of GOD: for GOD cannot be tempted with evil, neither tempteth HE any man:"

15.You are never tempted by GOD, only Satan. GOD will never set you up to sin, do wrong, or fall.

16.Wherever there is iniquity and transgression, Satan has a legal right to set you up to fall and fail. He has a legal right to tempt you.

17.Satan cannot just tempt you. He has to have something to tempt you with, and he uses the uncleanliness of your blood and your mental desires.

18.Satan will always show you something:

a. Need for flesh.
b. What you want for your flesh.
c. Things that will make you feel good.

20.Satan comes to or in our weakness.

21.**(Mark 1:13)** "And He was there in the wilderness forty days, tempted of Satan"

22.**(Luke 4:2)** "Being forty days tempted of the devil. And in those days, He did eat nothing: and when they were ended, He afterward hungered".

23.**(Hebrews 4:15)** "For we have not an high priest which cannot be touched with the feeling of our infirmities; but was in all points tempted like as we are, yet without sin".

24.**(Hebrews 4:15)** "but was in *ALL POINTS TEMPTED* like as we are, yet without sin".

25.Jesus had to go through the fleshy temptation as a man to prove that we could overcome any temptation.

26.**(Hebrews 2:18)** "For in that which He Himself suffered *when* He was tempted, He is able to help those who are tempted".

27.There are five ways to overcome temptation when you are being setup to fall:

1. Recognize your shortcomings.
2. Never OPENLY position yourself to be tempted.
3. Watch/Pay attention.
4. Build up your resistance.
5. Take your way out.

28.**(I Corinthians 10:13)** "There hath no temptation taken you but such as is common to man: but GOD is faithful, WHO will not suffer you to be tempted above that ye are able; but will with the temptation also make a way to escape, that ye may be able to bear it".

29.When it comes to temptation, you must know how to take your way out. GOD will always give you a way out. Because GOD knows what you can and cannot handle.

30.Your getting out is running quickly or deliverance. Prayer will reveal your exit strategy, and prayer will give you the strength to get out. People who do not pray will be weak to resistance or the exit plan.

Temptations
Questionnaire

1. Why do attacks come?

2. What do you do with prayer when it comes to attacks?

3. Explain what temptations tempt.

4. Explain why GOD will never tempt you.

5. Explain how Jesus was "in all points tempted".

Lesson 2
Trials

1.**(James 1:2-3)** "My brethren, count it all joy when ye fall into divers temptations; 3 Knowing this, that the trying of your faith worketh patience".

2.Trials come to:

a. Prove your faith
b. Expose your attitude, whether it is good or bad.

3."Try/trials" means *"to prove."* Prove means *"to convince."* Trials prove the amount of y our faith. Trials prove the strength of our faith.

4.Trials come to convince you. What you need to see about faith and yourself.

You must prove what you:

a. Have learned.
b. What you believe in.
c. Whom you believe in.
d. You must be convinced in whom you trust.

5.Faith is the plans and the wills of GOD in His written word or spoken word that must be believed and carried out.

6.What are trial? They are attacks on your:

a. Health
b. Finances
c. Family
d. Marriage
e. Death

7.Job experienced all types of trials. Everything was naturally tried in his life. Job had to prove his faith and attitude.

8.*"My brethren, count it all joy when ye fall into divers temptations."* We must understand each word in this scripture:

a. Joy – spiritual Contentment
b. Fall – out of nowhere
c. Divers – different kinds
d. Temptations – situations

10.Saints must be content when out of nowhere come different situations. For the proving or convincing of the word. you will have learned and believed, exposed, or developed your right attitude.

11.**(James 1:2-3)** "My brethren, count it all joy when ye fall into divers temptations…"

12.They are called temptation because they are DONE by Satan, but, ALLOWED and REGULATED by GOD.

13.**(Job 1:8)** And the Lord said unto Satan, hast thou considered My servant Job, that there is none like him in the earth, a perfect and an upright man, one that feareth GOD, and escheweth evil?

14.GOD will never let your trial be bigger than your faith. Faith is based on the word you have learned, received, and believe.

15.The only way your trial is bigger than your faith, is if you get your own self in the situation.

16.**(Matthew 14:22-33)**" When Peter was walking the water, he got himself into something that was bigger than faith'.

17.There are two types of wind/storms in your life:

a. ***Contrary – controlled.***
b. ***Boisterous-out of control.***

18.Your wind will be out of control if you go beyond your faith level. You will have a boisterous

19.**(Isaiah 54:17)** "No weapon that is formed against thee shall prosper".

20.A ***"weapon"*** is a personal attack. ***"Prosper"*** means to overcome. GOD will not let your person attack/trial overcome you.

21.He had Israel to go through the wilderness, because they were not prepared for war. Fighting at that time would have overcome them.

22. The second reason for a trial is to expose your attitude.

23.**(James 1:2)** "Knowing this, that the trying of your faith worketh patience'. *" Patience"* means attitude. *"Worketh"* means develop.

24.Trials will expose your bad attitude. Trials will develop your right attitude. "IF YOU LET THEM"

25.The things Satan wants us to do in a trial is:

a. Give up.
b. Give in.
c. Act up.

26. **(Job 2:9)** "Then said his wife unto him, Dost thou still retain thine integrity? Curse GOD and die.

27.**(I Peter 1:7)** "That the trial of your faith, being much more precious than of gold that perisheth, though it be tried with fire, might be found unto praise and honour and glory at the appearing of Jesus Christ".

28.The whole purpose of a trial, a situation on your faith, is to see if it can stand the test of time. Your faith must hold out until the end. Trials are about what you believe, attitude, and endurance.

29.Because, when the trial is finished, the reward is at the end. THE REWARD IS NOT WHEN YOU WANT IT.

30.**(Job 42:10,12)** “And the Lord turned the captivity of Job, when he prayed for his friends: also, the Lord gave Job twice as much as he had before”.12 So the Lord blessed the latter end of Job more than his beginning.

Trials
Questionnaire

1. Explain the word "prove".

2. Explain a way that trials will attack your health in detail.

3. Explain a trial being regulated by GOD.

4. What is the only way a trial can be bigger than your faith?

5. Explain the difference between the two winds.

Lesson 3
Tests

1.**(Genesis 22:1-2)** " And it came to pass after these things, that GOD did tempt Abraham, and said unto him, Abraham: and he said, Behold, here I am.2 And HE said, Take now thy son, thine only son Isaac, whom thou lovest, and get thee into the land of Moriah; and offer him there for a burnt offering upon one of the mountains which I will tell thee of'.

2.The third attack is Tests. *"Test"* come to prove/manifest your obedience:
  a. How available you are to obedience.
  b. How committed you are to obedience.
  c. What you can handle concerning obedience.
  d. How trustworthy you are concerning obedience.

3.Obedience is your willingness to do:
  a. HIS total general written word.
  b. A direct spoken word.
  c. HIS will for your life.

4.When you test something, you prove it will work. Obedience test to see if you will do what you are supposed to do.

5. **(Genesis 22:1-2**) "And it came to pass after these things, that GOD did tempt Abraham." The word "*tempt*" means test.

6.GOD tested Abraham's obedience:
  a. First time, HE tested his obedience when HE told him to leave his kindred **(Genesis 12:1-4)**
  b. Second time was when HE told him to send Ishmael away. **(Genesis 21:10-14)**
  c. This time, it was to sacrifice his son. **(Genesis 22)**

7.Your obedience is tested on many different levels. Each level of your obedience brings you:

a. Closer to GOD.
b. Closer to your destiny.

8.General obedience brings you closer to GOD. Specific obedience brings you to HIS will, your purpose and destiny.

9.Obedience will bring you to purpose. And purpose will bring you to your destiny. Purpose is what you were created to do. Destiny is your lifetime fulfillment.

10.It has been said *"you will know your purpose by what you enjoy"*. That is not true, look at the Bible.

11.GOD will put your true purpose in your heart, as you yield to obedience. Obedience runs you into purpose. Purpose runs you into destiny.

12.The disciples ran into their purpose as they yielded to obedience. ***(Matthew 4:19 (fishers of men)***

13.You see, most of us are looking for something to just enjoy, or a check, not purpose.

14.**(Matthew 22:14) "**Many are called (summoned), but few are available, yielded to obedience. Once you yield, HE will put that thing in your heart. Once GOD can put it in your heart, it isn't a job, it's purpose".

15.**(Isaiah 1:19)** "If ye be willing and obedient, ye shall eat the good of the land".

16.*"Willing"* means available. *"Obedient"* means to die to your own will.

17.*"Good"* means value. *"Eat"* means fulfill your source. *"Land"* means possession.

18.Every stage, or level of obedience, is an assignment. Every assignment opens another door to favor. Every level of favor opens another door to purpose. Every level of purpose opens another door to destiny.

Tests

Questionnaire

1. What is obedience concerning a test.

2. What does your obedience bring you to?

3. What is the difference between purpose and destiny?

4. Explain assignment.

5. How did the disciples come into their purpose?

Work Cited

1. The Strong's Exhaustive Concordance of the Bible

2. The Holy Bible King James Version

3. Holman Concise Bible Commentary

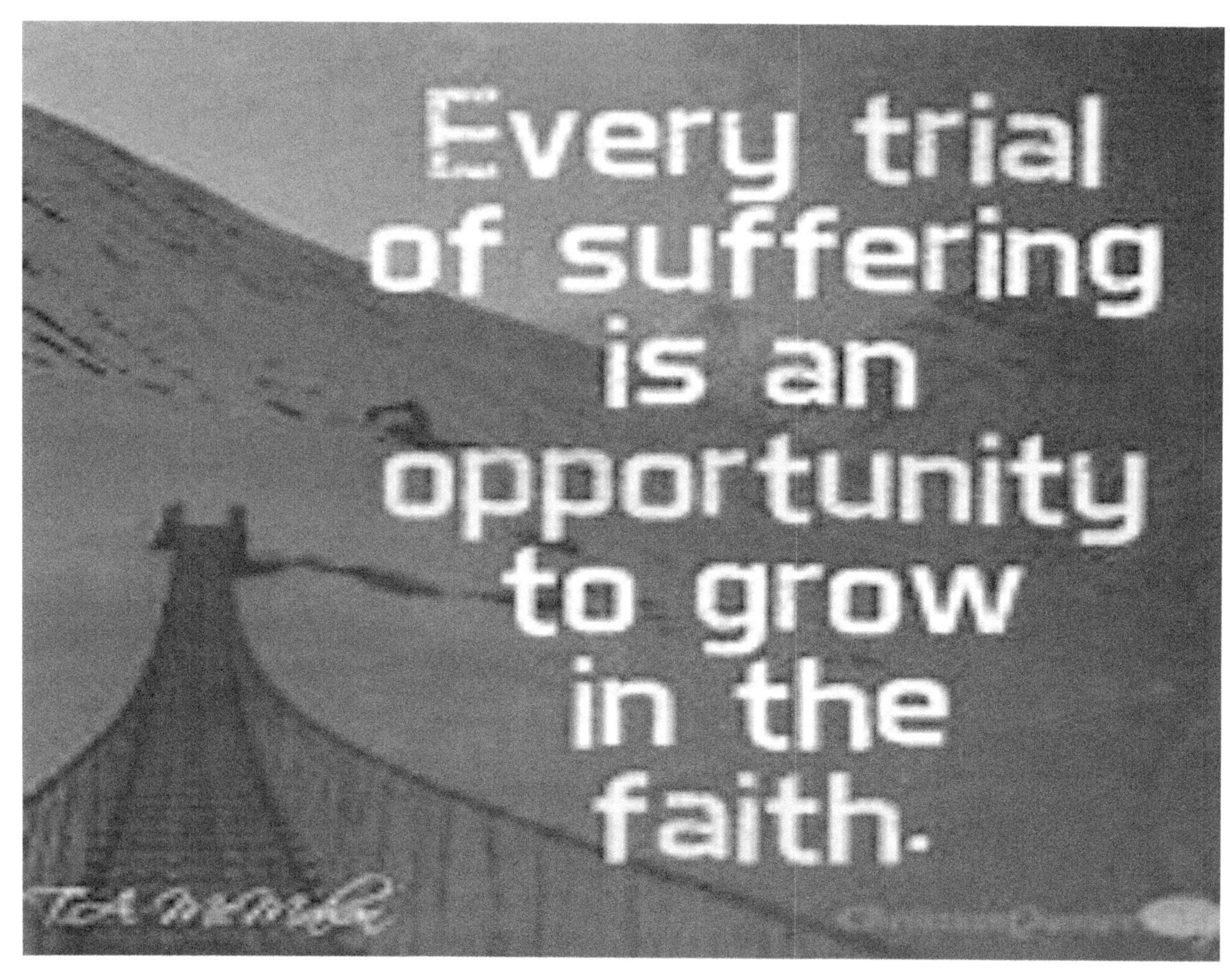
Every trial
of suffering
is an
opportunity
to grow
in the
faith.

WHAT SHOULD I GET OUT OF SUFFERING?

Safe Haven Interdenominational Bible College and Training Institute

PO Box 457

Zebulon, NC 27597

WHAT SHOULD I GET OUT OF SUFFERING?

Table of Contents

Lesson 1
Perfected In Suffering

1. **(1 Peter 5:10)** "But the GOD of all grace, who hath called us unto His eternal glory by Christ Jesus, after that ye have suffered a while, make you perfect, stablish, strengthen, settle you".

2. You must remember it is not just about suffering, but it is what one should get out of suffering. Don't waste suffering. If you do not get out of suffering what you should get, all of that pain and discomfort was for nothing.

3. Again, suffering means to be under a form of hardship or affliction. Also, the suffering has a time limit on it that is why the scriptures declares *"After that ye have suffered a while"*.

4. There are five major things that you must get out of suffering:
   1. GOD must perfect you.
   2. Establish you.
   3. Strengthen you.
   4. Settle you.

5. The word *"perfect"* means to complete. Whenever you suffer in any area, it means that something is missing or broken. Something is incomplete.

6. Something is incomplete in your finances, marriage. your family, even our ministry. If you are going to take advantage of suffering. you allow GOD to complete that specific thing in your life.

7. Jesus came to suffer for us because something was missing in our lives and that was salvation. Because of the fall of Adam and Eve we were incomplete in our relationship with GOD.

8. Moses had to g o to the back side of the mountain to complete his relationship with GOD. He had to suffer and then have that personal encounter at the burning bush to be complete.

9. Joseph had to go to prison to complete something in his life. Even though he had a great word in his dream about his leadership position, he was yet to complete.

10.If you do not complete something in your suffering it will later be an open door for the enemy to have a field day in your life. The devil did not just set that person up. It was something left incomplete that gave the enemy free reign in their lives.

Perfected In Suffering

Questionnaire

1. What does the word *"perfect"* mean?

2. What will happen if you do not get out of suffering what you should?

3. If you do complete something in your suffering, what will happen later?

Lesson 2
Established in You

1. **(1 Peter 5:10)** "But the GOD of all grace, who hath called us unto His eternal glory by Christ Jesus, after that ye have suffered a while, make you perfect, stablish, strengthen, settle you".

2. The second thing that must get you out of suffering is that GOD must establish you. The word *"establish"* means direction. Suffering should put you on the right path.

3. Sometimes it will take suffering to show you were headed in the wrong direction. Paul was headed in the wrong direction. GOD had to knock him down on the road of Damascus to get his personal attention.

4. Your finances, your ministry, your marriage, many things were headed in the wrong direction, so GOD will use suffering to redirect you.

5. GOD will take suffering to stop you before you are too far off course. There are people who do not realize they are being used and directed by the enemy. Therefore, GOD must stop them somewhere before it is too late.

6. **(Psalm 37:23)** "The steps of a good man are ordered by the LORD: and he delighteth in his way".

7. GOD is always trying to order the steps of GOD's people, but we often walk in rejection. Therefore, GOD must knock us down sometimes to get us back on the right path.

8.GOD has a certain place and times that he is always trying to get his people. It is just a matter of time as to whether not he can get them there.

9.(Proverbs 3:6) "In all thy ways acknowledge him, and he shall direct thy paths".

10.Suffering comes to make us acknowledge GOD so that he can get us on the right path. The words acknowledge means to look intently.

11.GOD will use suffering to get your attention so that you will look to him and he can redirect quickly.

Established in You
Questionnaire

1. What does the word *"establish"* means?

2. GOD will use suffering to stop you before you are what?

3. Suffering come to make us acknowledge who?

Lesson 3
Established in Suffering

1. **(1 Peter 5:10)** "But the GOD of all grace, who hath called us unto His eternal glory by Christ Jesus, after that ye have suffered a while, make you perfect, stablish, strengthen, settle you".

2. The third thing that GOD desires for all of us to get out of suffering is that he can strengthen us. The word "strengthen" means to be empowered.

3. GOD wants to empower you for what you have been through and what is to come.

4. GOD wants to give you what you need to be victorious. There are certain levels of power you can only get with suffering.

5. Again, GOD will empower you for where you are now and where you are going.

6. There are certain places you can only get in GOD with suffering and there is a certain amount of empowerment you need for what you are going to face.

7. When Joseph came out of prison, he was empowered to be in the second position or command with Pharaoh. But it took suffering at first to get him there.

8. **(Psalm 27:14)** "Wait on the LORD: be of good courage, and he shall strengthen thine heart: wait, I say, on the LORD" .

9. As you wait on the Lord, you embrace the timing of suffering. In the meantime, you are being strengthened. In waiting you are always getting

stronger concerning your situation. It just does not seem like it, because you can't really see anything that is going on at that time.

10. After David went through all of his field training by staying in that area to suffer with his father's sheep, he was then empowered to begin his kingship. He was ready to fight the giant. He was ready to go head-to-head with a real enemy.

11.After David had suffered years dealing with Saul as king, dealing with the hatred and meanness of this man, he then was ready to take over the complete kingdom.

Established in Suffering Questionnaire

1. What does the word *"strengthen"* mean?

2. What happened when Joseph came out of prison?

3. What happens while you are waiting?

Lesson 4
Settled in Suffering

1. **(1 Peter 5:10)** "But the GOD of all grace, who hath called us unto His eternal glory by Christ Jesus, after that ye have suffered a while, make you perfect, stablish, strengthen, settle you".

2. The next thing that GOD will do in your suffering is settle you. The word "*settle*" actually means to position you properly. There is destiny and purpose in so many people's lives, but they must let GOD settle them.

3. They must come to the place that GOD can settle them in their finances, marriage, and ministry, but it must be done first with suffering.

4. After Joseph suffered in prison, he got settled in his position again as second in command. But it first came with suffering. There are a lot of people in the body of Christ who will never get settled because they will not finish the suffering process.

5. When you have finished your suffering, you do not have to work for it, GOD will simply position you there.

6. He will open the door on that job, he will give you the financial blessings, he will give you the car, he will give you the house, because GOD is ready to settle you.

7. You see after Job finished his suffering GOD settled him back in position. But he did just settle in, he settled in with double of what he originally had. But it took suffering to get him there.

GOD settled Abraham into being the father of many nations. But he had to go through the phases of suffering first. It was not about his suffering; it was about getting himself ready for the position that GOD had for him.

8. It is so sad to see so many people who will never get to their real position because they will not prepare for the position that GOD has for them. They will not complete the suffering assignment.

9. **(1 Peter 4:19)** "Wherefore let them that suffer according to the will of GOD commit the keeping of their souls to him in well doing, as unto a faithful Creator".

10. Satan will attempt to run you crazy while you are in the midst of your suffering. That is why so many will give up. Because they do not understand they are trying to use their mind instead of understanding the spiritual side of things.

11. All you have to do again is commit the keeping of your mind to the power of GOD.

Settled in Suffering
Questionnaire

1. What does the word “settle” mean?

2. What happen after Job’s suffering?

3. Why is it that most people will not get their position?

Lesson 5
Matured In Suffering

1. The last thing that suffering does for us, is mature us. Maturity means to simply grow up. There are many immature Christian, and it is through suffering that maturity is developed.

2. (Genesis 37:5-11) "And Joseph dreamed a dream, and he told it his brethren: and they hated him yet the more. [6] And he said unto them, Hear, I pray you, this dream which I have dreamed: [7] For, behold, we were binding sheaves in the field, and, lo, my sheaf arose, and also stood upright; and behold, your sheaves stood round about, and made obeisance to my sheaf. [8] And his brethren said to him, Shalt thou indeed reign over us? or shalt thou indeed have dominion over us? And they hated him yet the more for his dreams, and for his words. [9] And he dreamed yet another dream, and told it his brethren, and said, Behold, I have dreamed a dream more; and behold, the sun and the moon and the eleven stars made obeisance to me. [10] And he told it to his father, and to his brethren: and his father rebuked him, and said unto him, what is this dream that thou hast dreamed? Shall I and thy mother and thy brethren indeed come to bow down ourselves to thee to the earth? [11] And his brethren envied him; but his father observed the saying.

3. Joseph was very immature that is why he told his brothers and his father his dream. He did not realize that was not something that he should have expressed at that time.

4. Again, GOD had to allow him to go through much suffering to mature him. He was going to be trusted with a very important position. Therefore, maturity was a necessity.

5. When Jacob went away to and meet his future father in-law, it was through all of the suffering that he had to go through with him that he learns to grow up.

6. (Hebrew 6:1) "Therefore leaving the elementary teaching about the Christ, let us press on to maturity, not laying again a foundation of repentance from dead works and of faith toward GOD"

7. It is through the suffering that you must press toward maturity. When people grow up during suffering, it positions them to never repeat that suffering again.

8. (Hebrew 5:14) "But solid food is for the mature, who because of practice have their senses trained to discern good and evil".

9. It is through suffering that you become trained and disciplined in many areas too. Most of them discern good and evil.

10. Don't let your suffering be in vain. We must grow up.

Matured In Suffering
Questionnaire

1. What does "maturity" mean?

2. What happens when people grow up during suffering?

3. It is through suffering that you become what?

Matured In Suffering
Assignments

(All homework, practical, and scripture information, must be on a separate sheet of paper. If it is written on this paper, there is a 50% deduction from your grade automatically.) Homework, practical, and Bible observation must be a paragraph long or more).

Homework
Give an example of someone suffering because of a permissive will.

Practical
Explain a care that most mothers carry causing them to be continuously stressed out.

Homework
Explain an infirmity in your life, explain regulation and timing with the infirmity.
Homework

Homework
Explain an area where leadership usually fall into temptation.
Explain an area where you know you are stuck in the wilderness because of rejecting the true will of GOD.

Give a detail example of how you will know that you have gone through the death experience.

How do you know you are in the glorified experience?

Homework
How will you know when suffering is not complete?

Homework
Explain an area where suffering will show you that you are off track.

Name ____________________

Site ____________________

Instructor ________________

Date ____________________

Matured In Suffering
Test

(Each Question is Worth 10 Point)

1. Explain suffering for sin.

2. Explains afflictions being subject to the grace of GOD.

3. What is a burden?

4. What is a “yoke”?

5. What does it mean to “take no thought for your life”?

6. What does it mean for an infirmity to come from Satan but be regulated by GOD?

7. What is the wilderness experience?

8. What is the garden experience?

9. Explain the word “prove”,

10. What is the difference between purpose and destiny?

Made in the USA
Middletown, DE
10 July 2024

57085851R00250